REUTERS FINANCIAL GLOSSARY

REUTERS FINANCIAL GLOSSARY

SECOND EDITION

Published by **Pearson Education**
London · New York · San Francisco · Toronto · Sydney · Tokyo · Singapore
Hong Kong · Cape Town · Madrid · Paris · Milan · Munich · Amsterdam

PEARSON EDUCATION LIMITED

Head Office:
Edinburgh Gate
Harlow CM20 2JE
Tel: +44 (0)1279 623623
Fax: +44 (0)1279 431059

London Office:
128 Long Acre
London WC2E 9AN
Tel: +44 (0)20 7447 2000
Fax: +44 (0)20 7447 2170

www.financial-minds.com
www.reuters.com

....

First published in Great Britain in 2000
This edition published 2003

© Reuters Limited 2003

ISBN 1 903 68436 6

British Library Cataloguing in Publication Data
A CIP catalogue record for this book can be obtained from the British Library

Library of Congress Cataloging-in-Publication Data

Reuters financial glossary -- 2nd ed.
    p. cm.
  ISBN 1-903684-36-6 (pbk.)
    1. Finance--Dictionaries. I. Reuters Ltd.

  HG151.R48 2003
  332'.03--dc21

                            2003048227

10 9 8 7 6 5 4 3 2

Designed by Sue Lamble
Typeset by Pantek Arts Ltd, Maidstone, Kent
Printed and bound in Great Britain by Biddles Ltd, of Guildford and Kings Lynn

The Publishers' policy is to use paper manufactured from sustainable forests.

CONTENTS

FOREWORD

The world of business, finance and economics has its very own vocabulary – one that can seem daunting at times, even to a seasoned professional. Now, with more people than ever before confronting business issues in their personal and professional lives, the *Reuters Financial Glossary* has become an indispensable tool for making sense of the language.

Reuters reputation as the world's leading news and information company is built on a global network of more than 2,500 financial market experts within our editorial operation. Our journalists make it their business to understand, then explain, the terminology used in markets and business around the globe. And through this Glossary you too can now tap into their expertise.

This is the second edition for the public of *Reuters Financial Glossary* and it has been completely overhauled and updated. In this edition we have added more than 500 new terms, keeping pace with the rapidly changing world in which we all live. We have also added many new worked examples and graphics to help illustrate complex terms, calculations or formulas.

For the first time, this edition of *Reuters Financial Glossary* also includes three important sections – on the economy, company analysis and financial accounting – which expand beyond simple definitions to give you more detail, relevant background and useful examples.

And when you're on the move, you can also access this Glossary online at **www.reuters.com/glossary**.

Whether you are trading in the markets for a living or are just an interested bystander, we trust you will find this book a useful companion.

Geert Linnebank
Editor in Chief
Reuters

LIST OF FIGURES

A

AAA/Aaa Top rating for bonds of the highest quality. Awarded by the main rating agencies: Standard & Poor's, Moody's and Fitch IBCA.
▶ *See also* Credit Rating, Moody's and Standard & Poor's.

AB Swedish company title: abbreviation of Aktiebolag.

Above the Line A gain or loss from a company's normal business activities, shown in the profit and loss account and affecting the balance sheet.
▶ *See* Below the Line, Extraordinary Item, Exceptional Item.

ABS Asset-backed Securities. Securities collateralized by assets such as car loans and credit card receivables which can be seized if the debtor defaults. ABS are created by the process of securitization whereby banks pool types of loans and use them as collateral or security against a bond issue.
▶ *See also* Securitization.

Acceptance House An acceptance house guarantees payment of trade bills used to finance trade deals and goods in shipment. It 'accepts' the bills by agreeing to pay the bill at a discounted rate at a specific future date. Its profit is the difference between the discounted amount it guarantees to pay and the full amount of the trade bill that it undertakes to collect from the original creditor.

Accretion An increase in the notional principal amount of a financial insrument over its life. For example the accounting of capital gains on a bond, bought at a discount, in anticipation of receipt of its full value at maturity.
▶ *See also* Amortization.

Accretive A company is described as being accretive if it achieves growth through internal expansion or acquisition.

Accruals Estimates of a company's costs that have been incurred but have not yet been paid. They appear on the profit and loss account and on the balance sheet.

Accrued Interest The interest accruing on a security since the previous coupon date. If a security is sold between two payment dates, the buyer usually compensates the seller for the interest accrued, either within the price or as a separate payment.
▶ *See also* Coupon, Simple Interest.

Accumulation/Distribution Analysis A technical analysis indicator that measures the difference between the cumulative amount of buying pressure (accumulation) and the cumulative amount of selling pressure (distribution).
▶ *See also* Technical Analysis.

ACI Association Cambiste Internationale. The Financial Markets Association in English. The professional umbrella organization for a large number of national associations of foreign exchange dealers (cambistes).
■ **www.aciforex.com** ■

Acid Test Also known as the quick ratio. Indicator of a company's ability to meet its short-term liabilities, calculated like a current ratio by measuring a company's current assets relative to its liabilities.
▶ *See* Quick Ratio.

Acquisition The purchase by one company of another, for cash, an exchange of shares, or a combination of both. The process, also known as a takeover, can be friendly and have the agreement of the acquired company. Or it can be hostile, when the target rejects the approach and tries to resist being acquired. A takeover or acquisition is usually done with the help of an investment bank and its M&A, or mergers and acquisition, division.

Acting in Concert Investors working together to achieve the same goal, e.g. to buy all the stock they need to take over a company or purchase the minimum needed so that they can legitimately make an open bid to buy outstanding shares. Sometimes acting in concert is considered illegal. Also known colloquially as a concert party.
▶ *See also* Warehousing.

Active Fund Management A fund is actively managed when securities selection is based on specific ideas and research about individual companies or financial instruments. The overall composition of the fund mirrors decisions made at the micro level. It is the opposite of passive management in which a fund aims to match the performance of a market or index, and its constituents mirror the composition of that market or index.

Activity Indicators Indicators that show where an economy is in the business cycle. Activity indicators include industrial production, capacity utilization and volume of retail sales.
> ▶ *See also* Business Cycle and Economic Indicators.

Actuals Also called physicals. Refers to the physical commodities available for shipment, storage and manufacture. Actuals available for delivery are traded for cash on a spot or forward basis.

Actuary A specialist in statistics and the mathematics of risk, often focused on insurance risks and premiums.

ADB Asian Development Bank. A multilateral development finance institution, with headquarters in Manila, dedicated to reducing poverty in Asia and the Pacific. Owned by member countries, mostly from the region. ▧ **www.adb.org** ▧

ADR American Depositary Receipt. The form in which shares of foreign companies are usually traded on US stock markets. An ADR is issued by a US bank and represents a bundle of shares of a foreign corporation held in custody overseas. Trading in ADRs rather than the underlying shares reduces administration and trading costs, both for companies and for investors.

AE Greek company title: abbreviation of Anonymi Eteria.

AFDB African Development Bank. A development finance organization based in Abidjan, Ivory Coast. Its aim is to reduce poverty and promote social development among its regional members.
▧ **www.afdb.org** ▧

Affiliate Two companies are affiliated when one owns less than a majority of the voting stock of the other or if both are subsidiaries of a third company.
> ▶ *See also* Associate, Subsidiary.

African Development Bank *See* AFDB.

After-hours Dealing Dealing taking place after the official close of business on the trading floor of an investment exchange.

AG German company title: abbreviation of Aktiengesellschaft, a joint-stock company.

Against Actuals ▶ *See* Exchange for Physical.

Agent Bank Bank appointed by members of an international lending syndicate to protect lenders' interests during the life of a loan.
> ▶ *See also* Syndicate.

Aggregate Demand Total demand for goods and services in an economy. Everything that is consumed by households or governments, exported, or used as an investment good to produce other products.
It comprises:

- consumption by households
- investment spending by companies and households
- local and central government spending on goods and services
- demand for exports from overseas consumers and companies.

Aggregate Risk Total exposure of a bank to any single customer for both spot and forward contracts.

Aggregate Supply Total supply of goods and services in the economy available to meet aggregate demand. The supply consists of domestically produced goods and imports.

AGM Annual General Meeting. Called some time after the financial year-end, inviting shareholders to vote acceptance of the company's annual report, balance sheet and final dividend. Companies often use the meeting to tell shareholders about corporate business prospects in the early months of the new financial year.
▶ *See also* Annual Report, Balance Sheet.

AIM Alternative Investment Market. A UK market for smaller or high-risk companies that do not qualify for a full listing on the London Stock Exchange. ■ **www.londonstockexchange.com** ■

AIMR An international non-profit organization of more than 50,000 investment practitioners and educators in more than 100 countries, which aims to promote professional excellence and integrity.
■ **www.aimr.com** ■

Alexander's Filter A technical analysis tool that measures the rate of rise or fall in prices in terms of a percentage price rise or fall over a set period. Buy signals are interpreted by a sufficiently fast rate of increase while sell signals are indicated by a fast rate of decrease.
▶ *See also* Technical Analysis.

All Ordinaries The All Ordinaries Share Price Index or 'All Ords' is the benchmark index for the Australian stock market. It is a capitalization-weighted index consisting of over 300 stocks. ■ **www.asx.com** ■
▶ *See also* Capitalization-weighted Index.

Alpha In the context of stock returns, alpha measures the risk-adjusted performance of a security or fund. It is the return on a security in excess of what would be predicted by a risk/return model.
▶ *See also* CAPM.

Alternative Investment Market ▶ *See* AIM

American Depositary Receipt ▶ *See* ADR.

American Option An option which can be exercised at any time during the life of the contract, up to and including the expiry date, in contrast to European options which can be exercised only on the expiry date. A variation, called the 'semi-American', is where options can be exercised on only a set number of dates before expiry.

American Petroleum Institute ▶ *See* API.

AMEX American Stock Exchange. ■ **www.amex.com** ■

Amortization The reduction of principal or debt at regular intervals. This can be achieved via a purchase or sinking fund. The term is also used to describe the depreciation of fixed assets; the opposite of accretion. ▶ *See also* Depreciation.

AN Norwegian company title: abbreviation of Ansvarlig Firma.

Analyst Generic term used to describe someone who analyses company data, economic data or price charts, in order to make trading recommendations.

Annual General Meeting ▶ *See* AGM.

Annual Rate The comparison of the average level of a given rate, e.g. inflation, in the current year with the average in the previous year. The benefit of this measure is that it smoothes out unusually large or small changes that may have occurred for short periods during the year.

Annualized Rate An annualized rate plots the change in an indicator over the whole year if the latest monthly or quarterly figure is presumed to persist for the rest of the year. It is calculated by multiplying one month's change by 12 to produce the annualized rate, or one quarter's rate by four.

Annual Report A status report on the current condition of a company. Issued once a year for shareholders to examine before the annual general meeting.

Annuity An investment that pays a given stream of income for a fixed period of time. Some annuities pay that income during the lifetime of the holder.

Anti-trust Laws US federal legislation to prevent business monopolies and restraint of free trade.

APCIMS   Association of Private Client Investment Managers and Stockbrokers. A UK trade association. ■ **www.apcims.co.uk** ■

APEC   Asia-Pacific Economic Co-operation. Organization aimed at promoting regional trade and economic co-operation. ■ **www.apecsec.org.sg** ■

API   American Petroleum Institute. US oil industry institution which provides key weekly data on US petroleum consumption and stock levels. ■ **http://.api-ep.api.org** ■

API Gravity   Universally accepted scale, adopted by the API, to express the specific gravity of oils. It serves as a rough measure of quality. The higher the API gravity number, the richer the yield in premium refined products.
   ▶ *See also* API.

ARA   Amsterdam/Rotterdam/Antwerp area. An oil cargo offered with cost and freight ARA means that ports within this area can be considered for delivery.
   ▶ *See also* C and F.

Arbitrage   The action of profiting from the correction of price or yield anomalies in markets. Often this will involve taking a position in one market or instrument and an offsetting position in another. As prices or yields move back into line, all positions may be profitably closed out. An arbitrageur is an individual or institution practising arbitrage.

Arithmetic Average   Simple average, equal to the sum of all values divided by the total number of values.

Around Par   Foreign exchange term used in the forward market when the points are quoted either side of par, i.e. one side of the quotation being at a discount, the other side at a premium.

ARPU   Average Revenue Per User. A measure used by telephone and media companies. A high ARPU spreads fixed costs and increases profit margins.
   ▶ *See also* Fixed Costs.

AS   Czech or Slovak company title: abbreviation of Akciova spolecnost.

A/S   Danish company title: abbreviation of Aktieselskabet.

ASA   Norwegian company title: abbreviation of Aksjeselaskap.

ASEAN   Association of South East Asian Nations, which aims to enhance economic progress and increase stability in the region. Members are Brunei, Indonesia, Laos, Malaysia, Myanmar, the Philippines, Singapore, Thailand and Vietnam. ■ **www.aseansec.org** ■

Asia-Pacific Economic Co-operation ▶ *See* APEC.

Asian Development Bank ▶ *See* ADB.

Asian Option ▶ *See* Average Price/Rate Option.

Ask A market maker's price to sell a security, currency or any financial instrument. Also known as an offer. A two-way price comprises the bid and ask. The difference between the two quotations is the spread.
▶ *See also* Bid.

Asset Allocation The process of distributing investment funds among different kinds of assets, such as stocks, bonds and cash, to achieve the highest expected returns for the lowest possible risk.

Asset-backed Securities ▶ *See* ABS.

Asset Management Also known as liability management, this is the function of controlling assets and liabilities to achieve the optimum return and reduce risk.

Assets Assets are tangible items of value to a business such as factories, machinery and financial instruments, and intangible items such as goodwill, the title of a newspaper or a product's brand name. They appear on the company's balance sheet.

Asset Stripping Seeking a profit by buying a company, often when the market price is below the value of the assets, and then selling off all or some of the assets.

Asset Turnover ▶ *See* Capital Turnover.

Assign To transfer ownership to another party. It usually involves signing a document. In derivatives markets assignment refers to the act of exercising an option.
▶ *See also* Exercise, Option.

Associate Formed when two or more companies engage in partnership or joint venture projects.

Association Cambiste Internationale ▶ *See* ACI.

Association of South East Asian Nations ▶ *See* ASEAN.

At Best A buy or sell order indicating it should be carried out at the best possible price available at that moment.

ATM Automated Teller Machine, or cash machine. An automated dispenser of cash and banking services.

At Par When a security is selling at a price that is equal to face value.

At the Money An option is described as being at the money when the exercise price is approximately the same as the underlying price. 'At the money' options may also be either in or out of the money. The term is used to describe the exercise price nearest to the actual trading price of the underlying financial instrument on which the option is based.
▶ *See also* In the Money, Option, Out of the Money.

Attributable Profit Total earnings of a company less expenses, attributable to the shareholders.

Auction A public sale of a security whereby the issuer invites authorized dealers to make bids in price or yield until the full amount of the issue is sold.
▶ *See also* Dutch Auction, Non-competitive Bid Auction.

Audit An official examination of a company's accounts.

Auditors Accountants who carry out the official examination of a company's accounts.

Authorized Capital The maximum number of shares that can be issued under a firm's articles of incorporation. This can be increased only with shareholders' approval.

Average Price/Rate Option An option whose settlement value is based on the difference between the strike price of the option and the average of the spot rates of the underlying instrument on which the option is based, over the life of the option. The averaging can be agreed to be taken at any point in the life of the option and readings can be at any specified interval and frequency. Also known as an Asian option.
▶ *See also* Option, Strike Price.

BA   Norwegian company title: abbreviation of Bergenset Ansvar.

BA   Bankers' Acceptances. Sometimes known as time drafts, these are bearer-form short-term non-interest-bearing notes sold at a discount, redeemed by accepting banks for full face value at maturity.
▶ *See also* Bill of Exchange.

Backlog   Orders for goods or services that have not yet been fulfilled. They can be measured in cash terms, or by the number of days of normal production it would take to clear them. The level of backlogs is an important indicator of whether an economy is growing or not. Falling backlogs may be a sign that new orders are dropping and the old ones are being fulfilled, and that producers are less willing to hold large stocks or inventories.

Back Month   The futures or options contract being traded that is furthest into the future and is thus furthest from expiry.
▶ *See also* Futures, Option.

Back Office   The department in a financial institution that processes deals and handles delivery, settlement and regulatory procedures.
▶ *See also* Front Office and Middle Office.

Back-to-back Loans   Arrangement whereby a loan in one currency is set against a loan in another currency. It can be used to avoid or overcome exchange risks and exchange controls. Also known as parallel loans.

Back-up Facility   Typically, a bank line of credit used to provide back-up liquidity should an issuer be unable to bankroll the outstanding commercial paper.

Backing and Filling   Numerous small rises and falls in a market, usually speculative but showing no major overall change in price levels.

Backpricing   Price-setting method in the metal market, whereby a consumer with a long-term contract has the option of fixing the price for a proportion of his contract on the valid LME settlement price.
▶ *See also* LME.

Backwardation In commodity markets, backwardation is a situation where the cash or near delivery price rises above the price for forward delivery. The forward price is usually higher than the cash price to reflect the added costs of storage and insurance for stocks deliverable at a later date. Shortage of supply is often to blame for backwardation, because demand for the spot or cash product rises sharply, but the futures price stays steady because more supplies are expected in the future. The opposite of backwardation is contango.
▶ *See also* Contango, Futures.

Bad Debt When a business recognizes that a debt is unlikely to be repaid, the debt is written off as an expense in the profit and loss account.

Balance of Payments A summary record of a country's net international economic transactions including trade, services, capital movements and unilateral transfers.

Balance of Trade Monetary record of a country's net imports and exports of physical merchandise. It can be negative, showing that a country is importing more than it exports, or positive, showing it exports more than it imports.

Balance Sheet An accounting statement of a company's assets and liabilities, provided for the benefit of shareholders and regulators. It gives a snapshot, at a specific point of time, of the assets that the company holds and how the assets have been financed.
▶ *See also* Assets, Liabilities.

Balanced Budget The situation in a government's budget where its expenditure matches revenue. Also known as a neutral budget.
▶ *See also* Budget.

Balloon Loan A loan that consists of regular monthly payments with one large (balloon) payment at maturity.

Banc Assurance A combination of banking and insurance products offered in continental Europe.

Bank Bill A bill of exchange issued or accepted by a bank. It is thus more acceptable than a normal trade bill of exchange because the risk is less and the discount is accordingly also smaller.
▶ *See also* Bill of Exchange.

Bank of England The UK's central bank. ■ **www.bankofengland.co.uk** ■

Bank for International Settlements ▶ *See* BIS.

Bank Negara Malaysia Malaysia's central bank. ■ **www.bnm.gov.my** ■

Bank Return Weekly or monthly statement issued by a central bank summarizing its financial position.

Bankruptcy A court proceeding in which the assets of an insolvent company or individual are liquidated.
 ▶ *See also* Insolvency, Solvency.

Bar Chart A type of chart, widely used by technical analysts and traders, that represents price information on a vertical bar. The top of the bar is the highest price and the bottom of the bar the lowest. A dash on the left-hand side of the bar denotes the opening price and a dash on the right-hand side the closing price. (Figure 1.)
 ▶ *See also* Technical Analysis.

Barrels Volume measurement of liquid in the petroleum industry, equal to 42 US gallons or 35 imperial gallons or about 0.136 tonnes, depending on specific gravity.

Barrels per Day Recognized worldwide as bpd. It is a measure of the flow of crude oil production from a field or producing company or a country.

Barrier Option An option, which is activated or deactivated once the price of the underlying financial instrument reaches a set level, known as the barrier. It can be categorized into either trigger or knockout options.
 ▶ *See also* Options.

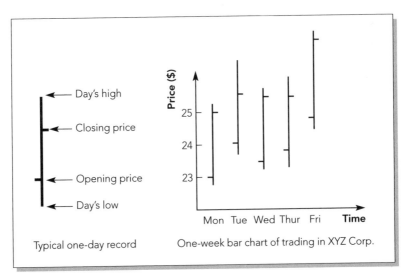

FIGURE 1 Bar chart

Barter The exchange of goods or services where no money is paid. Also known as counter trade.

Base Currency The currency that forms the base of a quotation, i.e. the denominator expressed as a unit of one (or sometimes a hundred). For example, the base currency in a US dollar/euro quotation is the dollar, whereas the base currency in the dollar/sterling quote is the pound.

Basel Committee A committee of the Bank for International Settlements that formulates broad supervisory standards for best banking practice and supervision, including setting the minimum capital standards for banks.
▶ *See also* BIS.

Basel Rules or Basel Accord Guidelines set by the Basel Committee of the BIS on the amount of capital that banks need to cover risks of default on their loan portfolio, or other problems with their operations. The riskier the loan portfolio the higher the capital requirements.
▶ *See also* BIS, Basel Committee.

Base Metals Major industrial non-ferrous metals other than precious metals and minor metals; notably copper, lead, tin, zinc, aluminium, nickel.
▶ *See also* Minor Metals, Precious Metals.

Base Year/Base Date The year chosen to set an index at 100. Any year can be chosen as a base year, but it is generally desirable to use a fairly recent year; widely used in the compilation of macro-economic data.

Basis The difference between a futures prices and the corresponding under-lying cash price. Basis is normally quoted as cash price deducted from futures price of the nearest delivery month. There is a high degree of correlation between cash and futures prices but the basis is not con-stant. A basis trade exploits the expected movements in basis. Basis is likely to reduce and eventually to shrink to nothing as the futures contract approaches its expiry date. (Figure 2.)
▶ *See also* Backwardation and Contango.

Basis Point One hundredth of a percentage point, or 0.01, the standard market measure for interest rates and bond yields.

Basis Risk The risk that the price of a future will vary from the price of the underlying cash instrument as expiry approaches.
▶ *See also* Convergence.

Basis Trading ▶ *See* Cash and Carry Trade.

Bear A market player who believes prices will fall. Bears will sell a financial instrument which they do not own and then make a profit by repur-chasing it at a lower price.
▶ *See also* Bull.

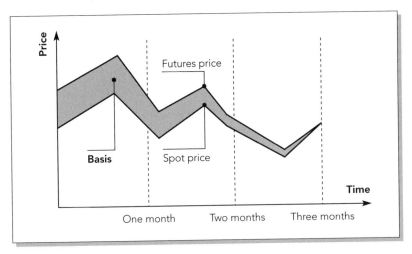

FIGURE 2 Basis

Bearer Shares/Bearer Bonds Securities which confer ownership with a simple certificate, with no central register of owners. The dividends or interest payments are claimed from a paying agent, by presenting coupons clipped from the ownership certificate. Bearer bonds are as portable and almost as anonymous as cash, making them highly desirable to thieves.

Bearish Holding a belief that prices will fall. A bearish sentiment in the market will therefore push prices lower. The opposite of bullish.
▶ *See also* Bullish.

Bear Market A market in which prices have been falling for a prolonged period. Opposite of a bull market.
▶ *See also* Bull Market.

Bear Raid An attempt to push down the price of a security, usually by short selling.
▶ *See also* Short.

Bear Trap A false signal that a rising trend will end and that the market will resume previous falls. Short sellers are trapped by rising prices and have to cover their positions by buying stock at higher prices.

Bed and Breakfast Deal The sale of a share and its repurchase shortly after the beginning of a new tax year. This allows shareholders to register a capital loss or profit for tax purposes while retaining ownership of the shares.

Beige Book A survey of the outlook for the US economy published eight times a year by the Federal Reserve Board. Also known as the Tan Book. ■ **www.federalreserve.gov/FOMC/BeigeBook/2002** ■

Bells and Whistles Additional features of a security designed to attract investors and/or reduce issuer costs.

Bellwether An instrument or indicator that is generally seen to be an indicator of the overall market, economy or sector's performance. From the lead sheep of a flock, which is belled.

Below the Line A term used to describe when an exceptional item is recorded separately in a company's profit and loss account.
   ▶ *See also* Extraordinary Item.

Benchmark A standard used for comparison. A benchmark security is usually the most recently issued security in good size. It sets the standard for the rest of the market. A benchmark issue is highly liquid.

Beta Beta records how volatile and risky investing in an individual stock is compared with the risk of the equity market as a whole. Beta measures how much the individual stock's excess return (the amount it earns in dividends and capital gains compared with a short-term money market rate) varies in comparison with movement in the excess return of the market as a whole (usually represented by the market's benchmark index). Beta compares excess return with short-term government paper because the latter investment is regarded as risk free. If the market's excess return rises by one percent and the stock's excess return rises during the same period by the same one percent then the stock's beta is one. The higher the beta the riskier the stock, reflected in its greater required return. A stock with a beta of more than one tends to be riskier than the market. A stock with a beta of less than one is less risky. High beta stocks tend to be in cyclical sectors such as property and consumer durables. Low beta stocks, also known as defensive stocks, tend to be in non-cyclical sectors such as food retailing and public utilities. Betas for individual stocks can vary according to whether the overall market direction is upwards or downwards. A stock may be riskier in a falling market than a rising market.

Bhd Malaysian company title: abbreviation of Berhad.

Bid A market maker's price to buy a security or instrument.

Bid–Ask Quote A two-way price comprises a bid, or the price at which a dealer is willing to buy, and an ask (or offer) at which a dealer is willing to sell. The bid, by definition, is always below the ask and is always the first quoted price. The difference between the two quotes is known as the spread. A spread between the best bid and best offer is called 'the touch'.
▶ *See also* Ask, Bid.

Bid Market A market in which there is more interest from buyers than sellers. Opposite of offer market.
▶ *See also* Offer Market.

Big Board Colloquial name for the New York Stock Exchange.
▶ *See also* NYSE.

Big Figure The stem of a rate. The big figure of 2-7/8 or 2.4253 is two. When quoting a price, dealers may only refer to the points (in foreign exchange) or to fractions (in money markets) and omit mention of the big figure. In the US, the big figure is known as the handle.
▶ *See also* Handle.

Big Mac Index A light-hearted index devised by *The Economist* magazine which compares the price of McDonald's Big Mac burgers, a fast food staple available around the world, as a guide to whether currencies are overvalued or undervalued. It's based on the assumption that similar goods should cost the same wherever they are purchased. If the prices are different there is an anomaly in the valuation of the local currency. For example, if a Big Mac costs $1 in Washington and 20 pesos in Ruritania then the dollar/peso exchange rate should be 20 pesos to the dollar. If it's out of line then the peso is either overvalued or undervalued on the basis of purchasing-power parity, which says exchange rates should move towards a level which equalizes the price of an identical basket of goods. Critics say the Big Mac index ignores the effects of taxes, profit margins and the price of raw materials in different countries.

Bill A short-term debt instrument with a maturity usually no longer than two years, although terminology varies from country to country. Bill is often a shorthand reference to Treasury bills, which are short-term government debt. Medium-term debt instruments are notes and longer-term instruments are bonds. In some markets a note has a maturity of two to five years and a bond has a maturity longer than five years, but usage varies.

Bill of Exchange Old financial instrument used to finance international trade. A bill of exchange is an order to pay a specified amount of money to the holder of the bill either at a set future date (a time draft) or on presentation of the bill (a sight draft). Also known as eligible bills, commercial bills, trade bills and BAs.

Binary Option An option that pays out a fixed amount if the underlying financial instrument which the option is based reaches the strike level either at expiry, or at any time during the life of the option. Also called all-or-nothing option, digital option or one-touch option.
▶ *See also* Option, Strike Price.

Binomial Model An option pricing formula suggested by Cox, Ross, Rubinstein and Sharpe and used primarily to calculate the value of American-style options.
▶ *See also* American Option, Option.

BIS Bank for International Settlements. An international organization that fosters international monetary and financial co-operation and serves as a bank for central banks and international financial organizations. It accepts deposits from central banks and also makes short-term loans to them. The BIS is concerned with safeguarding the stability of international financial markets and ensuring that all banks have sufficient capital to support their operating needs. It acts as a forum for regular meetings of the central bank governors of the G10 group of major industrialized countries. The Basel Committee of the BIS sets standards and guidelines for best banking practice. ■ **www.bis.org** ■
▶ *See also* Central Bank, G10, Basel Committee.
■ **www.bis.org/cbanks.htm** ■ (lists central bank websites)

Black & Scholes Model A widely used option pricing formula for European style options, which have a fixed expiry time, created by Fischer Black and Myron Scholes in 1973. It allows assessment of the value of a call option at any particular time up to expiry.
▶ *See also* Option.

Black Market Economy Transactions not officially recorded due to tax evasion.

Block Trading Large transactions usually performed by institutional buyers or sellers.

Blue Chip Stock A generic term for the stocks of major companies with sound earnings and dividend records and above-average share performance. Blue chip stocks are also known as income stock. Named after high-value poker chips, which were traditionally blue.
▶ *See also* Stock.

Blue Sky Laws State laws in the United States aimed at protecting the public against securities frauds. They require new issue offerings to be registered and full financial details provided. The phrase is thought to derive from a reference by a Supreme Court judge that some investment schemes had about as much value as a patch of blue sky.

BOE Bank of England. The UK's central bank.
 ▪ **www.bankofengland.co.uk** ▪
 ▶ *See also* Central Bank.

Bollinger Bands Used in technical analysis. Bollinger bands are lines plotted one standard deviation above and below the moving average of the closing prices. A standard deviation measures price volatility so these bands narrow and widen in line with volatility – narrow in calm markets and wide in volatile markets. The narrowing of the bands often indicates the start of a new trend, which is confirmed when prices break and close out of the band. Bollinger bands may be used with any price chart but are most commonly used with bar charts. (Figure 3.)
 ▶ *See also* Bar Chart , Technical Analysis, Standard Deviation.

Bolsa A Spanish and Portuguese term for stock exchange.
 ▶ *See also* Stock Exchange.

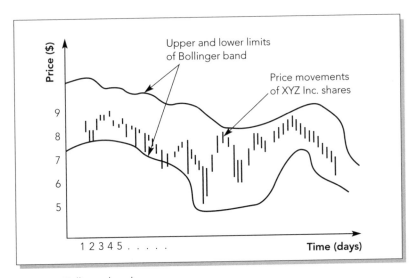

FIGURE 3 Bollinger bands

Bond A bond is a legal contract in which a government, company or institution (the borrower) issues an IOU certificate, which promises to pay holders a specific rate of interest for a fixed duration and then redeem the contract at face value on maturity. In theory bonds are safer than equities because they have a fixed maturity and are repaid before any payments are made to shareholders. But if a company fails, its bond holders suffer just as much as its shareholders.
▶ *See also* Convertible Bond, Bearer Shares/Bearer Bonds, Bullet Bond, Fixed Income, Senior Secured Debt.

Bond Equivalent Yield A calculation that converts the yield of a money market instrument, such as a Treasury bill, into the equivalent yield of a Treasury bond in order to compare efficiency. Yields on Treasury bills are expressed as a discount from face value and their maturity is often less than a year, so a calculation is needed to convert their yield into the equivalent annual yield of a bond.
▶ *See also* Money Market.

Bond Indenture The complete contract specifying all the terms and conditions of a bond issue.

Bond Washing When a bond-holder sells a security-cum-interest and buys it back after the coupon is paid so as to convert the interest income into a capital gain. This is worthwhile only where lower tax rates apply to capital gains.
▶ *See also* Bond, Coupon.

Bonus Issue When a company transfers money from its reserves to its permanent capital it makes a free issue of shares to shareholders. These new shares are then distributed to the existing holders in proportion to their existing holdings. Also known as capitalization issue, a free issue and a scrip issue.

Book A trader's record of purchases and sales in one or more financial instruments. Talking a book also means a trader commenting favourably or unfavourably on a financial instrument depending on whether he is long or short in that instrument. The 'books' is also a colloquial term referring to the overall accounting records of a business.
▶ *See also* Matched Book, Unmatched Book.

Book Building An exercise by an investment bank, which is lead-managing a new issue to ascertain the likely levels of demand for a security at different prices. It is designed to prevent an issue being undersubscribed because of a large discrepancy between the issue price and the price at which the security starts trading on the secondary market.

Book Entry Securities registered by the issuer. This usually occurs in computerized form with no physical issues, thereby reducing paperwork, expenses and simplifying transfer of ownership.

Book Price The value at which assets were originally entered in the books of a company's balance sheet.

Book Runner The investment firm responsible for looking after the administration of a new bond issue. The book runner is responsible for tasks such as inviting others to subscribe and allocating bonds to subscribers.

Book Value The value at which fixed assets are listed in the balance sheet. Effectively the original purchase cost minus any allowance for depreciation.

Book Value per Share ▶ *See* BVPS.

Borrowing Requirement The net amount of money needed by a government to finance budget deficits and maturing debt.

BOT Buoni Ordinari del Tesoro. Italian Treasury bills with maturities of three, six and 12 months, issued at a discount.

Bottom Fishing When an investor buys a company's shares at a time when he believes they are unlikely to fall much further. Also, when a company buys up loss-making competitors or purchases their assets.

Bottom Line The final cost or result of a project or action. The term derives from companies' profit and loss accounts in which the bottom line shows the extent of the profit or loss after all income and expenses have been accounted for. In contrast with the top line, which shows net sales or total revenues of a company.

Bottomry Authority given to a banker to dispose of goods pledged as security against a loan. For example, the pledging of a ship as collateral against emergency loans needed for repairs, with a commitment to repay the loan on safe completion of the voyage. If the ship's owner fails to repay the loans the bank can exercise bottomry and dispose of the ship.

Bottom Up An investment strategy that relies on stock picking, rather than trying to achieve a balanced weighting in various sectors. If a fund uses a bottom-up approach, it will focus on the performance and management of individual companies rather than general economic or market trends. The opposite of top down.

▶ *See also* Top Down.

Bought Deal Commitment from an underwriter or lead manager to purchase the whole issue of a security for resale to the secondary market. This method transfers the risk of being unable to sell a whole issue at the offering price from the issuer to the underwriter.

Bourse French term for stock exchange.
> ▶ *See also* Stock Exchange.

Brady Bonds These bonds originated as syndicated bank credits to developing countries, denominated in the major European currencies. During the economic recession of the early 1980s many developing countries ran out of foreign currency to meet their payments on these loans. To restore confidence in the borrowers, much of this debt was converted into negotiable bonds backed by the US Treasury, under a scheme introduced in 1989 by the then US Treasury Secretary Nicholas Brady. ■ **www.emgmkts.com/research.bradydef.htm** ■

Break-even Point The level at which an existing position in a market will produce neither a loss nor a gain. In company reporting terms the break-even point is where total sales exactly match total fixed and variable costs, so profit is zero. It can also be used for the point where total turnover exactly matches fixed costs.
> ▶ *See also* Fixed Costs.

Breakout A term used in technical analysis to describe when a price climbs above a resistance level (usually its previous high) or falls below a support level (usually its previous low). Breakouts usually occur when a trend line or formation is broken.
> ▶ *See also* Technical Analysis.

Brent Brent blend is a benchmark crude oil from the UK North Sea against which other crude oils are priced. It is widely used as an indicator of the price of oil beyond energy markets. It is traded on forward markets and is the basis of futures and options contracts listed on the International Petroleum Exchange in London.
> ■ **www.eia.doe.gov/emeu/cabs/northsea.html** ■
> ▶ *See also* Dated Brent, IPE, WTI.

Bretton Woods An agreement signed in 1944 at Bretton Woods, New Hampshire, USA, to effect a post-war international monetary system. This was the origin of the International Monetary Fund (IMF) and the World Bank. The system was based on fixed exchange rates combined with temporary financing facilities to overcome crises. In 1971 the dollar ceased to be convertible into gold and the Bretton Woods system exchange rate system was superseded by floating currencies.
> ▶ *See also* IMF and World Bank.

Bridging Bridging, or a bridging loan, is short-term financing made available pending arrangement of intermediate or long-term financing.

Broadening A term used in technical analysis. A price formation with the appearance of a horizontal triangle, with the apex on the left and the base at the right. The trend lines are widening so the base gets wider. Peaks and troughs get successively higher and lower, showing a market that has lost its way. (Figure 4.)
▶ *See also* Technical Analysis.

Broken Date Any trading date falling outside the standard periods traded in the forward markets. Also known as odd date.
▶ *See also* Forwards.

Broker Brokers act as agents for buyers and sellers, for which they charge a commission, or brokerage. There are two main categories of brokers: inter-dealer brokers who only work with specialist market makers, and client or agency brokers who deal on behalf of institutional or retail clients.

Brokerage The commission or fee charged by a broker. In the US, this term is commonly used to refer to a brokerage firm.

B/S Buy after sell limit order. Two orders treated as one, the first order being to sell. If done, the buy order becomes valid.
▶ *See also* S/B (Sell after Buy) which is the reverse limit order.

Bt Hungarian company title: abbreviation of Beteti tarsasag.

BTAN Bons à Taux Annuel Normalisés. French coupon-bearing, fixed-rate Treasury bills with two- and five-year maturities.

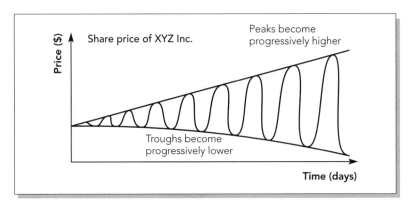

FIGURE 4 Broadening

B2B Business to Business trading of goods and services on the internet.

BTF Bons à Taux Fixe et Intérêts Précomptés. French discount Treasury bills with maturities of 13, 26 and 52 weeks. Occasionally, four- and seven-week BTFs are issued outside the calendar and are similar to the US cash-management bills.

BTP Buoni del Tesoro Poliennali. Italian fixed-rate Treasury bonds with maturities of between three and 30 years.

Buba ▶ *See* Bundesbank.

Bubble A ramping up of asset prices to such a degree that a major reversal or crash is expected.

Bucket Shop A fraudulent brokerage selling overpriced shares with little underlying value. They usually operate by telephone sales, often from another country. Also known as a boiler room, a reference to the cheap premises from which such brokerages work. A bucket shop can also be a brokerage that accepts commissions to trade shares at a certain price, then carries out the order at a different price to its advantage, pocketing the difference.

Budget An itemized forecast of the incomes and expenditure of a government or company for a given future period.

Budget Deficit The amount by which spending exceeds revenues. It usually refers to government spending and revenues.
▶ *See also* Budget.

Budget Surplus The amount by which revenues exceed spending. It usually refers to government spending and revenues.
▶ *See also* Budget.

Buffer Stock Stock of commodities held by an international organization that will aim to stabilize prices and supplies by buying and selling from its stockpile.

Building Society A British financial institution which pools deposits from savers to provide mortgage financing for house purchases.

Bulge Bracket The group of underwriters who have sold most of a new securities issue. They usually come first on a tombstone advertisement.
▶ *See also* Tombstone.

Bull A market player who is confident that share prices will rise and buys a financial instrument with a view to selling it at a higher price. The opposite of a bear.
▶ *See also* Bear.

Bulldog Bond A bond denominated in sterling, issued in the UK by a foreign borrower.
  ▶ *See also* Bond.

Bullet Bond A bond which pays a fixed rate of interest and is redeemed in full on maturity. It is also known as a straight or fixed bond because it has no special features. The name derives from the printers' symbol of a 'bullet point' or large dot, used to identify the bonds in price lists.
  ▶ *See also* Bond, Maturity, Vanilla Bond.

Bullet Redemption ▶ *See* Bullet Bond.

Bullion Precious metal in non-coin form such as ingots, bars or wafers.

Bullish Holding a belief that prices will rise. A bullish sentiment in the market will therefore push prices higher. The opposite of bearish.
  ▶ *See also* Bearish.

Bull Market A market in which prices have been rising for a prolonged period, fuelled by the prevalent view that share prices will continue to rise and that higher prices are justified. The opposite of bear market.
  ▶ *See also* Bear Market.

Bundesbank The Bundesbank, or Buba as it is sometimes known, is the Frankfurt-based German central bank.
  ▪ **www.bundesbank.de** ▪
  ▶ *See also* Central Bank.

Bundesobligationen (BOBL) German federal government notes with maturities between two and six years, also known as Kassen. Effectively replaced by Schätze in 1988.

Bunds German federal government bonds issued with maturities of up to 30 years.
  ▶ *See also* Bond.

Bunny Bond ▶ *See* Multiplier Bond.

Burn Rate ▶ *See* Cash Burn.

Bushel A measure of volume. In the UK, it equals 8 imperial gallons or 36.4 litres for corn, fruit, liquids, etc. In the US it equals 35.3 litres. The weight of a bushel varies according to the commodity involved.

Business Cycle Regular fluctuations in overall economic activity over time. The cycle has four distinct elements: recession, recovery, peak and slowdown. Business cycles tend to be anywhere from five to 10 years peak to peak.

Business Risk The risk that a company may not produce the sales and earning growth as forecast.

Busted Convertible A convertible issue of little value because the underlying stock has fallen below the conversion price.
▶ *See* Convertible Bond, Convertible Shares.

Butterfly Spread An option strategy involving the simultaneous sale of an At The Money Straddle and purchase of an Out Of The Money Strangle. Potential gains will be seen if the underlying financial instrument on which the option is based remains stable while the risk is limited should the underlying move dramatically.
▶ *See also* At the Money, Option, Out of the Money, Straddle, Strangle.

Buy Back The purchase by a company of its own shares in the open market, usually based on the belief that the shares are undervalued and that buying them will provide a better investment return than putting cash into the underlying business of the company. In theory the buy-back will reduce the number of shares in the market and increase the value of the remaining ones. Also known as a share repurchase. It effectively returns to the shareholders the cash held in company reserves which already belongs to them.

Buy-side Used to describe financial institutions whose primary business is to make investments either for themselves or on behalf of other investors. The opposite of sell-side, the financial institutions whose primary business is trading.

BV Dutch company title: abbreviation of Besloten Vennootschap.

BVBA Belgian company title: abbreviation of Besloten Vennootschap met Beperkte aansprakelijkheid.

BVPS

Book Value Per Share. Book value equals total assets minus total liabilities. Book value per share (BVPS) equals book value divided by the number of shares outstanding. It is the same as shareholders' equity.

BVPS is used in the calculation of the price/book ratio (share price divided by BVPS). Price/book is the ultimate measure of how much investors think a company's assets are worth. A price/book ratio should be higher than one; otherwise the market is pricing

▶

the assets below their replacement value. Companies with price/book ratios well below one automatically become takeover targets, as sector rivals will consider launching a bid for their stock rather than investing in new plant and equipment. Price/book is especially relevant for capital-intensive manufacturing firms. Service industry companies with few fixed assets typically trade at high price/book ratios.

Formula for BVPS: (Assets – Liabilities)/Number of shares outstanding.

Formula for price/book ratio: Share price/BVPS.

Example

The Old Rope Corporation has total assets of £1,407 million and total liabilities of £1,260 million. The difference, £147 million, is Old Rope's book value, which is also known as net asset value or shareholders' equity.

Book Value = 1,407 – 1,260 = 147 million

Book Value Per Share = 147 million/350 million shares outstanding = £0.42

Share price £1.50

Price/book ratio: 1.50/0.42 = 3.57

▶ See also Assets.

CAC-40 The principal French stock index covering 40 French equities, although the newer CAC-General, which covers 100 stocks, is more widely used. Both of these indices are capitalization-weighted averages. The CAC-40 is the basis for index futures and options traded on the MATIF and MONEP exchanges in Paris. ■ **www.bourse-de-paris.fr** ■
▶ *See also* Capitalization Weighted Index, MATIF, MONEP.

Cache A cache is a software function that allows frequently accessed data or pages to be stored on a user's PC to save time connecting to a network.

CAGR Compound Annual Growth Rate. Year-over-year growth rate of an investment over a certain period of time.

Calendar Spread ▶ *See* Horizontal Spread.

Call An option that gives the holder the right to buy an underlying instrument at an agreed price within a specified time. The seller or writer has the obligation to sell the underlying instrument if the holder exercises the option.
▶ *See also* Option, Put.

Callable A callable bond gives the holder the right to early redemption at a given redemption price, on a given call date.
▶ *See also* Puttable.

Call Money Interest-bearing deposits repayable on demand. This covers both domestic money markets and Euromarket funds. Also known as day-to-day money or sight money.
▶ *See also* Money Markets.

Call Provision A clause in a bond's indenture, granting the issuer the right to buy back all or part of an issue prior to the maturity date.

C and F Cost and Freight. A term used to indicate when both the costs of the goods and freight charges are included in the price of a commodity.
▶ *See also* CIF.

Candlestick Chart A type of price chart widely used by technical analysts. Candlesticks capture the same price information as a bar chart: the open, high, low and close. A thick box (known as the body of the candle) joins the open and close values. Thin lines on either end of the body (known as shadows) join the high and low prices. If the open value is higher than the close value, the body of the candle is solid or coloured. Conversely, if the close is higher than the open then the body of the candle is clear, white or unshaded. (Figure 5.)

▶ *See also* Bar Chart, Technical Analysis.

CAP The Common Agricultural Policy. This European Union policy was designed to stabilize commodity markets within Europe and ensure regular supplies at reasonable prices while guaranteeing farmers' income. It is implemented through a complex mix of price support mechanisms and export restrictions.

▶ *See also* EU, Green Rates.

Cap A derivative that protects the holder from an increase in interest rates. Caps normally have a life of between two and five years and the option can be exercised at regular intervals during that time. Should the underlying interest rate be higher than the strike level for the set period, the holder can exercise the option and receive a cash settlement. The size of the settlement is determined by the difference between the strike level and the underlying interest rate.

▶ *See also* Derivatives, Floor, Strike.

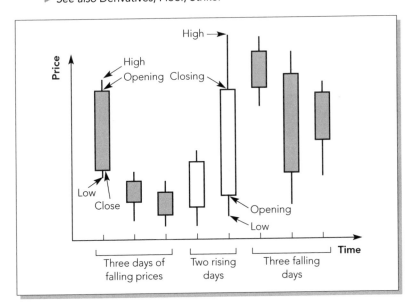

FIGURE 5 Candlestick chart

Capacity Utilization A macro-economic ratio that compares actual output to potential output, the maximum possible production in a given period of time, using existing plant and equipment.
▶ *See also* Macro-economics.

Capex ▶ *See* Capital Expenditure.

Capital Economists define capital as assets, other than labour and land, that are required for production. In financial markets capital refers to the financing instruments used principally to acquire capital goods – in particular it refers to debt instruments and equity.
▶ *See also* also Debt, Equity.

Capital Account An account in the balance of payments that records movements of capital between domestic and foreign residents. The capital account records changes in the asset and liability position of domestic residents. It covers flows such as loans and investments.
▶ *See also* Balance of Payments, Current Account.

Capital Adequacy A requirement for banks to have a minimum amount of capital to support their operations. In 1988, central banks from the G10 countries agreed to move towards one standard of capital adequacy. The BIS (Bank for International Settlements) rules determine how much and what type of capital commercial banks can raise in the financial markets and what type of loans they are allowed to make.
▶ *See also* Basel Rules, BIS, G10, Tier One.

Capital Allowances The amount of expenditure for capital equipment that can be set against tax.

Capital Asset Pricing Model ▶ *See* CAPM.

Capital Base The issued capital of a company, plus reserves and retained profits.

Capital Controls Government measures that restrict or bar the sending of capital outside a country. The threat of such controls can cause investors and fund managers to withdraw their funds, a reaction known as capital flight.

Capital Employed Capital used by a particular company in its business. It may refer to net assets but often includes bank loans and overdrafts.
▶ *See also* Capital.

Capital Expenditure Payment for the acquisition of a long-term asset. Often known simply as Capex.

Capital Flight The withdrawal of large amounts of money from a country. It may be caused by such things as political instability, currency depreciation, new regulations and taxation or fears of government restrictions on movement of capital.

Capital Gain Profit from selling or transferring assets at a higher price than their initial cost. Inflation and currency movements can affect the real capital gain.

Capital Goods/Equipment Fixed assets such as plant and machinery used to manufacture goods.
▶ *See also* Capital.

Capital Intensive A project or production process that uses a relatively large amount of capital.
▶ *See also* Capital.

Capital Investment Investment in capital equipment, such as buildings, plant or machinery. For example, the building of a chemical refinery would be capital intensive and require large capital investment.

Capitalization The total market value of a company's issued share capital. Calculated as the number of shares multiplied by the price of one share.
▶ *See also* Share, Stock.

Capitalization Issue An issue of shares – free to the shareholders – that results from a company transferring money from its reserves to its permanent capital. New shares are distributed to the existing holders in proportion to their holdings. Also known as a bonus or scrip issue.
▶ *See also* Scrip Issue, Share, Stock.

Capitalization-weighted Index A weighted average of the price of constituent stocks. Each stock is weighted according to its market capitalization relative to the total index.
▶ *See also* Stock Index, Market Capitalization.

Capital Loss Loss when the sale of an asset yields less than the acquisition cost.

Capital Markets ▶ *See* Capital.

Capital Ratios Ratios set by capital adequacy rules of the Bank for International Settlements. Commercial banks are required to set aside capital equal to eight percent of assets judged to be at risk. Some assets, such as loans to central banks, carry a zero percent risk weighting. At the other extreme, pure corporate loans are judged as being a 100 percent risk.
▶ *See also* BIS, Capital Adequacy.

Capital Reserve A part of shareholders' funds that comes from a revaluation of capital assets and not from the normal operations that are recorded in the profit and loss account.

Capital Risk The risk that a company's share price falls in value or becomes worthless, resulting in a loss of capital.
▶ *See also* Risk.

Capital Turnover A measure of how capital intensive a business is. It measures total sales (or turnover) divided by the capital employed in the business. The smaller the number the more capital is required for a given amount of sales. Also known as Asset Turnover.

Capitulation A sudden and final wave of selling at the bottom of a bear market, when all the bulls have given up hope of price rises.
▶ *See also* Bear, Bull.

CAPM Capital Asset Pricing Model. A model that tracks the relationship between risk and expected return. It stipulates that the return on a risky asset is equal to the risk-free rate plus a risk premium. The risk premium is the stock's beta multiplied by the difference between the market rate of return and the risk-free rate.
▶ *See also* Beta.

Capped Note A floating rate instrument with a cap that places a maximum coupon rate on the issue.
▶ *See also* Cap.

Captive Insurance Company An insurance company owned by the company or companies whose risks it insures. Using a captive company brings costs and tax advantages so they are often used when a company considers itself large enough to insure its own risks.

Carries A London Metal Exchange term for simultaneously matching purchases of one delivery with the sale of another. In other markets, these are termed straddles or switches.
▶ *See also* LME, Straddle, Switch.

Carrying Charge The cost of holding commodities, over and above the purchase price. It includes the cost of storage in warehouses and insurance against damage. When commodities are due to be delivered to fulfil the terms of a futures contract the carrying cost also includes charges for ensuring their quality, including sampling, weighing and repairing damage. Also used to describe a futures market where price differentials between delivery months fully reflect insurance, storage and interest costs.
▶ *See also* Futures.

Cartel A group of businesses, organizations or countries who agree to influence the price or supply of goods. Such a group has less power than a monopoly. In the US a cartel is sometimes called a trust.

Cash Collective term for ready money (coins and banknotes) at the bank and in hand, together with short-term deposits and other liquid assets.

Cash and Carry Trade An arbitrage position that typically comprises a long cash position together with a short position in its respective futures contract. The trader buys the cash (or physical) commodity, such as coffee, and at the same time sells a futures contract which promises to deliver the same amount of coffee at a future date. This will make him a profit as long as the cash price, plus the cost of storing and insuring the coffee (the cost of carry) until the futures contract falls due, is less than the money received for selling the futures contract. Arbitrageurs buy cash and 'carry' the commodity for delivery later against the future contract. Also known as basis trading or buying the basis.
▶ See also Arbitrage, Basis, Futures.

Cash Burn The rate at which a new company uses up its cash resources or venture capital when it has yet to produce a positive cash flow. The burn rate is usually expressed as the amount of capital used up per month.

Cash Commodity A physical commodity, such as bags of coffee or bushels of wheat, as distinct to a commodity derivative, such as a future or option, which is a paper contract derived from the physical commodity.
▶ See also Derivatives.

Cash Cow Something that generates a strong and steady flow of income, usually a product or a business.

Cash Crop A crop grown for sale is a cash crop, whereas a crop grown for food is a subsistence crop.

Cash Dividend A dividend paid in cash to a company's shareholders. Cash dividends are distributed from current earnings or accumulated profits.
▶ See also Dividend.

Cash Equivalent An asset that is so easily and quickly convertible to cash that holding it is equivalent to holding cash. A Treasury bill is considered cash equivalent. This term is also used to describe an alternative method of liquidating a position, whereby the seller provides the cash equivalent to the buyer rather than the security itself. Settling by cash equivalent is a much simpler process than providing the underlying bonds or shares. It is usually done when the counter party to a deal has no interest in owning the underlying securities but wishes to protect himself against interest rate or market moves.
▶ See also Cash.

Cash Flow Cash flow is the sum of pre-tax profits and depreciation allowances and is a key figure in a company's financial statement. The term is also used to describe the stream of funds received by a bond holder from the periodic receipt of interest payments.

Cash Flow Statement The cash flow, or flow of funds, statement shows how the operations of a company have been financed during the accounting period, and how the financial resources have been used.
▶ *See also* Cash Flow.

Cash Instruments ▶ *See* Cash Markets.

Cash Management Bills Treasury bills with maturities ranging from a few days to six months and issued on a discount basis. They are auctioned in the same way as Treasury bills, although not on a regular cycle, and can be announced as late as the auction day itself. Non-competitive bidding is not authorized for these bills.
▶ *See also* Treasury Bill.

Cash Markets A generic term used to describe markets in underlying financial instruments such as currencies, bonds and shares, as opposed to markets in derivative instruments such as futures, options and swaps. The term is also widely used in foreign exchange and debt markets to describe trading in debt instruments (bills, bonds, bankers acceptances etc.) with maturities of 12 months or so.
▶ *See also* FX.

Cash Ratios The proportion of cash and related assets to liabilities. A bank's cash ratio is that of cash to total deposits.
▶ *See also* Cash.

Cash Settlement Cash settlement is the most common method of settling financial futures. It involves closing out the position as opposed to physically delivering the underlying financial instrument or commodity. Also used to describe a transaction that settles the same day as the trade day.
▶ *See also* Futures, Closing a Position.

CBOE The Chicago Board Options Exchange is the world's largest marketplace for listed options, specializing in equity options.
■ **www.cboe.com** ■
▶ *See also* Option.

CBOT The Chicago Board of Trade is the world's oldest futures exchange and specializes in financial and agricultural futures. ■ **www.cbot.com** ■
▶ *See also* Futures.

CD Certificate of Deposit. A CD is a receipt for, and promise to repay, funds deposited at a bank or other financial institution. CDs have a fixed maturity and a specified interest rate. They are quoted on an interest-bearing face-value basis rather than at a discount, and interest is paid at maturity.
▶ *See also* Maturity, Money Market.

CDO Collateralized Debt Obligation. An asset-back security which uses a portfolio of bonds or loans as collateral, or security. A sponsor uses the portfolio to set up a special purpose investment vehicle which issues securities or CDOs, sometimes with a higher credit rating than any of the individual underlying assets. There may be reduced transparency in assessing the underlying risks.
▶ *See also* ABS (Asset-backed Securities).

Central Bank A central bank is the major regulatory bank in a nation or group of nations' monetary system. Its role normally includes control of the credit system, the issuing of notes and supervision of commercial banks. It also manages the exchange reserves and the value of the national currency, and acts as the government's banker, e.g. the Bank of England, the Federal Reserve and the European Central Bank.

CEO Chief Executive Officer. An executive title often held by the chairman of the board, the company president or another senior officer.

Cereals Commonly traded crops such as wheat, oats, barley, rye, rice, maize (corn), millet and sorghum.

Certificate of Deposit ▶ *See* CD.

Certificate of Indebtedness A United States Treasury debt obligation which has a maturity of one year or less, similar to a Treasury bill. The certificate has a fixed coupon with a set rate of interest, in contrast to the Treasury bill which pays interest by being sold at a discount from face value. The customer base for certificates includes banks, corporations and wealthy individuals.
▶ *See also* Coupon, Treasury Bill.

CFA Chartered Financial Analyst. A qualification awarded by the Association for Investment Management and Research which gives proof of competence and ethical standards.
▶ *See also* AIMR.

CFO Chief Financial Officer. An executive position, the CFO is responsible for handling a company's funds and financial planning.

CFTC Commodities Futures Trading Commission. The US government agency responsible for regulating domestic futures and options exchanges and their members. ■ **www.cftc.gov** ■
▶ *See also* Futures, Option.

Chaebol Generic name for diversified South Korean business conglomerates. Singular and plural, the word is the same.

Channel Lines Lines on a technical analysis chart connecting highs and lows that run parallel to each other. If either line is broken, it may indicate a substantial move in the direction of the breakout. (Figure 6.)
▶ *See also* Technical Analysis.

Chapter 7 Under US insolvency laws Chapter 7 deals with involuntary liquidation, where creditors petition to have a debtor judged insolvent by a court. It gives wide powers to a court-appointed interim trustee to operate the debtor business to prevent loss.
▶ *See also* Insolvency.

Chapter 11 An arrangement under US insolvency laws by which a debtor who is unable to pay his debts remains in possession of his business and in control of its operations unless a court rules otherwise. The arrangement allows debtors and creditors considerable flexibility in working together to reorganize the business.
▶ *See also* Insolvency.

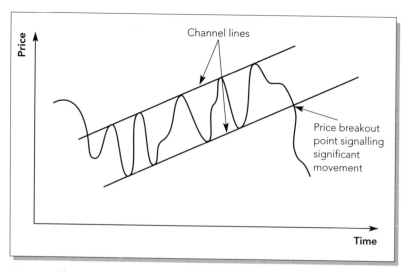

FIGURE 6 Channel lines

Charting Used in technical analysis, charting is a set of techniques used to plot volume, open interest, price movements, settlement prices and other indicators to anticipate share price movements.
   ▶ *See also* Technical Analysis.

Chartist An analyst who uses charts to plot historical trends of share prices. By following trendlines and recognizing patterns, chartists try to predict trends in markets.
   ▶ *See also* Technical Analysis.

Chart Points Price points or updates on a chart which are connected to form a continuous line.
   ▶ *See also* Technical Analysis.

Cheap Rich and Cheap refer to the pricing of a security in the primary market, relative to comparable existing securities in the secondary market. It is measured using standard deviation. A new issue is considered to be cheap if it is inexpensive compared to the rest of the market.
   ▶ *See also* Standard Deviation, Secondary Market.

Cheapest to Deliver ▶ *See* CTD.

Chinese Wall Rules designed to prevent price-sensitive information seeping between dealing, fund management and corporate finance operations within the same investment house. For example, it would not be considered appropriate, and in some countries it is illegal, for a corporate finance team to notify its own in-house share dealing department of an impending takeover bid.

Choice Price A firm price, where the dealer quotes one single price to a client regardless of whether that customer is buying or selling from the dealer. In effect the bid price (at which the dealer buys) and the offer price (at which he sells) are exactly the same, so there is no spread between the two. He is quoting at a zero spread. Also called either way.
   ▶ *See also* Ask, Bid and Spread.

Churning Excessive buying and selling on a customer's portfolio, allowing the broker who controls an account to earn extra commission. For a market as a whole it can refer to a period of heavy turnover with no clear market trend.
   ▶ *See also* Broker.

Cia Spanish company title – abbreviation of Compania; and Portuguese company title – abbreviation of Companhia.

Cie French company title – abbreviation of Compagnie.

CIF Cost, Insurance and Freight. Used to indicate when insurance and freight charges as well as the cost of the goods, are included in the price of a commodity.
▶ *See also* C and F.

Circling The pre-selling of an issue by taking orders from prospective customers.

Circuit Breakers Breaks in trading, imposed by exchanges, when prices have fallen by a certain percentage. Circuit breakers are designed to restrict panic selling.
▶ *See also* Limit Up/Down.

City London's financial centre is known as The City, also called the Square Mile.

Clean Price Basically, this is the quoted price of a bond, but its correct definition is the present value of the cash flow of a bond excluding accrued interest.
▶ *See also* Dirty Price.

Clearing Bank A bank that is a member of a national cheque clearing system. To clear a cheque means to process it so that the payee receives its value. Such systems can also involve clearing financial orders and standardized payment instructions such as standing orders.

Clearing House A clearing house is the administrative centre of the market through which all transactions are cleared. In addition to administering trades, the clearing house guarantees the performance of contracts. It becomes the counter party to both the buyer and seller of a contract when a trade has been matched, thereby greatly reducing counter party risk. Other functions include making sure that underlying financial instruments or commodities are actually delivered to fulfil futures contracts, and maintaining the margin accounts.
▶ *See also* Margin.

Clearing System A system that facilitates the transfer of ownership of securities and arranges custody.
▶ *See also* Clearstream and Euroclear.

Clearstream An international system for the clearing, settlement and custody of securities, created in 2000 by the merger of Cedel International and Deutsche Borse Clearing ■ **www.clearstream.com** ■
▶ *See also* Clearing System, Custody, Settlement.

Closed-end Fund A fund in which there is a fixed amount of authorized share capital, and new shares may not be created on demand. Known as Closed-ended Publicly Quoted Funds in the US and Investment Trusts in the UK.

Closing a Position The delivery of underlying financial instruments or commodities against a future or option contract. The offsetting of a long or short position in a market by making an offsetting trade in the other direction. A trader would close a short position by buying the same instrument, or close a long position by selling it.
▶ *See also* Long, Short.

CLS Bank A bank set up by leading trading banks, with the support of central banks and the BIS (Bank for International Settlements), to settle foreign exchange transactions on a global basis. CLS, or Continuous Linked Settlement, is designed to remove the Herstatt Risk of default by one party in a foreign exchange deal. ■ **www.cls-services.com** ■
▶ *See also* BIS, Herstatt Risk, Settlement.

CME The Chicago Mercantile Exchange was the first futures exchange to trade financial futures. It specializes in short-term interest rate futures and currency futures. ■ **www.cme.com** ■
▶ *See also* Futures.

CMO Collateralized Mortgage Obligations. A security sold to investors with collateral based on property mortgages. Cash flows from mortgages, and their maturity dates, vary widely. If they are pooled and CMOs are issued against their collective value, it becomes possible to calculate an overall cash flow and make predictable payments of interest.
▶ *See also* Securitization.

Co Widely used abbreviation for company; also Dutch company title.

COB Commission des Opérations de Bourse. French stock market regulator. ■ **www.cob.fr** ■

Cocktail Swap A mixture of different types of Swaps. A Cocktail Swap will often be incorporated to spread the risk on major financing.
▶ *See also* Swap.

Co-financing Finance jointly provided for a country both by commercial banks and an international financing institution such as the IMF or the World Bank. The participation of the international institution lends confidence to the commercial lenders.

Coffee, Sugar and Cocoa Exchange ▶ *See* CSCE.

Coincident Index An index of economic indicators whose movements closely coincide with the overall cycle of economic activity. Along with lagging and leading indicators, this index highlights the speed and size of growth or shrinkage in an economy.
▶ *See also* Lagging Indicators, Leading Indicators.

Coincident Indicators Coincident economic indicators measure economic factors that change at the same time as the overall economic cycle. They include such things as retail trade volume and industrial production. Leading indicators, on the other hand, measure factors that change ahead of changes in the overall economic cycle and are used to predict changes in overall output and activity in an economy. Leading indicators include such things as share prices, new orders for investment goods, housing construction orders and the index of consumer confidence. Lagging indicators are economic indicators that follow a change in the economic circle. They include such things as labour costs and interest rates.

Collar A derivative instrument which fixes interest payments within a certain range by combining a long cap and a short floor. The premium generated from the sale of the floor may completely or partly finance the premium to be paid for the cap.
▶ *See also* Cap, Derivatives, Floor.

Collateral Assets used as a form of security for bond issuances. In case of default by the borrowers, the lenders (bondholders) have the legal right to claim those assets and sell them off to repay the loan.

Collateralized Mortgage Obligations ▶ *See* CMO.

Combined Option An option comprising at least one call and one put. The components may be exercised or traded separately, although they are originally dealt as one. These strategies may be designed to take advantage of a particular view on the market or to reduce outgoing premium costs. Two common examples of combination options are strangle and straddle strategies.
▶ *See also* Call, Option, Put, Straddle, Strangle.

COMEX Commodity Exchange Inc., a New York exchange that trades principally in metal futures. ■ **www.nymex.com** ■
▶ *See also* Futures.

Commercial Banks Financial institutions that operate in wholesale and retail banking and allied markets. Commercial banks attract customer deposits and offer cheque-clearing facilities. They are known as clearing banks in the UK or money-centre banks in the US. They are allowed to borrow from their respective central banks when they need short-term funds. Commercial banks contrast with investment or merchant banks which specialize in raising funds for companies rather than concentrating on lending and the mechanics of money transmission.
▶ *See also* Central Bank, Investment Bank.

Commercial Paper ▶ *See* CP.

Commission House A term used in futures markets to describe a firm that buys and sells contracts for the accounts of customers. Its income is generated by the commission charged for its service.
▶ *See also* Futures.

Commission Merchant A term used in futures markets to describe a firm or individual that makes a trade on behalf of another member of an exchange or for a non-member client, but who carries out the trade in their own name and becomes liable as principal.
▶ *See also* Futures.

Commitment Fee A fee paid by a borrower for a lender's commitment to make funds available.

Commitments of Traders A monthly report by a US regulatory authority called the Commodities Futures Trading Commission, which shows the total open positions held by large-volume traders, speculators, hedgers and small position traders.
▶ *See also* CFTC, Open Interest.

Commodity A natural raw material used as a foodstuff or in manufacturing. Classified in the following groups:
- oil and gas
- metals
- grains and oilseeds
- soft commodities such as sugar, cocoa, coffee and tea
- plantation crops such as rubber and palmoil; cotton and wool.

Exchange-traded commodities are quoted in specific lots of a specific quality for specified delivery, and usually also trade in forward, futures and options contracts. Commodities traded outside organized exchanges usually change hands by direct contact between individual producers and individual end-users. The contracts are tailor-made for each deal and are often signed for a long-term continuing supply.

Commodity Agreement An agreement between producer nations to regulate the output and price of a particular commodity. Producers may agree to limit exports through a quota arrangement, stockpile production or reduce output or plantings. Sometimes action is prompted by market prices reaching a certain level, or trigger price. Commodity agreements rarely have more than limited, short-term success.

Commodity Exchange Inc. ▶ *See* COMEX.

Commodities Futures Trading Commission ▶ *See* CFTC.

Common Stock Common stock, or ordinary shares, represent ownership in a limited liability company. These are companies in which the owners' liabilities are limited to the shareholders' funds and the shareholders usually appoint directors to manage the company on their behalf. Holders of common stock are entitled to dividends when they are declared. They have the last claim on the assets and income of a company, after other creditors have been paid.

COMPANY

MEASURING A COMPANY

You need to measure a company in two ways. The **words in bold** are explained more fully under their individual entries.

1 Look at flows in and out of the business as measured in the **profit and loss account**, or income statement of a company.

2 Look at the size and economic health of a business at a particular moment in time as seen in the **balance sheet**.

1 The profit and loss account

For most companies **listed** on a **stock exchange** profit and loss accounts are published at least once a year, more usually twice a year, and increasingly four times a year to match standards in the United States. Each figure in that statement has a comparative figure from the previous period or year, so you can check whether business is expanding or shrinking, getting better or worse. You can compare a **profit** for the second quarter to that of the first quarter, but this can be misleading when there are strong seasonal influences on a company's business, such as a burst of sales in the spring for a company selling camping equipment. It is sometimes better to compare one quarter's performance with the same quarter in the year before, to compare like with like.

Within the profit and loss account the first thing to take a look at is the company's **sales**, which are also known as **revenues** or **turnover**. This is a crude measure of how much business the company has done in a given period, and it shows whether the company is growing or shrinking. But size isn't everything in sales. A supermarket will have very large sales because that's the nature of its business, whereas a small company selling specialized software may have relatively small sales but may make large profits and have very low costs.

The next thing to look at is **operating costs**, otherwise known as the cost of sales. What does it cost to produce those goods or services that appear in the sales figures? These costs include raw materials, labour, and sales and administration costs. The supermarket may have very large operating costs. Because it has to buy in everything it sells, its operating margin, or the difference between sales and costs, may be very slim. The software company may have very low operating costs, perhaps just the price of two software writers in a garage, so its operating profit margin may be very high.

The difference between sales and cost of goods sold is the **gross profit**. But that is not what is left for distribution to shareholders. The company first has to pay **interest charges**, or the cost of borrowing, for loans used in the business. The supermarket may have very high interest costs because it has borrowed large amounts to build stores and distribution depots, while a software company may not have borrowed at all. Analysts watch the level of a company's **interest cover**, or how many times interest payments are covered by profits.

Companies also need to set aside cash for **depreciation** of **fixed assets** such as building or vehicles and for **amortization** charges to write off **goodwill**. What's left is the **pretax** or **operating profit**. Then the taxman takes his slice. What's left is the **net profit**, sometimes known as **attributable profit** because it belongs to the shareholders. The **net profit margin** is the net profits expressed as a percentage of overall sales.

Some of that net profit may be earmarked for **preference shareholders** and for **minority interests** so the net profit makes allowance for those claims. The net profit is easier to understand if the figure is expressed as **earnings per share**. There is the possibility that the amount of profit attributable to current shareholders will be reduced or diluted by possible claims from other shares that may be issued through such things as **options** and **warrants**. So profit is sometimes expressed as **fully diluted**

▶

(profit divided by all current and possible ordinary shares). This makes allowances for any new shares that have been issued and makes it easier to see whether earnings have gone up or down.

Cash earning may have doubled but the number of shares may have trebled through a **rights issue** or through a **bonus** or **scrip issue**, so the earnings per share may have fallen. Companies usually publish the number of shares outstanding to give details of changes.

Shareholders are keenly interested in what happens to net profits. Will they be retained in the company as reserves for use as a resource to fund further growth? Or will they be distributed to shareholders in the form of dividends?

Analysts are interested in a company's **dividend cover**, or the ratio of profits to dividends, to see whether a company can afford to make the cash distribution to shareholders, and whether it is being mean or generous in comparison with similar companies in its market sector. Companies with no need for funds for further expansion may distributed most of their net profit in dividends. Those that are expanding rapidly may choose not to make a dividend distribution at all. The shareholders may settle for capital appreciation of the company and an increase in the price of their shares, rather than a stream of income from dividend payments.

As well as looking at the operating profit and the net profit (the **bottom line** figure), analysts look at several measures of profitability in between. They can look at earnings before interest and taxation (**ebit**) or earnings before interest, taxation, depreciation and amortization (**ebitda**). The latter removes the effects of **extraordinary charges**, such as the **goodwill** costs of an acquisition, but may mask serious problems of over-expansion.

2 The balance sheet

Measuring the flows of cash in and out of a business from the profit and loss account can be irrelevant if you don't take into account the size and economic health of a company at that particular moment in time. In order to get a meaningful overview you need to examine the **balance sheet**, which is usually issued in a detailed form once a year and published in the **annual report**. The balance sheet shows where the money has come from and what it has been spent on. There are always two sides to a balance sheet – the **liabilities** or debts, which show the source of a company's funds, and the **assets**, which show where the money has been spent.

On the liabilities side of the balance sheet the company's first source of funds is **equity** raised from its shareholders through the sale of shares. Listing on a stock exchange facilitates an **initial public offering**, but a company can also raise money through a **share placing**. It may return to the market to raise further funds through a **rights issue**. The company usually enlists the help of an **investment bank** to raise those funds.

Part of the profits are retained by the company to be employed by the company instead of being distributed to the shareholders in the form of dividends. These are known as **reserves**. Shareholders' equity plus reserves are known as **shareholders' funds**.

The company also has borrowings or debt, in the form of bank overdrafts, short-term borrowing facilities or long-term **bonds** and **debentures**. In the case of a company failure the debt must be repaid before the shareholders have any claim on the company's assets, so the shareholders take a greater risk than the debt holders. Analysts watch a company's **debt-to-equity ratio**. A company with large debts relative to its equity may be perceived as a more risky investment. It may have to continue making large interest payments and debt repayments even in a downturn, whereas a company funded largely by equity can suspend dividend payments.

The company is also partly funded by its creditors who have committed funds to the company by supplying raw materials and services that have not yet been paid for. Again, analysts watch the **quick ratio**, or the relationship between short-term assets and short-term liabilities, to see whether the company may run into short-term funding problems.

Analysts also watch whether a company has negative or positive **cash flow** overall. They want to know whether its activities are producing cash or consuming cash too rapidly, known as a **cash burn**. It may be sensible for a company to consume cash when it is rapidly expanding, but that is not a situation that can continue indefinitely.

The assets side of the balance sheet shows where the money has gone. It is usually spent on fixed assets such as land and buildings, on raw materials and stocks of semi-finished and finished goods, on debts that have not yet been paid by its debtors, and on keeping available a certain amount of cash.

Competition Commission The UK regulator of monopolies, mergers and anti-competitive activities. ■ **www.competition-commission.org.uk** ■

Competitive Bid Auction An auction method commonly used to issue government bonds, with underwriters submitting bids for certain amounts. The bonds are then allocated according to the level of demand at rates determined by the level of the bids. The highest bids are allocated their requests in full. The remaining bids are met in descending order until the issuer has sold the required amount of bonds.
▶ *See also* Dutch Auction, Non-competitive Bid Auction.

Compound Annual Growth Rate ▶ *See* CAGR.

Compounding A process whereby the value of an investment increases exponentially over time due to compound interest.
▶ *See also* Compound Interest.

Compound Interest The interest amount earned on the original principal and on the accumulated interest. Compounding annually means that there is only one period each year in which interest is calculated. For example, if £100 is deposited with annually calculated interest at 10 percent, after one year there will be £110. Where simple interest always calculates the rate from the initial amount invested (giving £120 after two years, £130 after three etc.), compound interest calculates the 10 percent from the previous year's total (giving £121 after two years and £133.10 after three). The extra £3.10 is the compound interest.
▶ *See also* Simple Interest.

Compound Option An option on an option. It grants the holder the right to buy or sell an option at a set price on a predetermined date. If the first option is exercised, the underlying option will then behave as a standard option. Compound options offer the opportunity of highly geared investment. Speculative investors lay down relatively little amounts of cash for the compound option and can then decide whether to lay out more cash to buy the underlying option, and finally can decide whether to lay out the cash to buy the underlying financial instrument.
▶ *See also* Gearing, Option.

Concerted Intervention Pre-arranged simultaneous intervention in foreign exchange markets by several central banks. This usually happens at the behest of one single central bank which is trying to maintain a target rate for its currency. The intervention may be designed to strengthen or weaken a currency as a matter of deliberate policy, or to fight off speculative currency flows.
▶ *See also* Intervention.

Concert Party ▶ *See* Acting in Concert.

Conditionality Economic conditions imposed on a country when it draws funds from the IMF (International Monetary Fund). The conditions often spell out requirements for economic policy, government spending and taxation and exchange rate policy.
▶ *See also* IMF.

Conference Board A US organization that disseminates research about management and the marketplace, including a monthly survey of consumer confidence. It is a not-for-profit organization.
▪ www.conference-board.org ▪

Conglomerate A company comprising diverse and often unrelated subsidiaries.

Consensus Estimates Averages of the estimates of a company's future performance supplied by a number of analysts. Consensus estimates cover figures such as growth in earnings per share, dividends and price/earnings ratios. Also known as early estimates.

CONSOB Commissione Nazionale per la Società e la Borsa. Italy's official body for regulating and supervising companies and stock exchanges.
▪ www.consob.it ▪

Consolidated Balance Sheet A report showing the financial position of a company and its subsidiaries. Also known as a consolidated account.
▶ *See also* Balance Sheet.

Consolidation Phase A sideways move in a market that generally remains at the same level despite minor rises and falls. Trading is usually at a low and steady volume.

Consortium A group of companies that have joined together to promote a common project.

Consumer Confidence Consumption is a major influence on an economy. The willingness of consumers to spend is closely watched as an indicator of future economic performance. It is measured by an index of consumer confidence.

Consumer Price Index ▶ *See* CPI.

Consumption The proportion of national output consumed by individuals and households, in contrast with government consumption, investment and net exports.

Contango A situation where futures prices are progressively higher the further the maturity date is from spot. The increase reflects the added cost of storage and insurance for commodities delivered further into the future. Contango is the normal relationship between spot and futures price and is the opposite of backwardation.
▶ *See also* Futures, Backwardation.

Contingent Liability A charge that a business expects to pay, contingent on future events.

Contingent Option An option for which the holder only pays the premium if the option is exercised. Contingent options are zero-cost unless exercised.
▶ *See also* Option.

Continuation In technical analysis, a sideways movement in price shown on a chart which is likely to be simply a pause in an underlying trend, possibly to correct an overbought or oversold condition. The next move will be in the direction of the main trend.
▶ *See also* Technical Analysis.

Contract for Difference The exchange of a fixed price asset for a floating price asset. In foreign exchange markets the term is used to describe the settlement of the difference between a contract rate and the eventual settlement rate.
▶ *See also* FX.

Contract Grades Standard grades for each commodity, which must be observed when commodities are delivered against futures contracts. Most contracts have a number of grades or qualities. If the delivered commodities vary from the contract grades then the price will be at a premium or discount when delivery actually takes place.
▶ *See also* Futures, Premium.

Contract Month The month in which delivery is due under a futures contract, i.e. when the contract expires.
▶ *See also* Back Month, Futures, Premium.

Contrarian Someone who moves or acts in the opposite direction to the general trend. A contrarian investor buys stock when the rest of the market is selling.

Convergence The process by which a futures price moves toward the price of the underlying instrument as expiry approaches. Also, the movement of interest rates in applicant countries towards those prevailing in the currency bloc which they are aspiring to join. This is a new factor in the market trading of the countries that want to join the Eurozone.
▶ *See also* Basis Risk, Futures.

Conversion The process of converting a convertible security, such as a bond or preferred stock, into common stock.

Conversion Ratio The ratio for the convertibility of a preferred share into a fixed number of common shares, or from a convertible bond into the underlying shares.

Convertible Arbitrage Buying convertible bonds and selling short the shares into which they can be converted.
> *See also* Arbitrage, Convertible Bond, Short.

Convertible Bond A bond that is convertible into a fixed number of an issuing company's stock at a pre-set conversion price. This price is usually at a premium over the current or average price, but purchasers of the convertible bond hope that the price of the underlying stock will rise. Because of the prospect of possible capital gains on the shares, the bond can carry a lower coupon, or nominal rate of inter-est. Convertible bonds may often be used for arbitrage by traders who can make money by spotting differences between the valuation of the bond and the underlying shares.
> *See also* Arbitrage, Bond, Coupon.

Convertible Preference Share A preference share that can be converted into common shares at a fixed conversion price. Preference or pre-ferred shares entitle a holder to a prior claim on any dividend paid by the company before payment is made on ordinary shares.
> *See also* Preference Share.

Convexity Like duration, convexity is a measure of the price sensitivity of a bond. It measures the change in modified duration for a change in yield.
> *See also* Duration.

Core Capital ▶ *See* Tier One.

Corp Widely used abbreviation for corporation.

Corporate Dealer A dealer or group of dealers responsible for advising and dealing with corporate customers of their bank who have direct access to the trading room.

Corporate Finance Bank departments which advise corporate clients on all aspects of balance sheet risk management, including interest rate and currency exposures.

Corporate Settlement The market standard for settlement and delivery, five business days or seven calendar days from the trade date. Also known as regular way settlement.

Correction A correction in technical analysis refers to a price movement in the opposite direction of the trend. Corrections can occur on both the up- and downside of a trend. The market ultimately reverts from a correction to the overall trend.
▶ *See also* Technical Analysis.

Correlation A statistical tool that measures the degree to which two variables move together. A correlation of 1 means that the two variables move together exactly, while a correlation of –1 means that the variables move in exactly the opposite direction from each other.

Corto The 'corto', or short, is the amount of pesos the Mexican central bank withdraws from the local money market on a daily basis to control liquidity. An increase in the corto reduces liquidity and leads to higher interest rates.

Cost and Freight ▶ *See* C and F.

Cost, Insurance and Freight ▶ *See* CIF.

Cost of Carry The difference between the interest generated on a cash instrument such as a bond or a Treasury bill and the cost of funds to finance the position.
▶ *See also* Positive Carry, Negative Carry.

Cost of Sales ▶ *See* Operating Costs.

Cost to Close A calculation of what the cost would be of having to liquidate outstanding contracts at the prevailing market rates. Used in forward foreign exchange revaluations.

Counter Clockwise Used in technical analysis, this is a chart that plots price against volume over the a given number of periods. Price/volume patterns can be identified and strategies can be planned, based on pattern repetition.

Counter-cyclical Stock A stock whose market value moves against the rise and fall of the economy. Typically, shares of companies that produce necessities for which demand remains relatively constant irrespective of economic cycles, such as food retailers.
▶ *See also* Cyclical, Cyclical Stock.

Counterparty Risk ▶ *See* Credit Risk.

Counter Trade The exchange of goods or services where no money is paid. Also known as barter.

Country Risk Risks associated with lending funds to, or making an investment in, a particular country. Also known as sovereign risk.

Coupon The interest paid on a bond expressed as a percentage of the face value. If a bond carries a fixed coupon, the interest is paid on an annual or semi-annual basis. The term also describes the detachable certificate entitling the bearer to payment of the interest.

▶ *See also* Bullet Bond, Bearer Forms.

Coupon Stripping Detaching the coupons from a bond and trading the principal repayment and coupon amounts separately, thereby creating zero coupon bonds.

▶ *See also* Zero Coupon Bonds.

Coupon Swap ▶ *See* Swap.

Covariance A statistical term for the correlation of two variables multiplied by the individual standard deviation for each of the variables. Covariance measures the degree to which two variables move in the same direction.

▶ *See also* Correlation, Standard Deviation.

Covenant A promise in a formal agreement that some activity will or will not be carried out. In a debt agreement a breach of covenant may mean that the whole debt is immediately due. Covenants can cover issues as varied as dividend payments, gearing ratios or the amount of working capital.

Covered Bond A bond which has other financial instruments, such as mortgage loans, pledged as security against default.

Covered Call Writing An option strategy combines a short call position and a long position in the underlying financial instrument or share. By owning the underlying instrument on which the option is written, the call is covered if exercised because the instrument can be delivered. The strategy may be followed by institutions such as pension funds with large holdings of underlying assets.

▶ *See also* Option.

Covered Warrant A warrant issued by a bank that enables the holder to buy shares in another company at a future date, for a price that is generally above the current market price of the share. Used as a trading instrument. For example, Merrill Lynch might issue covered warrants on shares of General Motors. They are covered because the issuer will hold at least some of the underlying stock into which the warrants may be exercised. Covered warrants are aimed principally at international investors looking for geared exposure to a specific stock, basket of stocks or even an entire index.

▶ *See also* Share, Stock, Warrant.

CP Commercial Paper. This is a short-term unsecured promissory note that is issued for a specified amount and matures on a specified date. CP is a negotiable instrument, typically in bearer form. CP, like CDs (Certificates of Deposit), are a means of raising working capital. In terms of funding costs, the issue of one or another should make no difference since both will produce comparable yields. However, CP tends to be issued with maturities of 30 days or less, to avoid competing with the CD market.
▶ *See also* Bearer Shares/Bearer Bonds,CD.

CPI Consumer Price Index. The CPI is a measure of retail inflation. It is calculated by collecting and comparing the prices of a set basket of goods and services, as bought by a typical consumer, at regular intervals over time. Also known as a Retail Price Index.

Crack Spread A calculation showing the theoretical market value of petroleum products that could be obtained from a barrel of crude after the oil is refined or cracked.

Crash A dangerously steep fall in economic conditions or asset prices, such as the Wall Street Crash of 1929. A crash leads to a sudden fall in confidence in investment and the economy. Companies and individuals reduce consumption and investment as they try to repay debt borrowed to buy assets which have fallen steeply in value. That leads to further drops in demand for credit and threatens the overall level of economic activity.

Crawling Peg A currency system which allows a gradual depreciation or appreciation in an exchange rate, usually to adjust for inflation.

Credit Card A card that allows the holder to make purchases on borrowed money, repayable at varying intervals and at varying rates of interest. A widespread and popular means of obtaining credit for goods and services in developed economies, particularly the United States.
▶ *See also* Debit Card.

Credit Crunch ▶ *See* Credit Squeeze.

Credit Derivatives Derivative instruments created to separate the credit risk of a borrower from overall market risk. A purchaser of a bond buys a credit derivative to cover the risk of the bond's debtor defaulting. Effectively the seller or writer of the credit derivative is providing an insurance policy against default. Credit derivatives can provide cover against a sudden widening of the bond's yield spread over Treasuries, a deepening of its price discount, bankruptcy, insolvency or default.
▶ *See also* Derivatives.

Credit Line An agreement by which a bank lends or borrows money up to a specified limit for a set period. The limits on this borrowing are known as credit limits.

Credit Rating Credit ratings measure a borrower's creditworthiness and provide an international framework for comparing the credit quality of issuers and rated debt securities. Rating agencies allocate three kinds of ratings: for issuers, for long-term debt, and for short-term debt. Of these, issuer credit ratings are the most widely watched. They measure the creditworthiness of the borrower including its capacity and willingness to meet financial obligations. A top rating means there is thought to be almost no risk of the borrower failing to pay interest and principal. The higher the rating, the less the borrower will need to pay for funds. The top credit rating issued by the main agencies (Standard & Poor's, Moody's and Fitch IBCA) is AAA or Aaa. This is reserved for a few sovereign and corporate issuers. The naming and designation of ratings varies according to each agency. But they all fall into two broad groups – investment grade and speculative (junk) grade. ■ www.moodys.com ■ ■ www.standardandpoors.com ■ ■ www.fitchratings.com ■
   ▶ *See also* AAA, Credit Watch, Downgrade, Moody's, S&P.

Credit Risk The risk that an issuer might default on a payment or go into liquidation. Also known as counter party risk.

Credit Squeeze A credit squeeze occurs when the supply of money is unable to keep up with demand, causing interest rates to rise and exacerbating the borrowing position. A credit squeeze can also be a government-imposed situation to rein in excessive spending in macro-economic terms. An extreme squeeze can be a credit crunch.

Credit Watch When a credit rating agency announces that it is putting a borrower on credit watch it is giving notice that it expects shortly to issue a lower or higher credit rating.
   ▶ *See also* Credit Rating.

CRL Portuguese company title: abbreviation of Cooperativa de Responsabilidad Limitada.

Cross In the US, a cross is where the broker acts for both the buyer and seller of a security in the same deal. This is also known as an agency cross or dual agency, or in the UK it is known as a put through. Cross can also refer to a practice, usually illegal, where the buy and sell orders for a stock are offset by a broker without being recorded as a trade on the exchange. The risk is that either the buyer or the seller will not receive the fair market price.

Cross Border Activities in the financial and economic sector that involve movement of goods or negotiations across national borders.

Cross Currency Settlement Risk ▶ *See* Herstatt Risk.

Cross Default Clauses Cross default clauses are triggered automatically when a lender declares that a loan is in default. Such clauses might mean that other loans and borrowing instruments made to the borrower by the lender – and by other lenders – are also in default.

Cross Listing Shares that are officially listed on more than one stock exchange and are therefore, traded freely away from their domestic centre. They can also appear in cross-border stock market indices.
▶ *See also* Share, Stock.

Cross Rate The exchange rate between two currencies, neither of which is the US dollar. However, cross rates are often calculated from the exchange rate of each currency against the dollar.

Crude Oil Oil produced from a reservoir after any associated gas has been removed.
▶ *See also* Brent, WTI.

CSCE The Coffee, Sugar and Cocoa Exchange is a New York futures market that trades contracts in these three commodities. ▦ **www.csce.com** ▦

CTD Cheapest to Deliver. The security or commodity available in the cash market can be delivered most economically against a futures position.
▶ *See also* Futures.

Cum All Cum all means a buyer of shares is entitled to all the supplementary advantages attached to a share at the time.

Cum Dividend A term used to describe when shares are bought with the right to receive a dividend which has been announced.
▶ *See also* Ex-Dividend, Stock, Share.

Cumulative Method A method of voting rights which allows the ordinary shareholder to cast votes in any combination for a set number of positions being elected. There is no commitment to equally distribute the votes.
▶ *See also* Ordinary Share.

Cumulative Preferred Stock A type of preferred share that grants the holder the right to dividend arrears before any payments are made to holders of ordinary shares.
▶ *See also* Ordinary Share.

Currency Basket A bundle of foreign currencies gathered into a single unit, against which an exchange rate can be set. Often the representation of a foreign currency in the basket is weighted for the importance of its use in the country's trade. If 40 percent of a country's imports and exports are priced in US dollars then the dollar may comprise 40 percent of the basket against which that country's currency is valued.

Currency Board A strict exchange rate system in which a country pegs its currency firmly to another, such as the dollar or the euro. The currency board guarantees full convertibility of the country's notes and coins into the reference currency at a fixed exchange rate. Because of that guarantee the board cannot issue more notes and coins than it can match with its holdings of foreign currency. As a result the currency board's operations are automatic and passive. This system prevents the government financing its operations by printing money thereby creating inflation.

Currency Fixings In some markets, a daily meeting is held at which the rates for different currencies are officially fixed by adjusting the buying and selling level to reflect market conditions. The central bank of the relevant country often participates to influence the fix.

Currency Limit The maximum amount a dealer, a group of dealers, or a dealing room are allowed to trade in any particular currency.

Currency Risk The potential for losses arising from adverse moves in exchange rates.

Currency Swap ▶ *See* Swap.

Current Account A country's current account balance is the sum of the visible trade balance (exports and imports that can be seen) and the invisible balance (credits and debits for services of one kind or another, such as tourism, banking and insurance). It excludes flows produced by long-term borrowings or investment, which are counted in the capital account.
▶ *See also* Balance of Payments, Capital Account.

Current Assets A company's assets that can be realized easily or rapidly turned into cash. These include inventory (stock in trade), receivables (monies usually due within one year), cash (bank balances) and cash equivalents (marketable securities, government bonds etc.).

Current Coupon The prevailing coupon (interest paid on a bond, expressed as a percentage of the face value) on a floating rate note or other variable rate security.
▶ *See also* Coupon.

Current Earnings Current or recurrent earnings are those arising from normal company operations, including financial items, before extraordinary items and taxes. Current earnings are therefore the company's operating earnings (EBIT or earning before interest and taxes) plus or minus financial items. When analysts forecast earnings per share, they usually forecast current earnings, because they find it hard to predict extraordinary items and taxation.
▶ *See also* Consensus Estimates.

Current Issue ▶ *See* On-the-Run Issue.

Current Liabilities The short-term financial commitments of a company, such as accounts payable, taxation and dividends payable, usually due within 12 months.
▶ *See also* Assets/Liabilities.

Current Maturity The time remaining to maturity, an important factor in bond valuation.
▶ *See also* Maturity.

CURRENT RATIO

The current ratio is a measure of a company's ability to meet its short-term liabilities and is calculated by dividing the current assets by the current liabilities. Current assets are made up of cash and cash equivalents ('near cash'), accounts receivable and inventory, while current liabilities are the sum of short-term loans and accounts payable.

The current ratio's normal range is between 0.5 and 2.0, but this 'liquidity ratio' must be interpreted with caution. A high ratio could indicate that the company is sitting on too much cash, that it is owed a lot of money by its customers or that it needs to operate with huge amounts of inventory. A low ratio does not necessarily mean the company is a risky creditor. It could mean the company operates in an industry where cash payment is standard (such as restaurants, which typically have little or no accounts receivable), in an industry that operates without much inventory (most service sector companies) or an industry in which customers pay slowly (such as the building sector).

Formula: Current Assets/Current Liabilities

Example

The Old Rope Corporation's annual report shows the following figures, in millions of British pounds:

Current assets:	760
Cash at bank and in hand	45
Short-term investments	35
Accounts receivable	250
Stocks	430
Current liabilities	840

Current ratio: 760 / 840 = 0.9

▶ *See* Current Assets, Current Liabilities.

Current Yield A measure of the return to a bondholder, calculated as a ratio of the coupon to the market price. It is simply the annual coupon rate divided by the clean price of the bond.
▶ *See also* Clean Price, YTM.

Curve ▶ *See* Yield Curve.

CUSIP Unique identifying numbers assigned to US Treasury, federal, municipal and corporate securities by the Committee on Uniform Securities Identification Procedures. ▪ **www.cusip.com** ▪

Custody The storage and safekeeping of securities and the maintenance of accurate records of their ownership. Cross-border trading has produced a growing need for custody services both within countries and globally.
▶ *See also* Clearstream, Euroclear.

Cyclical A regular occurrence. Something that happens on a periodic basis.

Cyclical Deficit The portion of a country's budget deficit which is due to economic swings, with budget positions tending to deteriorate as economies slow, tax revenues fall and welfare spending rises. The cyclically-adjusted deficit strips out the impact that economic swings have on budgetary health.
▶ *See also* Structural Deficit.

Cyclical Stocks Stocks that are affected by economic cycles, such as property and consumer durables. Cyclical stocks are generally viewed to be riskier investments and carry a higher beta than non-cyclical stock.
▶ *See also* Beta, Counter-cyclical Stock.

Cylinder ▶ *See* Risk Reversal.

Daily Price Limit The maximum amount, fixed by an exchange, that prices are permitted to rise or fall in one day before trading on a contract is suspended. The daily limit is measured from the previous day's settlement price.

▶ *See also* Limit Up/Limit Down.

Daisy Chain A sequence of deals which trade a forward (or paper) cargo of Brent or Dubai cargo of crude oil ahead of receiving loading dates (known as turning wet). A daisy chain is also known as a paper chain.

▶ *See also* Brent.

Dated Brent Brent crude oil for prompt loading. Dated Brent is a cargo of crude that has been awarded its loading date. This occurs 15 days ahead of loading – or the nearest to 15 days allowing for non-trading days.

▶ *See also* Brent.

Dated Date Date from which interest begins to accrue on a new issue, frequently the issue date.

Dawn Raid Buying a large block of stock in a short time, usually for the buyer to position himself in a possible or actual takeover. The purchase often takes place at the start of a trading day.

▶ *See also* Stock, Share.

DAX 30 This is the most widely followed German stock index although it only consists of 30 blue-chip equities and is considered too narrowly based for performance measurement purposes. Like the S&P 500, the CAC-40 and the FTSE 100, this index is a market capitalization-weighted average index, rather than a simple average.

Unlike these other indices, which only measure change in market prices, the DAX attempts to measure the total return on German equities. In particular, the DAX includes dividend income and notionally reinvests any dividend income in additional equities in the same proportion as the index. Even if there is no net change in German equity prices it is possible for the DAX to rise because of the added value of an inflow of dividend income. Futures and options contracts on the DAX 30 are listed on EUREX. ■ **www.exchange.de** ■

▶ *See also* Capitalization-weighted Index, EUREX.

Day Traders Traders who buy and sell assets on their own account but always liquidate their positions at the end of the day. Day traders are known as scalpers in futures markets.

Daycount Conventions Every bond market has its own system of determining the number of days in a year and even the number of days between two coupon dates. These different methods are referred to as daycount conventions and are important when calculating accrued interest and present value (when the next coupon is less than a full coupon period away).
▶ *See also* Coupon.

DD Slovenian company title: abbreviation of Delniska Druzba.

Dd Croatian company title: abbreviation of Dionicko Drustvo.

DDM Dividend Discount Model. It values common stock as the sum of the present (discounted) values of its estimated future dividend payments. This model assumes that dividends paid in the future are worth less than their nominal value because of the effects of inflation. To compare them with dividends received today they must be discounted by the estimated rate of inflation. DDM is the share valuation model most readily comparable with bond evaluation, which discounts future coupon payments by an appropriate rate.
▶ *See also* Dividend.

Dead Cat Bounce A rise in the price of a financial instrument, or an overall market, after a prolonged fall. This is likely to be followed by renewed weakness because there has been no change in underlying market sentiment. Even a dead cat bounces if it is dropped from a great height.

Dealer An individual or company that trades financial instruments and takes positions for its own account.

Deal Limit The maximum amount that a dealer can trade per transaction. The limit is set by the financial trading house or institution that employs the dealer, taking into account trading expertise and track record and the institution's willingness to accept risk.

Debenture Bond, Debentures Long-term debt not secured by a specific property but which gives bondholders the claim of general creditors over all assets that are not specifically pledged elsewhere.

Debit Card A means of payment for consumer goods and services which allows retailers to draw funds directly from a consumer's bank account. Unlike a credit card it does not offer the possibility of purchasing using borrowed money.
▶ *See also* Credit Card.

Debt The supply of funds from a creditor to a debtor in exchange for interest and a commitment to return the funds in full at a fixed date in the future. Debt is usually in the form of financial instruments such as bonds, bills and notes. Creditors, who can be private individuals, banks or institutions such as pension funds and insurance companies, lend the money in the belief that the debtor will honour the obligation to pay the interest and eventually to repay the capital of the loan. Debt instruments have a defined life, a maturity date and normally pay a fixed rate of interest. All purchasers of debt have a supply of cash which is not immediately needed, on which they wish to earn interest until it is required for their own direct use. The interest is a payment for their willingness to forgo use of the funds for a fixed time.
▶ *See also* Bond, Bills, National Debt, Notes.

Debt/Equity Ratio A ratio that measures a company's debt relative to its equity. Calculated by dividing long-term debt by shareholders' equity.

Debt Financing Raising capital by selling debt instruments such as bonds, bills or notes.

Debt for Equity Swap When a debtor country, usually with economic problems or a deteriorating credit rating, uses its local currency to buy back its foreign debt at a discount in line with market conditions. Creditors then use that local currency to invest in companies in the debtor country, turning there debt into equity. The debtor country is then said to have securitized its debt. The term is also used when a company cannot meet payments on its debt and exchanges the debt for shares in the company.

Debt Service Ratio The proportion of a country's export earnings needed to cover interest and principal repayments of its foreign debts, particularly those owed by the public sector. A level of 20 percent is normally considered an acceptable maximum. Establishing the exact figure is often difficult.

Declaration Date ▶ *See* Expiry Date.

Default Failure to meet an obligation such as a payment of interest or principal. Technically, the borrower does not default. The initiative comes from the lender who declares the borrower is in default.

Defensive Stock Low beta stocks that are less risky than the overall market. Defensive stocks tend to be in non-cyclical sectors such as food retailing and public utilities, where sales do not fluctuate markedly throughout the economic cycle.
▶ *See also* Beta.

Deferred Coupon A bond that delays coupon payments for the first few years, paying them in a lump sum at maturity. It is aimed at investors who want delayed cash flow and who also seek a lower tax bill in early years when their income might be higher than in later years.
▶ *See also* Coupon.

Deficit The difference when expenditure is greater than income. Opposite of surplus.
▶ *See also* Surplus.

Deficit Financing Budgetary policy that produces a deficit and a resulting government borrowing requirement. It can be the direct result of positive government action or failure to control spending.

Deflation A fall in prices. Not to be confused with depreciation, which is a fall in value of a currency.
▶ *See also* Depreciation, Disinflation, Inflation.

Delivery Price The settlement price set by a clearing house for deliveries of commodities against futures contracts.
▶ *See also* Clearing House.

Delivery Versus Payment ▶ *See* DVP.

Delta A measure of sensitivity derived from an option pricing model. It measures how much an option's price will change for one unit of change in the underlying price.
▶ *See also* Option.

Delta Hedging A method used by option writers to hedge risk by purchasing or selling the underlying instrument in the spot market in proportion to the delta of their options position. Effectively traders are trying to remain neutral in a particular market.

Demerger When a company hives off some of its units into a wholly-owned separate concern, which may also be listed on a stock exchange. This can occur following a number of acquisitions of a similar nature that may diverge from a company's mainstream operations.

Depletion Depletion is an accounting measure that records the loss of value of a wasting asset, such as mines and gas reserves. In contrast, the reduction of the value of tangible assets is depreciation and the reduction of the value of intangible assets is amortization.
▶ *See also* Amortization, Depreciation, Assets.

Deposits ▶ *See* Fixed-term Deposit.

Depository A storage facility for securities registration and ownership documents.

Depository Receipts ▶ *See* ADR.

Depository Trust Corporation ▶ *See* DTC.

Depreciation
  1 Depreciation is an accounting measure that records the loss of value of an asset as a result of usage, the passage of time, or obsolescence. Depreciation is applied only to tangible assets, such as property and machinery. ▶ *See also* Amortization, Depletion.
  2 The loss in value of a currency, usually through the forces of supply and demand in the open market. In contrast with a devaluation, which is an administered downward change in a currency rate.

Derivatives Derivatives instruments are derived from underlying cash assets that can be bought, sold and traded in a similar way to shares or any other financial instrument. The pricing and performance of derivatives such as futures, options and swaps is largely based on the underlying asset. In practice, derivatives often drive the underlying market and the volume traded in certain futures and options contacts can outstrip the underlying cash market. Derivatives can be traded on an investment exchange, or directly by telephone or computer in an over-the-counter (OTC) market.
  ▶ *See also* Cap, Collar, Floor, Futures, Option, OTC Over-the-Counter, Swap.

Detachable Warrant Issued as part of a bond but then detached and traded separately in the secondary market. The warrant holder has the right to buy new equity or debt.
  ▶ *See also* Warrant.

Devaluation Formal downward adjustment of a currency's official par value or central exchange rate. Opposite of revaluation.

Dilution Reduction in the value of earnings and assets to existing holders of a company's shares caused by an increase in issued shares, which occurs when a rights or a bonus issue is made. In the US, fully diluted earnings per share are earnings after assuming the exercise of warrants and stock options and the conversion of convertible bonds and preferred stock.
  ▶ *See also* Bonus Issue, Rights Issue.

Dilutive The effect of reducing earnings per share by spreading the same amount of earnings among an increased number of shares.

Dirty Float A system where no official parities for currencies are declared or maintained. The central bank or national monetary authority does not publish details of a fixed target, e.g. four francs to the dollar. Instead it intervenes in foreign exchange markets to achieve an undisclosed target exchange rate. The target may be changed according to circumstances. Also known as a managed float.

Dirty Price Present value of the cash flow of a bond including accrued interest. Also known as gross price.
> ► *See also* Clean Price.

Discount Generally used to describe when something is selling below its normal price. An asset or fund is described as being at discount when its value is above its market price. In the money markets it is the action of buying financial paper at less than par value. In the foreign exchange markets it is a margin by which the forward rate falls below spot. In the futures market it is referred to as backwardation. Opposite of premium.
> ► *See also* Backwardation, Premium.

Discount Brokerage A brokerage firm that executes orders at a discounted rate of commission. Discount brokers tend to offer fewer client services than non-discount or full-service brokers. For example, they may not offer full research and investment recommendations.
> ► *See also* Broker.

Discounted Cash Flow Establishes the relative worth of a future investment project by assessing the expected cash flows from the project against its net present value. Cash flows in the future are discounted, or are estimated as worth less than current cash flows, because their real value will be eroded by inflation. Commonly used in valuing companies and as a component of equity valuation.

Discount House Term used in the UK to describe an institution acting as an intermediary between the Bank of England and the banking system.

Discount Rate The interest rate at which a central bank is prepared to lend funds to commercial banks, which supply government debt such as Treasury bills as collateral.
> ► *See also* Central Bank, Discount.

Discount Window The facility set up by central banks to provide funds to commercial banks as the 'lender of last resort'. Central banks lend at their discretion, and not as a right, to commercial banks at the discount rate.
> ► *See also* Central Bank, Discount.

Discount Yield The yield on a security that sells at a discount.

Discretionary Account An account for which the broker or bank has a discretionary power of attorney from the holder, either completely or within set limits, to manage on his behalf.

Disinflation A fall or slowing in the rate of inflation. Prices are still rising but at a slower rate than before. Not to be confused with deflation, which is when prices are falling.
▶ *See also* Inflation.

Disintermediation Process where borrowers or investors bypass banks and other financial intermediaries by directly issuing or buying securities.

Disinvestment Cutting capital investment by disposing of capital goods, such as plant and machinery, or by not replacing capital assets.

Distressed Debt Debt whose market rating has fallen sharply because the borrower has defaulted or is highly likely to default on repayments.

Distressed Securities Shares and bonds of companies which are in, near or emerging from bankruptcy.

Distributed Profits Profits distributed to shareholders via dividend payments.

Diversification Spreading investment risk by constructing a portfolio that contains many different investments whose returns are relatively uncorrelated. Risk levels can be reduced without a corresponding reduction in returns.
▶ *See also* Portfolio.

Dividend The part of a company's after-tax earnings that is distributed to the shareholders. The board of directors of the company recommends how much dividend should be paid out at its annual meeting and it is voted through by the shareholders. The dividend is neither automatic nor guaranteed for ordinary shareholders. The dividend can be in the form of cash or shares.

Dividend Cover The extent to which a company's dividend and/or interest payments are matched or exceeded by its earnings. Expressed as a multiple. The company's rating in the market increases as the multiple rises.

Dividend Discount Model ▶ *See* DDM.

Dividend Stripping A term used to describe a speculator's strategy whereby shares are purchased shortly before a dividend payment date, based on the belief that a much higher than normal dividend will be paid.
▶ *See also* Dividend.

Dividend Yield The ratio of annualized dividends to the price of a share. Dividend yields are widely used to measure the income return of a share. High yields may mean high dividends, or they may mean that the price of the share has fallen, making the ratio look impressive despite a poor market rating of the company. Low yields may mean that the company's share price is high in anticipation of rapid growth, or that the company is not distributing much of its earnings in dividends, preferring to keep cash for reinvestment in the business.

▶ *See also* Dividend.

DJIA Dow Jones Industrial Average. One of the oldest barometers of US equity markets. The DJIA or Dow Jones is watched by investors worldwide because it is the benchmark for equity prices in the world's largest stock market, and because of the importance of the US economy to the rest of the world. The index consists of only 30 of the largest US stocks listed on the NYSE. It is calculated as a simple arithmetic average of the constituent stock prices. There is no weighting for the market capitalization of the member companies, so that the same percentage change in the price of the smallest and of the largest constituents has the same effect on the index.

▧ **http://indexes.dowjones.com** ▧

▶ *See also* Arithmetic Average, NYSE, Dow Jones Industrial Average.

Doha Round A round of trade negotiations launched in Doha, Qatar under the auspices of the World Trade Organization.

▶ *See also* WTO.

Dollarization Adoption of the US dollar as the main currency across large parts of the economy. It can occur informally and without official approval, when citizens vote with their pockets, or formally when a country stops issuing its own currency and uses only foreign currency.

Domestic Final Sales Domestic final sales are a measure of gross domestic product, excluding additions to stocks and net international trade. It is a way of measuring how much is produced and actually consumed within a country, so it excludes production added to inventories and not immediately consumed. It also excludes the effects of a net trade deficit, because those goods have come from abroad, or a net trade surplus, because those goods have been exported abroad and not consumed at home.

▶ *See also* Balance of Trade, GDP.

Done Dealers' language: verbally confirms a deal.

Double Dip A second and subsequent drop in a market or an economy. When an economy slows, then starts to recover, only to falter and slow once more.

Double Top/Bottom A double top is a term, used in technical analysis, to describe a reversal pattern that occurs in a rising market. A typical top has two prominent peaks at about the same level. A double bottom is a reversal pattern that occurs in a falling market. It typically has two troughs at about the same level. (Figure 7.)
▶ *See also* Technical Analysis.

Double Witching ▶ *See* Triple Witching.

Dow The Dow Jones Industrial Average is the main benchmark US stock market index.
▶ *See* DJIA.

Down and In A trigger option that is activated when the price of the underlying instrument falls to a predetermined level. A type of barrier option.
▶ *See also* Option.

Down and Out A knockout option that is cancelled when the price of the underlying instrument falls below a predetermined level. A type of barrier option.
▶ *See also* Option.

Downgrade The reduction of credit rating for a borrowing institution or its debt instruments. Opposite to upgrade.
▶ *See also* Credit Rating, Upgrade.

Downsizing A euphemism for the process of reducing the workforce of an organization, which usually involves laying off a significant number of employees.

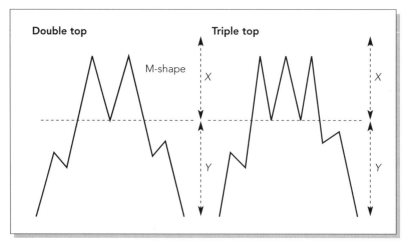

FIGURE 7 Double top/Triple top

Downstream Oil operations such as refining, transportation and marketing that take place after crude is produced.
▶ *See also* Crude Oil, Downstream.

Downtrend Generally used to describe a falling trend in prices. The term is used more exactly in technical analysis where a trendline links four successively lower price points to identify a downtrend.
▶ *See also* Technical Analysis, Trendline.

Dow Theory The term generally used to describe Charles Dow's ideas about stock market behaviour. Dow applied his ideas to the stock market averages (indices) he designed – the Dow Jones Industrial Average (DJIA) and the Dow Jones Transportation Average (DJTA). His theories are widely recognized to be the foundation to many modern technical anlaysis disciplines. Dow Theory is also used specifically to describe one of Dow's theories – that a major trend in the US stock market has to be confirmed by a parallel change in the DJIA and DJTA.
▶ *See also* Technical Analysis.

Dragon Bonds Bonds issued by Asian companies outside Japan and usually denominated in US dollars. Dragon bonds are usually short-dated, three to five years, and issued by companies who want to expand their range of investors from among Asia's rapidly growing economies.

Drawdown Taking delivery of funds made available from financial institutions. It can include credits from the IMF, eurocredits from banks, or corporate use of credit granted by a domestic bank.
▶ *See also* IMF.

DTCC Depository Trust Clearing Corporation. A US central depository for securities certificates and registrations. Used for Street Name or Nominee Account holdings. ▨ **http://dtcservices.dtcc.com** ▨
▶ *See also* Depository, Nominee Account.

Dual Currency Bond A bond that pays a coupon in one currency, but is redeemed for a fixed amount of another currency, often the dollar. Investors usually get an above-market coupon, but run the risk that, in this example, the dollar would fall below the exchange rate implied when the amount was fixed. These bonds are attractive to borrowers who operate in the redemption currency because they have no long-term exchange rate risk. For other borrowers, the guaranteed exchange rate can be used in a swap, for example, with corporations having liabilities in the currency of issue.
▶ *See also* Swap.

Dual Listing A company which is listed on more than one stock exchange.

Dual Pricing Identical product sold at different prices in different markets or countries.

Dubai Crude A leading benchmark crude oil produced in the United Arab Emirates, used in pricing sour crudes, predominantly for pricing Middle East crude exports to Asia.

Due Diligence Process The investigation process into the operation and management of a potential investment target or borrower to verify material facts. It is usually performed by investors or lead managers.

Duration A measure of the average maturity of a bond's cash flows from both coupons and principal repayment, or how long you have to wait to earn exactly half the expected total return in coupons and principal repayment. A zero coupon bond's duration would be the same as the maturity date because there are no coupons to take into account. Duration, quoted in years, indicates the average exposure to market risk. It allows bonds with different coupons and maturities to be compared. Bonds with higher durations face higher risk from changes in interest rates. Also known as Macauley Duration.
▶ *See also* Coupon.

Dutch Auction An auction where the price is lowered gradually – from a price well above the true value – until a responsive bid is seen. This then becomes the price at which the offering is sold. The US Treasury sells its Treasury bills using a similar basis where the bids are termed tenders.
▶ *See also* Treasury Bill.

DVP Delivery Versus Payment. The normal method of settling bond trades whereby delivery of the security is made on the same day as payment is effected.

DWT Dead weight tonnes. The measurement of a ship by the maximum weight it can carry, including cargo, fuel and stores. The weight is measured in metric tonnes (1000 kg or 2,204 lbs) or long tons (2,240 lbs).

Dynamic Time and Sales Alternative term for volume-weighted average price or VWAP.
▶ *See* Volume-weighted Average Price.

E

Early Estimates ▶ *See* Consensus Estimates.

Early Exercise When a security or option is exercised before its due maturity date. American-style options can be exercised at any time, allowing early exercise. European-style options can be exercised only at the maturity date.

Early Redemption The repurchase of a bond by the issuer before it matures.

Earnings Per Share ▶ *See* EPS.

Earnings Shock An earnings report that differs from analysts' expectations in their consensus estimates. An earnings shock often causes a substantial movement in the company's share price.
▶ *See also* Consensus Estimates.

EBT Earnings Before Tax.

EBIT Earnings Before Interest and Tax.

EBITDA Earnings Before Interest, Taxes, Depreciation and Amortization.

EBRD European Bank for Reconstruction and Development. A bank set up by the major industrialized nations to help centrally planned economies in 27 countries from central Europe to central Asia move to a free market in a democratic environment. It is owned by governments but invests mainly in private enterprise, usually with commercial partners. ▪ **www.ebrd.com** ▪

ECB European Central Bank. The bank sets monetary policy for the 'Eurozone' countries within the Economic and Monetary Union. It replaced the European Monetary Institute when the euro single currency was introduced. ▪ **www.ecb.int** ▪
▶ *See also* EU, EMU, Eurozone.

ECLAC United Nations Economic Commission for Latin America and the Caribbean. ▪ **www.eclac.cl** ▪

ECN Electronic Communications Network. Electronic stock markets which anonymously match buy and sell orders.

ECOFIN A regular gathering of EU economics or finance ministers. The main forum for co-ordination of economic and financial policy within the European Union.
▶ *See also* EU.

E-commerce Electronic commerce. A term used to describe all forms of buying and selling of goods electronically.

Econometrics The use of statistical and mathematical methods to verify and develop economic theories. Also covers the development of plans and implementation of policies based on economic findings.

Economic and Monetary Union ▶ *See* EMU.

Economic Indicators Published data that provide information on the state of an economy, such as gross domestic product, the consumer price index, money supply, the trade balance and unemployment. They can give clues about the future direction of output and demand, prompting reaction from consumers, governments, companies and financial markets. Leading indicators move ahead of the overall economic cycle; lagging indicators move afterwards and coincident indicators move at the same time.
▶ *See also* Lagging Indicators, Leading Indicators, Coincident Indicators.

Economic Risk The risk associated with changes in exchange rates or local regulations, which could favour services or products of a competitor.

Economies of Scale The theory that it is cheaper and more efficient to produce additional units of a product because the fixed costs of production, such as land and buildings, are spread over a larger amount of output. The marginal cost, or the cost of the last unit of production, drops as more output is produced.

ECONOMY
....

An overview of how economies are measured. The **words in bold** are explained more fully under their individual entries.

Size and growth
The size of a country's economy, or its total output of goods and services, is measured by the **gross national product** or **GNP**, representing all the output that the country and its nationals

own and control. GNP includes not only output produced within the country's boundaries, but also output overseas produced by the country's foreign investment or expatriate workers.

Gross national product can, however, overstate or understate what's actually happening inside the specific economy so a more commonly used measure of output is **gross domestic product** or **GDP**. That comprises all the output of goods and services produced within the country, even if some of it is produced by foreign capital and by foreign workers. A country such as Britain with large overseas investments will have a gross national product that is larger than its gross domestic product. Conversely an economy such as Saudi Arabia that uses lots of migrant labour will have a gross domestic product larger than its gross national product.

Not many people think of total GDP in currency terms when measuring an economy. It is unusual to state that the GDP of Norway is more than $160 billion. It's more usual to be aware of the relative size of economies, and to know that the US economy is about 60 times as large as Norway's. **GDP per head** gives a much clearer picture of relative wealth of nations, and on that measure Norway is slightly richer than the United States.

Even more important is the **real**, or inflation-adjusted, change in gross domestic product over a given period, which shows how quickly an economy is growing or shrinking. Real growth is measured by adding up the total output of goods and services and reducing that number by the **GDP deflator**, an official calculation of inflation. Growth is usually expressed as a percentage change. It can be the actual change in the period, or the **annualized** change in the period.

You can look at the overall size of an economy by measuring where income comes from – industrial production, agricultural production or the service sector. Or you can look at how output is consumed – by private consumption, public or government consumption, investment, or by being shipped abroad as net exports.

Some elements of GDP are easier to measure than others. **Industrial production**, or factory output, is relatively easy to assess and in most developed economies the change in industrial output is measured and published monthly. Agricultural output is less important to most economies, changes at a much slower seasonal pace and is subject to vagaries beyond the control of farmers. The service sector is also relatively hard to measure and requires estimates of output from sectors such as insurance, banking, the

▶

media and catering. There are other figures that give guidance on the level of industrial output, such as **stocks** (or inventories), new orders and **backlogs**.

On the spending side of the economy, the easiest factor to track is **consumption**, which is usually measured on a monthly basis through indices such as retail sales or the level of consumer credit. Economists and traders also want to know the likely pattern of future changes, so they watch closely for changes in indices of **consumer confidence**.

Government consumption can be tracked on a monthly basis through its own published figures. In theory it should be broadly predictable from figures published in the annual **budget**, and should not be subject to wild swings.

Investment is harder to track. It is often spent in large and unpredictable lumps. The final element of the consumption side of the national economy is net exports, which are tracked by **trade figures**.

Imports and exports of physical goods are relatively easy to track and monthly trade figures are an important indicator of the health of the economy. The measurement of trade in physical merchandise is added to figures on trade in **invisibles** to calculate the **current account** of the **balance of payments**. Movements in and out of the country of sums of capital for investment, borrowing and aid are measured in the **capital account**. The overall balance of payments comprises the current and the capital accounts.

Inflation

It is almost impossible to measure growth in an economy without knowing the rate of **inflation**. Measurements in money terms are useless because it is impossible to distinguish between **real** and **nominal** changes. Changes in prices, and in the level of inflation, can be measured at the retail level, using a **consumer price index**. Inflation can also be measured at other stages in the economy by capturing data on **wholesale** prices or factory gate prices.

Unemployment

The number of people in work and seeking work is a valuable measurement of economic activity. **Unemployment** figures are usually published monthly. Some economies also publish figures for employment, such as the non-farm payrolls in the United States. A related measure of the economy is the level of average earnings, which reflects supply and demand for labour.

Currency

The value of a country's currency and its relative movement against major traded currencies is a valuable indicator of the health of an economy. Some market analysts regard currency rates and interest rates as the best and most definitive signals. You need to know where a country has a **free-floating exchange** regime in which foreign exchange rates are set purely by supply and demand in the open market. If a country's currency does not float freely it may be fixed at a set **rate** which is defended by central bank intervention, the sale and purchase of foreign currencies to change rates. Or the currency may have a **dirty float**, with a rate defended only on certain occasions, or a **crawling peg** that allows controlled changes.

Balance of payments

The performance of a currency is largely affected by supply and demand, which in turn is dependent on the **balance of payments**. If a country is exporting more than its imports, and running a surplus on its balance of trade, then foreigners will want to hold its currency to buy its goods and the currency is likely to appreciate. Similarly if the country is an attractive place to invest then foreigners will demand its currency for **foreign direct investment** or **portfolio** investments. That influence will show up in the capital account of the balance of payments.

If the current and capital accounts are in deficit, or if there is a sudden loss of confidence in a country's economy, then the currency is likely to **depreciate** and may be subject to a formal **devaluation**. The pressure may show up first in a sharp drop in the country's **foreign exchange reserves**. If the pressure continues and the country is likely to run out of foreign currency to pay for essential imports it may have to turn to the **International Monetary Fund** for emergency assistance, which is usually granted only on strict conditions of economic reform.

Interest rates

Interest rates can be another major influence on a currency. High rates increase the reward for holding the currency and help to offset the risks of depreciation or devaluation. There is usually one key interest rate in an economy which acts as a benchmark for all other rates. In the United States it is the **discount rate**, which the Federal Reserve Bank charges to commercial banks for short-term loans. It is changed infrequently but gives important insight into the central bank's monetary policy and expectations. Markets also closely

▶

watch the **Fed funds rate**. Commercial banks borrow at that rate the funds they need to meet their **reserve requirements** with the central bank.

The overall level of interest rates in an economy often reflects the government's need to control **inflation**. High rates choke off demand for consumption and investment. Lower rates stimulate spending and can stimulate growth.

Budget

Interest rates can themselves be affected by the level of government spending, set out in its **budget**. If the government runs a large budget deficit, spending more than it collects in taxes, it can boost spending and inflation and can force up interest rates because of its competition for a limited supply of funds. Currency, equity and bond markets all watch closely for changes in government spending and tax collection, and the consequent changes in the overall budget deficit and level of government debt.

Money supply

At one time the money supply was a crucial economic indicator. Its importance has shrunk with the change of emphasis on controlling the economy through the price of money, or interest rates, rather than the supply of money.

EDSP The Exchange Delivery Settlement Price is the official closing price of a futures contract given by the futures exchange at the end of every trading day. This price is used for marking-to-market purposes and for calculating actual cash settlement amounts required on the expiry date or on the closing out of a futures position.

▶ *See also* Futures, Mark to Market.

Effective Exchange Rate A currency's composite exchange rate against other currencies. It is normally presented as an index intended to reflect the overall performance of a currency against its main trading partners on a trade-weighted basis.

▶ *See also* Index, Trade Weighted.

Efficient Market Hypothesis The theory that all available information about an asset is reflected in the price of that asset.

EFTA The European Free Trade Association has its headquarters in Geneva and comprises Iceland, Norway, Switzerland and Liechtenstein. It promotes free trade within its members' borders and has a customs union with the European Union. ■ **www.efta.int** ■

▶ *See also* EU.

EGM Extraordinary General Meeting. A company meeting of shareholders called for an extraordinary purpose such as the approval of a merger or a capital increase (in contrast with the annual general meeting, which is a routine meeting of shareholders to approve the accounts and dividend payments and to elect directors).

EIB European Investment Bank. The long-term financing body of the European Union. It raises funds in the market to foster regional development among the member nations and especially to aid less-developed areas on a macro-economic scale. It also provides soft loans to developing countries associated with the European Union.

■ **www.eib.org** ■

▶ *See also* EU.

Either Way ▶ *See* Choice Price.

Electronic Communications Network ▶ *See* ECN.

Elevator Pitch A summary of a business proposition, brief and succinct enough to be delivered in the time taken by an elevator ride, preferably with someone influential.

Eligible Bills A bill is said to be eligible when it can be delivered to a central bank at the discount window in return for funds.

▶ *See also* Bill of Exchange, Discount Rate, Discount Window.

Elliott Wave Theory A technical analysis theory, which states that the market follows a repetitive pattern, with each cycle made up of a five-wave rise followed by a three-wave fall. There are many different degrees of trend, but the Elliott wave theory categorizes nine different trends (or magnitude) ranging from a grand supercycle covering 200 years to a subminuette of only a couple of hours. The eight-wave cycle is constant, regardless of what degree of trend is being considered.

▶ *See also* Technical Analysis.

Embargo A temporary action taken by one country to halt shipment of goods into or out of another country.

EMBI Emerging Markets Bond Index. A benchmark bond market index produced by investment bank J.P. Morgan. The investment bank also produces the EMBI+, Emerging Markets Bond Index Plus which covers Eurobonds and US dollar local market instruments as well as the Brady bonds in the main EMBI.

■ **www2.jpmorgan.com/MarketDataInd/EMBI/embi.html** ■

Emerging Markets A term used to describe the financial markets of developing countries. Definitions vary of which countries are emerging and which are not. However, the emerging market indices compiled by the IFC and Morgan Stanley are often used as benchmarks.
▶ *See also* IFC, MSCI Indices, S&P/IFCI.

EMI European Monetary Institute. The EMI was a precursor to the European Central Bank.
▶ *See also* ECB (European Central Bank).

EMS European Monetary System. A system that links the member states of the European Union.

EMTA Emerging Markets Traders Association. An industry interest group which promotes fair, efficient and transparent trading of emerging market financial instruments. ▦ **www.emta.org** ▦

EMTN European Medium-term Notes; Medium-term notes issued in the Euromarkets. Medium-term notes are borrowings with terms of up to five years, typically issued on the same terms as commercial paper. Euromarkets are the international capital markets dealing in offshore currency deposits held in banks outside their country of origin.
▶ *See also* MTN, CP.

EMU Economic and Monetary Union. The single market within the European Union, which allows free movement of people, goods, capital and services. Stage three of Economic and Monetary Union saw the introduction of a single currency, the euro, in 1999, and the creation of the European Central Bank (ECB).
▶ *See also* ECB, EU, Euro.

Encryption A security measure designed to prevent electronically transmitted information from being accessed by anyone other than the intended recipient. Encryption involves coding the information in such a way that only the recipient can decipher it.

Enhanced Scrip Dividend A dividend to shareholders in the form of extra shares which have a market value greater than the value of the dividend. They can usually be sold immediately by the holder.
▶ *See also* Dividend.

Enlarged Access Method of allowing countries to bend some of the rules in lending by the IMF, provided they promise to undertake strong policy measures aimed at redressing payment imbalances.
▶ *See also* IMF.

Enterprise Value ▶ *See* EV.

Enterprise Zone Sites in depressed, mostly inner-urban areas, where companies are given favourable taxation treatment and are freed of various planning regulations.

EPS
......

Earnings Per Share. These are net profits divided by the number of ordinary shares outstanding. A company which earned an attributable profit of £10 million in the previous financial year and with two million shares outstanding has an EPS of five pounds.

Historical or trailing EPS are earnings per share for the last available financial year or quarter. Forecast EPS are earnings as forecast by analysts. A consensus forecast is an average or median figure derived from several individual forecasts. EPS is a key component of the Price/Earning ratio.

Formula: Net Profit/Shares Outstanding

Example

In the last complete financial year The Old Rope Corporation earned a net profit of £64 million. At the end of the year it had 350 million shares outstanding.

Old Rope's EPS = £64 million / 350 million shares = £0.183 or 18.3 pence per share.

The consensus forecast for net profit this year is £72 million, which divided by 350 million shares produces a forecast EPS of 20.5 pence.

The consensus forecast for net profit the following year is £85 million producing a forecast EPS of 24.3 pence.

▶ *See also* P/E Ratio.

Equity The shareholders' stake in a company. Equity markets are the markets in which shares or stocks are issued and traded.

Equity Financing Selling common or preferred stock to investors to raise funds.

Equity Options Options that give the holder the right, but not the obligation, to buy or sell a stock or share at a particular price on or before a certain date.

▶ *See also* Options.

Equity Risk Premium The extra return that the overall stock market or a particular stock must provide over the rate on Treasury bills to compensate for market risk. Treasury bills are regarded as risk free because they are guaranteed by the government.

Equity Swap A corporate takeover or merger that does not involve cash, but that is carried out by the exchange of shares in one company for those in the other. Sometimes shares in two companies will be swapped for equity in a third newly-created enterprise in a ratio reflecting the underlying assets or worth of the two companies merging.

ERA Exchange Rate Agreement. This is a foreign exchange derivative contract based on a synthetic or constructed forward in which settlement is based on the difference between two foreign exchange forward rates and not the spot rate. In contrast, a standard forward exchange agreement or FXA is based on the difference between the forward rate on the start date of the contract and the spot rate at settlement.
▶ *See also* Derivative, Forwards, FXA, Spot.

ERM Exchange Rate Mechanism. A system first created in 1979 to limit movements in the currencies of member countries of the European Union. A grid allows currencies to fluctuate within bands either side of their fixed central rates. New countries are supposed to enter their currencies in ERM-2, with its wide 15 percent bands, for two years before joining the Eurozone.
▶ *See also* Euro, European Union.

Escrow Money, property or financial instruments put into the care of a third party for delivery only when certain specified conditions are met. Such money is held in an Escrow account.

ETF Exchange-traded Fund. An investment vehicle which issues and trades shares representing an underlying basket of assets, typically the constituents of a major share-market index. ETFs allow small investors to diversify their risk over a broad spread of investments, tracking an index, while offering the flexibility of trading like a share.

EU European Union. The umbrella term introduced in the Maastricht Treaty to refer to the three-pillar construction in Europe of the European Community and two new areas of co-operation; common foreign and security policy, and justice and home affairs. It has taken over in common usage to refer to the Community in all its aspects.
■ http://europa.eu.int ■

EUREX The European Derivatives Exchange created in 1998 by the merger of the DTB and SOFFEX. ■ www.eurexchange.com ■
▶ *See also* DTB, SOFFEX.

Euribor Euro-denominated Interbank Offered Rate. The Europe-wide version of the London and Paris interbank offered rates, which are the rates that banks lend to each other in the money market. Euribor serves as a benchmark short-term interest rate for European money markets.
▶ *See also* FRN, LIBOR.

Euro The EU's single currency introduced in 1999 by the 11 Eurozone countries that joined stage three of EMU.
▶ *See also* EMU, Eurozone.

Eurobond Bonds issued by a country or company in a currency that is not their own, e.g. a Japanese company issuing a dollar bond. They are not subject to withholding tax and fall outside the jurisdiction of any one country. Not to be confused with euro-denominated bonds, which are bonds issued in euros.

Euroclear International clearing organization that provides clearance/settlement and borrowing/lending of securities and funds through a computerized book-entry system. The system covers both bonds and equities and serves major financial institutions in more than 80 countries. ■ **www.euroclear.com** ■
▶ *See also* Clearstream, Clearing House, Clearing System.

Eurocredits/Euroloans Large bank credits, usually in maturities of three to ten years, granted by international bank syndicates put together on an ad hoc basis. Lenders are almost exclusively banks and finance companies and these credits are not placed with private investors. Interest rates are calculated by adding a margin to interbank-offered rates and usually adjusted every three to six months. Funds for the loans are drawn from the Eurodeposit market.
▶ *See also* Eurodeposit.

Eurocurrency A currency that is held on deposit outside its country of origin. The most extensively used Eurocurrency is the Eurodollar.

Euro-denominated Interbank Offered Rate ▶ *See* Euribor.

Eurodeposits Fixed-rate deposits that are traded wholesale between banks. Eurodeposits have maturities that range from overnight to one year.
▶ *See also* Eurocredits.

Eurodollar A US dollar held on deposit outside the United States.
▶ *See also* Eurocurrency.

Euroland ▶ *See* Eurozone.

Euromarkets An overall term for international capital markets dealing in offshore currency deposits held in banks outside their county of origin.
▶ *See also* Eurobonds, Eurocredits, Eurodeposits.

Euronext An integrated cross-border European market for equities, bonds, derivatives and commodities created initially by the merger of exchanges in Amsterdam, Brussels and Paris. The exchange has its own stock indices, including Euronext 100 and Next 150.
▉ www.euronext.com ▉

European Bank for Reconstruction and Development ▶ *See* EBRD.

European Derivatives Exchange ▶ *See* EDE.

European Free Trade Area ▶ *See* EFTA.

European Investment Bank ▶ *See* EIB.

European Monetary Institute ▶ *See* EMI.

European Monetary System ▶ *See* EMS.

European Option An option that the holder can exercise only on the expiry date.
▶ *See also* American Option, Option.

European Union ▶ *See* EU.

Eurostat The statistics agency of the European Union.
▉ http://europa.eu.int/comm/eurostat/ ▉

Euro STOXX Shorthand for the Dow Jones Euro STOXX50, one of over 200 indices covering 16 stock markets in Europe compiled by Dow Jones. The Euro STOXX is used as a benchmark for tracking Europe's stock markets. It comprises 50 blue-chip European stocks.
▉ www.djindexes.com ▉

Eurotop 100/300 These are both pan-European stock indices compiled by FTSE International. The Eurotop 300 consists of Europe's largest 300 companies and is widely used as a benchmark for tracking the European stock market. The Eurotop 100 covers the 100 most traded large capitalization stocks. ▉ www.ftse.com ▉ ▉ www.reuters.com ▉

Eurozone (Euro Zone) A term used to describe the 11 EU countries that joined the third stage of EMU and adopted the euro. The Eurozone, or Euroland, countries are Austria, Belgium, Finland, France, Germany, Ireland, Italy, Luxembourg, The Netherlands, Portugal and Spain.
▶ *See also* EU, EMU.

EV Enterprise Value. A measure of how the share market values a company. It comprises market capitalization plus debt and preferred shares minus the company's holding of cash. Enterprise value divided by EBITDA is often used to measure the value of listed companies, because the EV includes a company's debt (and thus a measure of total cost in case of a takeover *and* the leverage involved), while the divider (EBITDA) focuses on the company's core earnings power, ignoring elements that may vary depending on local regulations.
▶ *See also* EBITDA.

EVA Economic Value Added. Conceived by consultants Stern Stewart & Co., EVA is a popular method of measuring a company's profitability. EVA is calculated by taking the total cost of capital from post-tax operating profit.

Even Lot A commodity trading unit governed by official exchange price quotations.

Ex Means excluding. Thus ex-cap, ex-div, ex-rights. Ex indicates that a buyer of shares does not receive a current capitalization issue, a current dividend or a current rights issue. It is opposite of cum dividend.
▶ *See also* Cum Dividend.

Ex-All Means a buyer of shares does not receive any of the supplementary benefits attached to a share at the time.

Exceptional Item An item that is within normal business activities, but is of unusual size. It is usually recorded separately in the profit and loss account.
▶ *See also* Extraordinary Item.

Excess Portfolio Returns The return on a portfolio over and above a 'risk-free' rate (such as the yield on US Treasury bills).
▶ *See also* Portfolio.

Exchange An exchange provides a safe environment in which market participants can trade. Regulated exchanges are like clubs in that they have approved members and a formal set of rules to govern members' behaviour.

Exchangeable Bonds Similar to convertible bonds but not linked to the shares of the issuer. They can be exchanged for shares in another company, which the issuer may already own.
▶ *See also* Convertible Bonds.

Exchange Controls Regulations to prevent or restrict certain foreign currency transactions, mostly by a country's nationals. Used to protect and maintain a country's financial position and the value of its currency.

Exchange Delivery Settlement Price ▶ *See* EDSP.

Exchange for Cash ▶ *See* Exchange for Physical.

Exchange for Physical This occurs where the buyer of a cash commodity transfers to the seller an equivalent amount of long-futures contracts, or receives from him a corresponding amount of short futures at an agreed price. Also termed exchange for cash, and against actuals.

Exchange Rate Agreement ▶ *See* ERA.

Exchange Rate Mechanism ▶ *See* ERM.

Exchange-traded Contract Standard futures and options listed and traded on a recognized exchange. The opposite to over-the-counter.
▶ *See also* OTC.

Ex-Dividend This indicates shares that have been bought without the right to receive the dividend, i.e. the seller retains the dividend.
▶ *See also* Cum Dividend.

Exercise To make use of the right possessed by the holder of an option. The option holder notifies the writer that they wish to exercise or assign their option. The writer is then obliged to the holder on the terms already agreed – they must buy or sell the underlying asset.
▶ *See also* Assign.

Exercise Price ▶ *See* Strike Price.

EX-IM Bank of Japan The Export-Import Bank of Japan, a state-owned bank that specializes in loans to developing countries. As a government-backed institution it can borrow on the Japanese markets at favourable rates.

Exit bond A long-term bond with a low interest rate, often issued by a less developed country, that gives the buyer the right of exemption from taking part in any subsequent rescheduling. Thus an exit bond allows an investor to convert his existing loans and offers a way out of sovereign lending when the bond is resold or when it matures.
▶ *See also* Rescheduling.

Exotic A term used to describe unusual or complicated financial instruments. The opposite of 'vanilla' instruments. In foreign exchange markets the term exotic is used to describe currencies of emerging market countries.
▶ *See also* Emerging Markets, Plain Vanilla.

Expiry Date The date on which delivery takes place on a futures contract. In options trading, it is the date on which a European option can be exercised.

> ▶ *See also* Futures and Options.

Exponential Moving Average A weighted moving average that gives more weight to recent price action.

> ▶ *See also* Moving Average.

Export Enhancement Programme A US programme that allows exporters to receive a subsidy to sell US products to foreign customers at world market prices. The US Department of Agriculture subsidises the difference between the world price and the higher domestic price – which exporters have to pay for the product – in the form of commodities from the Commodity Credit Corporation inventory or cash.

> ■ **www.fas.usda.gov/excredits/eep.html** ■

Export Quota A quota set under an international commodity agreement whereby exporting countries of a particular commodity accept limits on their exports. It is also a bilateral or multilateral agreement between countries governing exports of industrial or other goods.

> ▶ *See also* Commodity Agreement.

Exposure The total amount of credit committed to a borrower or a country. Effectively, the total amount at risk in the case of default. Banks can set rules to prevent overexposure to any single borrower. In trading operations, exposure is the potential for running a profit or loss from fluctuations in market prices.

Ex-Rights A term associated with a rights issue. It indicates when stocks are trading without rights.

> ▶ *See also* Rights Issue.

Extended Fund Facility Assistance given to IMF member nations with economies suffering from serious balance of payments difficulties caused by structural imbalances in production, trade and prices. Or alternatively, to those countries whose economies are characterized by slow growth and an inherently weak balance of payments position. Drawings can be made over a period of three years under conditions similar to IMF standby drawings. ■ **www.imf.org** ■

> ▶ *See also* IMF.

Extendible Bond A bond on which terms are reset for a further period beyond the initial maturity date. Typically both the borrower and the investor will have the right to redeem the bonds at these refixings.

Extraordinary Item A non-recurring item which shows gains or losses outside normal business activities. An extraordinary item is shown in the profit and loss account and affects the balance sheet. It can be, for example, the sale of property or loss from selling part of the company.
> ▶ *See also* Exceptional Item.

Extrapolation The process of determining a rate (or other variable) that lies beyond the range of known rates.
> ▶ *See also* Interpolation.

F

FA Abbreviation of Indonesian company title: Firma.

Face Value On a share certificate or bond, the face value is what appears on the face of the document. On a debt instrument, it is the amount to be repaid at maturity. On a share it is a purely nominal amount and has no relevance to the market value of the instrument. Face value is also known as 'par value' or 'nominal value'.

Facility Fee A payment made by a borrower to a lender for arranging a loan.

Failure Swing A term used in technical analysis with specific reference to the Relative Strength Index (RSI). A top failure swing occurs when the market is in an uptrend and the RSI is over 70 but the next peak fails to exceed the previous peak. Similarly, a bottom failure swing occurs if the market is in a downtrend and the RSI is below 30 but the next peak fails to fall below the previous peak.
▶ *See also* Technical Analysis.

Fair Average Quality ▶ *See* FAQ.

Fair Value A term used in the futures market that represents the cash price plus the net cost of carry. The fair-value calculation for an equities index future is different for every account. It can be defined as any of the following:
- the estimated premium over cash to allow for dividend flows and carrying costs
- the allowance for expected dividend flows and financing costs involved in holding the contract until expiry
- how much higher futures should be over a share index after balancing the attractive financing cost of futures against the dividends that shareholders receive
- accounts for financing costs and share dividends
- the difference between the interest on cash and the dividends paid on the index over the remaining life of the future.
▶ *See also* Futures, Carrying Charge.

Fallen Angels Bonds that were originally above investment grade, but which have subsequently fallen in credit quality.

Fannie Mae Federal National Mortgage Association (FNMA). A stock-holder-owned corporation that was established in 1938 and is sponsored by the US government. The FNMA's main purpose is to increase the affordability of home mortgage funds for low-, moderate- and middle-income buyers and it is the largest source of home mortgage funds in the United States. Fannie Mae provides funds to the mortgage market primarily by buying mortgages from mortgage origi-nators. These are then held in an investment portfolio or pooled for FNMA members. Purchases are financed by the sale of corporate obli-gations to private investors. ■ www.fanniemae.com ■

FAO The Food and Agriculture Organization is an offshoot of the United Nations, concerned with the agricultural, forestry and fishing indus-tries. ■ www.fao.org ■

FAQ Fair Average Quality. FAQ is an average grade based on samples that is used in the sale of agricultural commodities.

FASB The Financial Accounting Standards Board was established in 1973 to establish and supervise accounting rules in the United States. ■ www.fasb.org ■

FCM Futures Commission Merchant. An individual or legal entity who is registered with the Commodity Futures Trading Commission in the USA to seek business for execution on a listed commodity exchange.

FDI Foreign Direct Investment. In business, FDI implies long-term involve-ment, a degree of managerial control and possibly technical input from the investor.

FDIC ▶ *See* Federal Deposit Insurance Corporation.

Fed Shorthand for the US central bank.
    ▶ *See also* Federal Reserve System.

Federal Deposit Insurance Corporation A US federal agency, established in 1933, that provides limited guarantees for funds deposited with member banks. It also takes action to help banks merge or avoid fail-ure. ■ www.fdic.gov ■

Federal Energy Regulatory Commission ▶ *See* FERC.

Federal Home Loan Mortgage Corporation ▶ *See* Freddie Mac.

Federal Open Market Committee ▶ *See* FOMC.

Federal Reserve Board This board runs the Federal Reserve System, which controls US monetary policy and oversees the banking industry. Its seven governors are appointed for 14-year terms by the US president (with Senate approval), but each chairman's term is only four years, thereby allowing each president the possibility of influencing the choice of chairman. The FOMC, a sub-committee of the board, sets US interest rates.
▶ *See also* Federal Reserve System, FOMC.

Federal Reserve System Established in 1913, the Federal Reserve System is the central bank system of the US. Although its board is selected by the US president, it is considered to be an independent entity. It comprises the Federal Reserve Board, the 12 Federal Reserve Banks, their 24 branches and all national and state member banks. They regulate money supply, set reserve requirements, supervise printing of currency, act as a clearing house for the transfer of funds throughout the banking system and ensure that member banks meet Federal Reserve regulations. ■ **www.federalreserve.gov** ■
▶ *See also* Federal Reserve Board, FOMC.

Fed Funds Reserve balances deposited at the Federal Reserve Bank by US commercial banks. These funds can be lent out to other member banks to meet short-term reserve requirements and the rate at which they are lent is known as the Fed Funds rate. This is one of two key US interest rates, the other being the discount rate. Fed Funds can also refer to the money used by the Federal Reserve to pay for its purchases of government securities.
▶ *See also* Discount Rate, Federal Reserve System.

Feeds Animal foodstuffs are classified by the livestock for which they are designed: poultry, hog, dairy, cattle/sheep, speciality and small animal.

FERC Federal Energy Regulatory Commission. An agency within the US Department of Energy that oversees regulation of interstate natural gas pipelines and gas prices. ■ **www.ferc.fed.us** ■

Fiat Money Paper money issued by a government that is not convertible into gold or silver. It derives its purchasing power simply from the authority and reputation of the government.

Fibonacci Numbers A number sequence discovered by a thirteenth-century Italian mathematician Leonardo Fibonacci in which the sum of any two consecutive numbers equals the next highest number. The ratio of any number to its next highest number approaches 0.618 after the first four numbers. These numbers are used by technical analysts to determine price objectives from percentage retracements.
▶ *See also* Retracements, Technical Analysis.

Fiduciary Money Money held in trust and invested on behalf of a beneficiary. A fiduciary is one who holds assets for a beneficiary, such as an executor of a will.

FIFO First In First Out. A method of valuing stocks, or inventory, where the oldest stock is sold first.
▶ *See also* LIFO.

Fill or Kill FOK. An order to buy or sell a share that must be cancelled if not carried out immediately. FOKs are often used when an investor wants to buy a large quantity of stock at a particular price.

Final Dividend A dividend paid to shareholders by a company at the end of its financial year and authorized by shareholders at the annual general meeting.

Financial Accounting Standards Board ▶ *See* FASB.

Financial Centre A country's key location for international and domestic, commercial and government financial transactions. Financial centres are often in a country's capital, e.g. Tokyo, Paris, Brussels and the City in London, but financial centres in non-capital cities include New York, Chicago, Frankfurt, Milan, Hong Kong, Sydney, Toronto and Osaka.

Financial Intermediation Financial intermediaries bring together users of capital, such as businesses and governments, with suppliers of capital such as pension funds and private investors. The term is usually reserved for describing the activities of commercial and investment banks.
▶ *See also* Disintermediation.

The Financial Services Authority ▶ *See* FSA.

Financial Stability Forum ▶ *See* FSF.

Financial Year The year used for a company's accounting purposes. It can be a calendar year or it can cover a different period, often starting in April. It can also be referred to as the company's fiscal year.

Firm Order An order to buy or sell a share that can be executed without further confirmation. It can also mean a commercial order of goods which cannot be cancelled.

First Coupon The date on which an initial interest payment is due to the holder of a bond.

First Notice Day The first date on which the seller of a futures contract is authorized to give notice of intention to deliver actual financial instruments or physical commodities against that futures contract.
▶ *See also* Futures.

Fiscal Balance The balance of a government's tax revenues, plus any proceeds of asset sales, minus government spending. If the balance is positive the government has a fiscal surplus, if negative there is a fiscal deficit.

Fiscal Policy The budgetary policies through which a government influences the economy, such as changes in taxation and government spending.
> *See also* Monetary Policy.

Fiscal Year The accounting year for a government or a company, often starting in either January or April.

Fix The setting of an official price for a currency or commodity, often on a daily basis.

Fixed Assets Assets bought by a company for its continued use for a number of years, rather than for resale. There are three categories of fixed assets:
- tangible assets, such as land and equipment
- intangible assets, such as a company's logo or brand
- investments, such as stakes in joint ventures.
> *See also* Assets.

Fixed Capital Fixed assets that are purchased out of paid-up capital.
> *See also* Paid-up Capital.

Fixed Costs Company costs such as interest charges, insurance and rent, which do not vary with the level of production or sales. On the other hand, variable costs, such as raw materials and labour, do change with the level of production or sales.

Fixed Exchange Rate A system in which currencies have exchange values with fixed rate relationships (or parities) with the US dollar or other currencies.
> *See also* Bretton Woods, Floating Exchange Rate.

Fixed/Floating Bonds Bonds that pay both fixed- and floating-rate interest at different periods during their life.

Fixed Income The generic term for debt instruments (such as bonds and loans) which pay interest in the form of a coupon. The rate of interest is often fixed, hence the term 'fixed income'.
> *See also* Debt, Coupon.

Fixed Price Offer New issues are offered on either a tender or a fixed price reoffer basis. In the latter, the issue is marketed at a predetermined fixed price and coupon. Most new bond issues are offered on this basis.
> *See also* Tender Offer.

Fixed-term Deposit Deposits placed in the money markets with commercial banks for fixed periods by individuals, companies, banks or governments. These deposits are non-negotiable. They cannot be transferred or cashed in before maturity. Maturities can vary from overnight to one year.

▶ *See also* CD.

Flags/Pennants These price patterns, used in technical analysis, represent brief pauses after a sharp advance or decline that has gone ahead of itself. The market trades in a tight range for a while before running off in the direction of the main trend. Flags and pennants are among the most reliable continuation patterns in technical analysis and rarely produce a trend reversal. (Figure 8.)

▶ *See also* Technical Analysis.

Flat The price of a share or financial instrument that is neither rising nor falling; also called sideways. Also, a bond that is trading without accrued interest, such as a bond in default, and a position in a market, or a financial instrument, which is balanced – neither long nor short – are referred to as flat.

Flight to Quality A movement by investors to purchase safer (more secure and higher quality) securities, typically Treasuries. This normally occurs if investors are expecting political instability or a deterioration in economic activity.

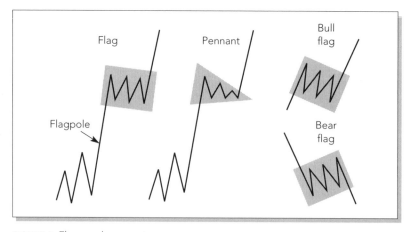

FIGURE 8 Flags and pennants

Floating Debt Debt with a floating interest rate as opposed to fixed.

Floating Exchange Rates A system in which currencies have no fixed parities and exchange rates. Prices are determined by supply and demand in the free market. A country's currency strengthens or weakens based on the underlying strength of its economy and its relationship with its trading partners. An overly strong currency can damage exports by making its goods too expensive for other countries to buy. A weak currency makes its exports cheaper to buy and its imports more expensive. A sudden weakening of the currency may signal economic instability.
▶ *See also* Bretton Woods, Fixed Exchange Rate, Measuring an Economy.

Floating Rate Bond A bond with a variable interest rate as opposed to a fixed rate.

Floating Rate Note ▶ *See* FRN.

Floor The trading floor of an exchange where dealers meet face to face to quote prices and deal. Alternatives to the trading floor are screen-based trading systems, or an over-the-counter system. Also, a type of derivative that protects the holder from a fall in interest rates. The holder, by exercising, receives a cash settlement representing the difference between the strike level and the underlying interest rate, should the latter be lower. Floors normally have a life of between two and five years. The option can be exercised at regular intervals (every six months, for example) during the life of the floor.
▶ *See also* OTC, Screen Trading, Cap.

Floor Broker The person responsible for accepting orders on an exchange floor and handing them on to a specialist or trader for execution.
▶ *See also* Exchange.

Flotation When a privately owned company needs new capital, it can raise the money by issuing shares to the public on the stock market and floating the company. Flotation is also known as 'going public' or making an IPO (Initial Public Offering).
▶ *See also* IPO.

FMA The Financial Markets Association is an umbrella organization for groups of foreign exchange dealers in various countries. Also known as the Association Cambiste Internationale (ACI).
▮ www.aciforex.com ▮

FNMA ▶ *See* Fannie Mae.

FOB A shipping term, which stands for Free on Board. If a price quote is FOB, the costs of the goods and the loading of the ship are included, but not the freight charges. This makes imports more directly comparable with exports.

FOK ▶ *See* Fill or Kill.

FOMC The Federal Open Market Committee. A 12-member policy committee of the US Federal Reserve Board that sets official US interest rates
and other Federal Reserve guidelines.
▩ **www.federalreserve.gov/fomc** ▩

Food and Agriculture Organization ▶ *See* FAO.

Force Majeure A force majeure clause is written into contracts to allow
contracting parties to be freed from their obligations in the event of
an occurrence that is outside their control, such as an earthquake,
hurricane or a serious labour dispute.

Forecast A projection of current trends using existing data. Forecasts are
widely used by business and financial planners, economists and stock
market analysts. Analysts' forecasts include price levels, company
earnings and economic indicators.

Foreign Acceptances Foreign acceptances are short-term non-interest-
bearing notes denominated in US dollars and backed by the credit of
foreign banks or agencies domiciled in the USA. They usually trade at
a yield premium over normal bankers' acceptances.
▶ *See also* BA (Bankers' Acceptances).

Foreign Bond A bond issued on the domestic capital market by a foreign
borrower and denominated in the domestic currency. These bonds
have different names according to the currency of issue, such as
Bulldog bond for sterling, Samurai bond for yen and Yankee bond for
US dollars.

Foreign Exchange Instruments used to make payments between countries.
▶ *See* FX.

Forex Widely used abbreviation referring to foreign exchange.
▶ *See also* Foreign Exchange.

Forex Club An umbrella title for the Forex organizations which have been
formed in various countries. The Forex Club is made up of groups of foreign exchange dealers who are linked by affiliation to the Association
Cambiste Internationale (ACI), or Financial Markets Association.
▶ *See also* ACI.

Forward Margin The discount or premium between the spot and forward
rates for a forward foreign exchange transaction. It represents the
interest-rate differential between the two currencies traded.
▶ *See also* Discount, Premium.

Forward Market Markets that deliver and settle on a date other than spot. The term is often used to describe the forward FX (Foreign Exchange) market, which is one of the most liquid forward markets.

▶ *See also* Forwards, Spot, FX.

Forwards A forward is an agreement to buy or sell a commodity or a financial asset at a specified future date for a fixed price. It is a completed contract and the commodity or financial asset will be delivered, unlike an option which gives a choice of whether or not to complete the trade at the later date. Unlike futures, forwards are not contracts with standard fixed terms. They are tailor-made between the buyer and seller for each deal and are traded OTC rather than on an exchange.

▶ *See also* Futures, OTC.

FRA A forward rate agreement is an interest-rate derivative that allows investors and borrowers to set the interest rate on a short-term investment or loan in advance for a predetermined period.

▶ *See also* Derivatives.

Franchise Permission to distribute or sell a particular brand of goods or services in a specific area. A particular business that has been set up to exercise such a right. For example, an individual McDonald's restaurant can be a franchise.

Franc Zone A zone that embraces a number of emerging markets, all of which originally linked their currencies to the French franc and now link to the euro, holding most of their currency reserves in euros. Convertibility of their currencies into the euro is guaranteed by the French exchequer. Members include Burkina Faso, Cameroon, the Ivory Coast, Niger, New Caledonia and French Polynesia.

Freddie Mac A nickname for the Federal Home Loan Mortgage Corporation. Various US savings institutions own the stock of this corporation, which purchases residential mortgages from lenders, forms bundles of securities backed by the pools of mortgages, and then offers the securities to the public.

▓ **www.freddiemac.com** ▓

Free Asset Ratio A way of seeing whether a life insurance company has enough assets to cover its potential liabilities. The Free Asset Ratio simply measures the market value of the company's assets to its liabilities. If the ratio is low the company has to be more cautious in its investments to make sure it has enough cash to cover maturing savings policies.

Free Cash Flow A company's operating cash flow minus what it spends on capital assets. Operating cash flow is simply the change in a company's net cash position during a given trading period.
▶ *See also* Operating Cash Flow.

Free Delivery Method of settlement in which the securities are delivered before payment is effected.

Free Float The proportion of a company's listed shares that are freely available for trading and are not restricted or unlikely to trade.

Free Floating Exchange Rate A currency exchange rate that is allowed to be set completely by market forces, in contrast with a managed exchange rate using devices such as a dirty float or a crawling peg.
▶ *See also* Dirty Float, Crawling Peg.

Free Issue When a company transfers money from its reserves to its permanent capital it issues free shares to existing shareholders. The new shares are distributed in proportion to their existing holdings. Also known as a capitalization issue or a scrip issue.

Free to Trade ▶ *See* W/I.

Free Trade Zone A designated area within a country in which businesses can operate free of customs duties or currency restrictions. Profits are usually tax-free for a set period. Also known as a free trade processing zone and a foreign trade zone.

Frictional Unemployment Unemployment caused by the time it takes workers to search for a job. This is sometimes inevitable in a changing economy.
▶ *See also* Unemployment.

FRN A floating rate note is a medium-term debt instrument that pays a variable rate of interest. The coupon is usually a premium to Libor (the London Interbank Offered Rate), the 'riskless' rate at which banks lend to each other, or its local equivalent such as Euribor. For example, the investor is promised a quarterly coupon of 125 basis points over three-month Libor.
▶ *See also* Coupon, Libor, Euribor.

Front-end Fees The lead and co-lead managers for a loan receive front-end fees from a borrower for making the arrangements, and servicing fees for administering interest payments and principal repayments.
▶ *See also* Lead Manager/Underwriter.

Front Office The Front Office describes the dealing and support staff in a financial institution who are closest to the buying and selling operation of a market.

▶ *See also* Back Office, Middle Office.

Front Running

1 An illegal practice whereby a trader deals on his own behalf ahead of carrying out a client's order to buy or sell shares or other financial instruments, when he knows that client's order is likely to change prices, or move the market.

2 Trading in shares by a brokerage house ahead of publication of its own research report which has not yet been widely disseminated.

Frozen Assets Assets, balances or credits temporarily blocked or immobilized due to political circumstances such as war or legal action.

FSA The Financial Services Authority is a government regulatory body for the financial services industry in the United Kingdom, including deposit-taking, insurance and investment business. It also educates the general public on personal finance topics.

▨ **www.fsa.gov.uk** ▨

FSF Financial Stability Forum. Set up in 1999 at the behest of the G7 finance ministers and central bank governors, the purpose of the FSF is to identify and oversee action to remove threats to the international financial system. Its members are regulators, central bankers and leading economists from the G7 and international financial organizations. ▨ **www.fsforum.org** ▨

FTSE 100 The FTSE 100 is the benchmark index for equity prices on the London Stock Exchange. Known as the 'Footsie' it comprises 100 of the largest UK stocks, by market capitalization, accounting for about 70 percent of stock turnover. The FTSE is a capitalization-weighted index and is the basis for index futures and options contracts traded on LIFFE. ▨ **www.ftse.com** ▨

▶ *See also* LIFFE, LSE.

FTSE Eurotop 100 An index of the 100 most-traded European stocks.

▨ **www.ftse.com** ▨

FTSE Eurotop 300 A benchmark index of European stocks, the FTSE Eurotop is made up of the largest 300 European companies by market capitalization ▨ **www.ftse.com** ▨

Fuel Oil Heavy distillates from the oil refining process. Used as fuel for power stations, industry and marine boilers.

Fully Diluted EPS An EPS (earnings per share) figure that is calculated by dividing earnings by a larger amount of shares than the number currently outstanding. It assumes the eventual full issue of all shares connected to convertibles, options, warrants and convertible preferred shares. This leads to a greater dilution of the EPS figure.

Fund A pool of money which is invested by a fund manager who then manages that money using a range of investment criteria.

Fundamental Analysis A method of forecasting prices based on research into company performance and basic economic, political and environmental factors such as supply and demand, economic statistics, government policies and the financial accounts of companies. Unlike technical analysis, fundamental analysis focuses on what *should* happen to prices, not what has happened to them in the past.
▶ *See also* Quantitative Analysis, Technical Analysis.

Fund Manager An individual or institution involved in investing funds for their own account or on behalf of others.

Fungible The term used to describe when one instrument is identical to, and therefore interchangeable with, another. A fungible bond is a new issue that has all the same specifications as an existing issue, other than price. If a bond is fungible, it can be exchanged for an existing bond with the same characteristics.
▶ *See also* Bond.

Futures A future is an undertaking to buy or sell a standard quantity of a financial asset or commodity at a future date and at a fixed price. Futures resemble forwards, but are standardized contracts (i.e. every futures contract has standardized terms that dictate the size, the unit of price quotation, the delivery date and contract months) and must be traded on a recognized exchange. Price movements are expressed in ticks (the smallest unit of price quotation). Delivery of a future is rare. As the delivery date draws near, most investors close out their positions by undertaking an equal and opposite trade. The futures markets bring together hedgers who wish to protect themselves against the rise or fall of prices, and speculators who are trying to benefit from such movements. A clearing house acts as the counter party in every transaction to protect against the risk of default, so the buyer and seller do not have to deal directly with each other. Futures developed as a method for establishing forward purchase prices and managing price instability caused by seasonal factors in agricultural markets. Today, interest rate and stock index futures attract the greatest volume.
▶ *See also* Clearing House, Forwards, Hedging, Margin, Option, OTC, Tick.

Futures Commission Merchant ▶ *See* FCM.

Futures Pit An area on the floor of a futures exchange where trading takes place by way of the Open Outcry system.
  ▶ *See also* Open Outcry.

Future Value The expected value of a payment (or series of payments) at a set date in the future, once it has been invested at a specific rate of interest until that date.

FX The Foreign Exchange markets that deal in the exchange of deposits in different currencies for varying effective 'value' dates. Most transactions are for 12 months or less, and are in the form of spot (cash), forwards, futures and options. FX rates refer to the number of units of one currency needed to buy another.
  ▶ *See also* Spot Market, Forwards, Futures, Option.

FXA A Forward Exchange Agreement is a currency derivative in which settlement is based on the difference between the forward rate on the start date of the contract and the spot rate at settlement.
  ▶ *See also* Derivatives, ERA.

FX Swap A foreign exchange swap is a simultaneous purchase and sale, or vice versa, of identical amounts of one currency for another with two different value dates (normally spot to forward). The two parties agree a currency exchange on one day and simultaneously agree to unwind or reverse that deal on a date in the future. Effectively, each party is given the use of an amount of foreign currency for a specific time. Each party is taking a view on the relative movements of currencies and interest rates between those two dates, in comparison with their current relative prices. The price of a swap is quoted in forward points. The deal locks in the price of holding or taking delivery of an amount of foreign currency at a future date, or allows arbitrage between spot and forward rates.
  ▶ *See also* Swap.

G

G3 The world's leading industrial nations – Germany, Japan and the USA.

G7 A forum for the world's leading industrial nations to meet and discuss policy. The G7 members are Canada, France, Germany, Italy, Japan, the UK and the USA.

G8 The G7 countries plus Russia.

G10 The G7 countries plus four others: Belgium, the Netherlands, Sweden and Switzerland. The group has 11 members but is still known as G10. It aims to co-ordinate monetary and fiscal policies for a stable world economic system.
 ▶ *See also* GAB.

G24 An informal grouping of 24 developing countries formed to represent their interests in negotiations on international monetary matters.
 ■ **www.g24.org** ■

G30 A private, non-profit group of industry leaders, bankers, central bankers and academics that discusses and studies international economic and financial market issues. The group meets twice a year, with guests. ■ **www.group30.org** ■

G77 An informal grouping of developing countries, initially with 77 members but now considerably expanded. It is designed to enhance their negotiation strength within the United Nations system and to promote economic and technical co-operation. ■ **www.g77.org** ■

GAAP Generally Accepted Accounting Principles are procedures and rules that define accounting practice. The United States uses GAAP, whereas Europe uses IAS, International Accounting Standards.
 ▶ *See also* International Accounting Standards.

GAB General Arrangements to Borrow. An agreement between the G10 nations to provide special credits to the IMF. The GAB needs the collective agreement of its members to be activated. Credits are separate from the IMF's normal resources
 ▶ *See also* G10, IMF, NAB.

Gamma The measure of change in the delta of an option compared with a price change in the underlying financial instrument on which the option is based.
▶ *See also* Delta, Option.

Gann Technical analyst W.D. Gann emphasized the proportionate influence of the time and duration of market movements as well as the influence of the size of price movements. Gann angles are specific angles used by technical analysts to draw trendlines from market price tops or bottoms. The most important Gann angle is the 45-degree line because it is seen as the perfect balance between time and price. A major reversal is usually indicated by a break of the 45-degree line.
▶ *See also* Technical Analysis.

Gap A mismatch between a bank's assets and liabilities. Also a term used by technical analysts to describe a break between price levels, indication a sharp price movement and leaving a gap on the charts. An upwards gap shows market strength and a downwards gap the reverse. A breakaway gap appears at the completion of key price patterns and often signals the start of a significant move. (Figure 9.)
▶ *See also* Technical Analysis.

Gapping The process of intentionally mismatching the maturities of assets and liabilities by borrowing short and lending long.

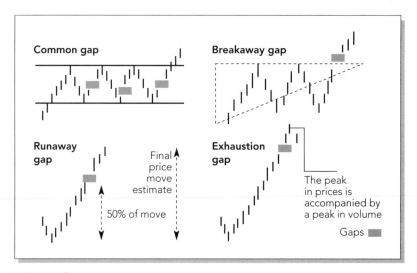

FIGURE 9 Gap

Garman Kohlhagen Model A currency option pricing formula similar to Black & Scholes but with separate conditions for domestic and foreign interest rates.
  ▶ *See also* Black & Scholes Model, Option.

GATT The General Agreement on Tariffs and Trade (Geneva) was founded in 1948 as an ad hoc Secretariat defined by a treaty between trading nations. The Secretariat was absorbed by the new World Trade Organization in 1995, but the GATT agreement remains as the WTO's underlying treaty document for trade in merchandise – albeit with many updates since 1948. ■ **www.wto.org** ■
  ▶ *See also* WTO.

GDP Gross Domestic Product is the total monetary value of all goods and services produced within a country. GDP does not include income from overseas investments and earnings or from remittances from nationals working abroad.
  ▶ *See also* GNP.

GDP per Head Total gross domestic product divided by the population gives us a figure for output per person. GDP per head is an effective way of comparing the relative wealth of two countries. For example, the United States' total GDP is 60 times larger than Norway's, but its GDP per head is slightly less.

GDP Deflator A price index applied to the cash or nominal estimates of gross domestic product in order to produce a more accurate or 'real' value of GDP. Deflators remove the effects of inflation, which boosts the nominal value of GDP but does not change the underlying real level of output.
  ▶ *See also* GDP.

GDR Global Depositary Receipts. Certificates issued by a bank in more than one country. They confer ownership of shares in a foreign company held in safekeeping by the bank. The certificates allow the underlying shares, which are traded in only one country, to be offered globally without the need to be registered on foreign equity markets.
  ▶ *See also* ADR.

Gearing
  1 The ratio of a company's debt to equity. Gearing is an indicator of a company's ability to service its debt. A company with a high proportion of debt to equity (high gearing) is more vulnerable to fluctuations in business activity. It therefore represents higher risk for equity holders and offers greater return. Whether gearing is acceptable or not is often judged by comparisons with companies in similar industries or sectors.

2 In derivatives markets, gearing is the measure of the amount of cash spent purchasing an option or a futures contract, compared to the actual value of the underlying position. The more highly geared the trading position, the greater the risk that a small change in market prices will completely wipe out the cash investment. That also means that a small change in market prices in the right direction can produce large profits in relation to the size of the cash investment. Gearing is also known as leverage.

▶ *See also* Derivatives.

General Accounting Office This office audits US government departments and examines the use of public funds. It is headed by the Controller General. ▨ **www.gao.gov** ▨

General Agreement on Tariffs and Trade ▶ *See* GATT.

General Arrangements to Borrow ▶ *See* GAB.

General Obligation Bonds A type of municipal security that is issued by US States, counties, special districts, cities, towns and schools.

Gensaki Market The Japanese market for medium-term bond financing, but it is also referred to as a repo market. Securities acting as collateral in these operations are both long-term bonds and Treasury bills.

▶ *See* Repos.

Geometric average A very precise way of measuring the average movement in security prices. To calculate the geometric average of a group of stocks multiply all of the prices and then take the nth root (where n equals the number of stocks that you are averaging).

▶ *See also* Arithmetic Average, Weighted/Unweighted Index.

Gilt-edged A term used to describe securities that carry little risk. Government bonds in both the UK and South Africa are known as gilts. The name comes from original UK government bond certificates which had gilded edges.

Ginnie Mae Government National Mortgage Association (GNMA). A wholly owned corporate unit of the US government whose chief function is to guarantee securities backed by pools of federally insured or guaranteed mortgages to aid secondary market liquidity. Its guarantees are known as GNMA pass-through certificates.

▨ **www.ginniemae.gov** ▨

▶ *See also* Securitization.

Given Dealers' language for when a bid has been hit, or accepted, by a counterparty.

▶ *See also* Bid, Broker.

GKO Short-term rouble-denominated Russian Treasury bill.

GmbH German company title: abbreviation of Gesellschaft mit beschränkter Haftung, a limited liability company.

GNMA ▶ *See* Ginnie Mae.

GNP Gross National Product. Total value of goods and services produced by an economy including income from overseas investments and remittances from nationals working abroad. If a country has heavy servicing charges on foreign debt or heavy dividend payments on foreign inward investment then its gross national product is reduced accordingly. Similarly GNP shrinks if a country makes large payments to an immigrant workforce.
▶ *See also* GDP.

Going Concern An accounting convention that presumes a company will continue to exist and trade normally. It allows accountants to value assets at their historic, or purchase cost, rather than at the lower level that would be achieved if the company was broken up.

Going Public The term for a privately owned company that seeks a listing on a stock exchange and issues shares to the general public. Also known as a flotation or issuing an IPO.
▶ *See also* Flotation, IPO.

Gold Standard A monetary system of fixed exchange rates whose parities were set in relation to gold. Under the system, central banks had to be able to exchange gold for any amount of their currencies. Most developed countries had abandoned the gold standard before the end of the Second World War.

Golden Handcuffs A financial bonus offered by a company wanting to retain an employee. Payment may be delayed or spread over several years.

Golden Hello A financial bonus offered to an employee on joining a company.

Golden Share A share that confers sufficient voting rights in a company to maintain control and protect it from takeover. The golden share prevents potential predators from buying shares and then using them to outvote the company's existing owners.
▶ *See also* Stock, Share.

Go Long/Short ▶ *See* Long, Short.

Good Delivery The delivery of an instrument in good time and with all relevant information in order, such as title, endorsement and legal papers.

Good Till Cancelled ▶ *See* GTC.

Goodwill Goodwill is the excess price paid for a company above the value of its assets and may cover intangible assets such as brand names. It is normally only recognized in the accounts of a company when it acquires another business as a going concern for a price that is higher than the book value of its capital and reserves. Negative goodwill is a gain when the price paid for a company is less than the value of its assets.

Government National Mortgage Association ▶ *See* Ginnie Mae.

Grace Period The time period agreed by the lender during which a borrower pays only interest and does not start to repay the principal.

Grades Standards set for judging the quality of a commodity.

Grains Traditional agricultural grains such as wheat, corn (maize), oats, barley, sorghum, rye and millet.

Greenfield Investment Investment in a start-up project, usually for a major capital investment such as a production plant, a refinery or a port. The investment starts with a bare site in a green field.

Greenmail Potential predators can buy shares in a company and threaten to take it over, or disrupt its management. The company can sometimes remove that threat by buying back the shares owned by the predators at a premium to market price, often in exchange for a commitment to limit their shareholdings in future.

Green Rates Green rates are accounting currencies used in assessing payments to farmers within the EU's Common Agricultural Policy (CAP). Under CAP, farmers are paid in agricultural units of account, and green rates were devised to convert these units of account payments into national currencies. They can only be revised by governments, which makes them far more stable than market rates and the number of green rates was sharply reduced by the introduction of the euro in 1999. Green rates only exist for those countries that remain outside the single currency.
▶ *See also* CAP, European Union, Euro.

Greenshoe Option A provision in the underwriting agreement for a share issue that allows the sale of additional shares to the public if demand is high. Named after the Green Shoe Company which first granted such an option. Sometimes known as an Over-Allotment Option.

Grey Market (Gray Market) An informal market in which investors buy and sell securities that have been formally announced or authorized but not yet allotted for settlement or delivery. These unofficial markets are also described as When Issued (W/I).
▶ *See also* W/I.

Gross Domestic Product ▶ *See* GDP.

Grossing Up An accounting practice that calculates the amount of income needed from an investment subject to tax, to equal the income from an investment that is not subject to tax.

Gross National Product ▶ *See* GNP.

Gross Price ▶ *See* Dirty Price.

Gross Profit Total profit before the deduction of tax and expenses.

GTC Good Till Cancelled. A limit order that remains valid until the limit is reached and the order is executed, or until the order is cancelled.

H

Haircut The difference between the actual market value and the value ascribed to the collateral used in a repo transaction.
▶ *See also* Repurchase Agreement.

Handle ▶ *See* Big Figure.

Hang Seng The Hang Seng Index (HSI) is the benchmark equity index for the Hong Kong Stock Exchange. The index is based on 33 blue-chip stocks, representing 70 percent of the capitalization of the Hong Kong exchange. ▨ **www.hsi.com** ▨ ▨ **www.hkex.com.hk/index.htm** ▨

Hard Currency A currency that can be traded and exchanged, and in which there is a general wide-ranging confidence.

Head and Shoulders Used in technical analysis, head and shoulders patterns are considered to be one of the most reliable of all major reversal patterns. The pattern consists of a major rally (the head) separating two smaller, though not necessarily identical, rallies (the shoulders). A neckline can be drawn connecting the bottom of the two shoulders and confirmation is normally accepted on a clear close below that neckline. The inverse head and shoulders is a mirror image of the head and shoulders. (Figure 10.)
▶ *See also* Technical Analysis.

Hedge Fund A private investment fund which typically aims to produce high returns from rapid, short-term market movements, often by taking very leveraged positions and using aggressive strategies such as short selling, swaps, derivatives, program trading and arbitrage. Usually restricted to financial institutions and wealthy individuals.
▶ *See also* Derivatives, Leverage, Program Trading, Short Selling, Swaps.

Hedging An action or strategy designed to minimize risk. A hedge often takes the form of a transaction in one market or asset, which protects against losses in another, e.g. a company buys an FX (foreign exchange) option to protect against the risk to its business of fluctuations in spot currency rates. Those pursuing hedging strategies are known as hedgers.
▶ *See also* Speculator.

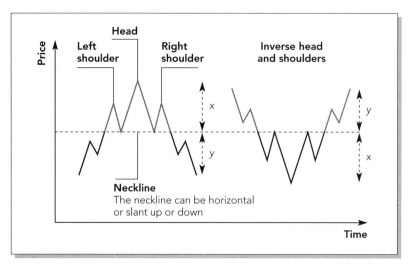

FIGURE 10 Head and shoulders

Hermes Hermes Kreditversicherungs Ag. A German state export insurance agency. ■ **www.hermes-kredit.com** ■

Herstatt Risk The risk that when dealing with an overseas client a bank may not be recover its funds if the counterparty defaults on its payment obligation. Named for the failed German bank Bankhaus Herstatt in 1974. Also called Cross-currency Settlement Risk.

High Low Open Close (HLOC) These represent the four most important types of price information which are displayed in most price displays and charts. High is the highest level at which a security or commodity has traded, while low is the lowest level. Depending on the instrument, it can be the high/low that day, that year or since price records began. Open/close are the opening and closing levels for any of those periods.

High Tech Stock The stock of companies involved in computer technology and advanced electronics.

HIPC Heavily Indebted Poor Countries. Those countries helped by the International Monetary Fund and World Bank's 'HIPC Initiative' which provides exceptional financial assistance to the poorest countries following sound financial policies, to help them reduce external debt.

Hire Purchase The purchase of a good by instalments, with ownership not conferred until the final payment is made.

Historical Cost The original cost of a company's assets, as distinct from replacement cost.

Historical Volatility A measure of volatility based on past price or yield behaviour. Beta measures volatility against the rest of the market.
▶ *See also* Volatility, Beta.

Hit Market talk for the acceptance of a specific bid or offer price by a counterparty.

HKMA Hong Kong Monetary Authority, effectively Hong Kong's central bank. ▨ **www.info.gov.hk/hkma** ▨

Holder of Record The name of the owner of a security as recorded in the issuing company's records.

Holding Company A company that controls one or more other companies, often by having a majority of the shares in each subsidiary. A holding company often has control over areas such as marketing and financial management, but not investment.

Horizontal Spread An option strategy that involves buying and selling contracts with the same strike price but different maturities, in view of expected moves in volatility. Also known as a calendar spread.
▶ *See also* Option.

Hostile Bid A bid for a company that is not supported by the senior management of that company.

Hot Stock A stock whose price suddenly rises or falls sharply.

Hyperinflation Inflation rising at 100 percent or more per year. Hyperinflation can become self-fuelling and can ultimately trigger an economic collapse.
▶ *See also* Inflation.

Hypothecation
   1 The pledging of assets to secure a loan.
   2 The dedication of the proceeds of a specific tax to a specific purpose.

IADB Inter-American Development Bank. The Bank promotes economic and social projects in Latin America and the Caribbean using loans and technical assistance. ■ **www.iadb.org** ■

IAS ▶ *See* International Accounting Standards Board.

IBRD The International Bank for Reconstruction and Development. An affiliate of the World Bank, it aims to reduce poverty in middle-income and creditworthy poorer countries by promoting sustainable development through loans, guarantees, and analytical and advisory services. It provides these countries with access to capital in larger volumes and on better terms than the international capital markets would provide. ■ **www.worldbank.org** ■

ICANN Internet Corporation for Assigned Names and Numbers. A private sector organization established by the US government, with the backing of governments around the world, to register and develop domain names for the internet.

ICC International Chamber of Commerce. The ICC groups chambers of commerce and business and banking associations from around the world. It has an arbitration court used for settling international business disputes. ■ **www.iccwbo.org** ■

ICCO The International Cocoa Organization. An industry organization that acts as a forum for discussions between cocoa producers and consumers. ■ **www.icco.org** ■

ICO The International Coffee Organization. A forum for discussions between coffee importing and exporting nations. ■ **www.ico.org** ■

ICSID The International Centre for Settlement of Investment Disputes. A World Bank affiliate founded in 1966 to mediate in disputes between government and private foreign investors to help promote increased flows of international investment. ■ **www.worldbank.org/icsid** ■
▶ *See also* World Bank.

IDA International Development Association. An affiliate of the World Bank that finances development projects and programmes on favourable terms in the poorest countries. ▓ **www.worldbank.org/ida** ▓
  ▶ *See also* World Bank.

IDB Inter-dealer broker. A broker who acts on behalf of market makers.

IEA International Energy Agency. Set up by the OECD to monitor oil supply and demand, and to supervise consumer levels of oil stocks. The 26 member countries are committed to taking joint measures to meet oil supply emergencies. ▓ **www.iea.org** ▓
  ▶ *See also* OECD.

IFC International Finance Corporation. An affiliate of the World Bank which promotes private enterprises in developing countries with a mixture of loans and equity financing. It charges market rates for its financing and aims to be a catalyst for additional private investment. ▓ **www.ifc.org** ▓
  ▶ *See also* World Bank.

IFO Business Climate Index. A closely watched indicator of German business conditions, based on a monthly survey of about 7,000 companies. It is widely seen as a barometer for economic conditions in the whole of the Eurozone.
  ▶ *See also* Eurozone.

IIF Institute for International Finance. A global association of leading banks and financial institutions. Created in 1983 in response to an international debt crisis, the IIF analyses risks in emerging market economies, serves as a policy forum on emerging markets' finance and regulation, and promotes collaboration between member firms and institutions such as the World Bank and regional development banks.
  ▓ **www.iif.com** ▓

Illiquid Markets or instruments are described as being illiquid, or lacking depth, if there is a shortage of buyers or sellers. This shortage makes it difficult to find a true price for an illiquid security. The opposite of liquid.
  ▶ *See also* Liquid.

ILO International Labour Organization. A UN-sponsored body that is concerned with labour issues. ▓ **www.ilo.org** ▓

IMF International Monetary Fund. The IMF is a specialized agency of the United Nations that has a wide-ranging brief to oversee the international monetary system and to promote exchange rate stability and international trade. It provides funds to member countries with bal-

ance of payments problems, to support their policies of economic adjustment and reform. It is funded by subscriptions from member states whose drawing rights and voting powers are accordingly determined by their subscriptions. ■ **www.imf.org** ■
▶ *See also* Bretton Woods.

IMM   The International Monetary Market. A division of the Chicago Mercantile Exchange that trades futures. ■ **www.cme.com** ■
▶ *See also* CME, Future.

Implied Volatility   The volatility implied in the price of an option. It is a measure of how much the market thinks prices will move given a known option price. It indicates the size, but not the direction, of the movement expected. Volatility is expressed as an annualized percentage.
▶ *See also* Volatility.

IMRO   The Investment Management Regulatory Organization. The UK authority responsible for regulating the fund management industry. ■ **www.imro.co.uk** ■

Inc.   (Incorporated) A US and Canadian company title. Incorporation is the process by which a company receives a charter and is allowed to operate as a corporation. This process must be recognized in the legal name, i.e. Inc.

Income   Money earned from investments, earnings or employment.

Income Statement ▶ *See* Profit and Loss Account.

Income Stock ▶ *See* Blue Chip Stock.

Incomes Policy   A broad term covers various direct forms of inflation control by a government. It can include a freeze or limitation on increases in prices, wages, dividends, investment income and rents.

Incremental Cost ▶ *See* Marginal Cost.

Index   A composite of values that is designed to measure change in a market or an economy. Indices are usually created by measuring the value of a number of securities, or an economic indicator, at a certain date and letting that value be represented by 100. Subsequent changes in the index can be easily perceived in comparison with that 100 base number.

Index Funds ▶ *See* Indexing.

Indexing   Creating a portfolio with a weighting that recreates and matches the performance of a broad-based index. Investment funds constructed in such a manner are known as index funds.
▶ *See* Index Tracking.

Index-linked Bonds Bonds in which the coupons are linked to a retail or consumer price index.

Index Tracking A process whereby a fund manager aims to reproduce the performance of a stock market index. A manager buys the shares that make up the index in the relevant proportions in which they are represented in the index.

Indications of Interest ▶ *See* IOI.

Indicators ▶ *See* Economic Indicators.

Indirect Quotation A foreign exchange term for the number of units of foreign currency that can be exchanged for one unit of domestic currency. The most common example of an indirect quotation outside the US is the sterling/dollar rate. US banks use indirect quotations in their international dealings but use direct quotations for domestic purposes.

Industrial Production A measure of the output of goods-producing industries, used as an indicator of the state of an economy.

Inflation Inflation is a persistent rise in the prices of goods and services, caused by too much money chasing too few goods. Inflation can be caused by an increase in money supply or demand due to government spending or the printing of money, or by a contraction in the supply of goods. Different types of inflation are defined by their cause. Demand-pull inflation is caused by excess demand in the economy, while cost-push inflation is caused by increased costs of production. The rate of inflation is often a primary policy target of governments, and of central banks given policy independence to achieve a target rate. Moderate inflation is common in economies and can be regarded as relatively benign. If all inflation is removed and an economy slips into deflation it can stunt consumption because consumers postpone purchases in the knowledge that goods will become cheaper. Deflation also stunts demand for credit and makes repayment of existing debts more difficult because the value of money is increasing.
▶ *See also* Deflation, Hyperinflation, Stagflation.

Inflation Risk The risk associated with the return from an investment not covering the loss in purchasing power caused by inflation.

Initial Margin The margin payment paid to a clearing house by both the buyer and the seller of a futures contract to protect against potential losses.
▶ *See also* Clearing House, Margin.

Initial Public Offering ▶ *See* IPO.

Inland Revenue The UK government department responsible for collecting tax.

Inland Revenue Service ▶ *See* IRS.

INSEE Institute National de la Statistique et des Études Économiques. The French National Statistics Institute, which collates and issues a number of government economic indicators. ■ **www.insee.fr** ■

Insider Dealing (or Insider Trading) Exploitation of inside or privileged information for profit in market transactions. This is illegal in many countries.

Insolvent A company becomes insolvent when it is either unable to pay its debts as and when they fall due, or when its liabilities, including contingent and prospective liabilities, exceed the value of its assets. The opposite of solvent.
▶ *See also* Solvent.

Institutional Investors Financial institutions, such as pensions funds and investment trusts, which invest large amounts of capital in financial markets on behalf of their clients.

In strike The designated point when a trigger option, such as a 'down and in' or an 'up and in', turns into a conventional option.
▶ *See* Down and In, Up and In.

Intangible Assets The non-physical assets of a company such as patents, copyright, a brand name, goodwill etc.
▶ *See* Assets.

Integrated Producer A metals producer that owns mines, smelters and refineries, and in some cases fabricating plants.

Integrated Services Digital Network ▶ *See* ISDN.

Inter-American Development Bank ▶ *See* IADB.

Interbank Market A term used to describe professional markets between banks. Most commonly used to refer to the wholesale market in foreign exchange, but also used for funds traded overnight to satisfy reserve requirements at the central bank.

Inter-dealer Broker ▶ *See* IDB.

Interest Bearing A term used to describe instruments that pay a given rate of interest on the principal amount, either in one payment (typically at maturity) or as a series of payments over the life. Also referred to as coupon bearing.

Interest Cover Interest cover, or income earning, expresses how many times a company's interest obligations could be met out of gross profits. It is calculated by dividing a company's pre-tax operating income by its interest obligations, for a given period.

Interest Rate The cost paid by a borrower to a lender over a period of time, often calculated annually. It is intended to compensate lenders for the sacrifice of losing immediate use of their money, for the inflationary erosion of buying power over the life of the loan, and for the risk involved in lending.

Interest Rate Differential The difference in yield between two comparable instruments denominated in different currencies. Used in forward foreign exchange pricing.

Interest Rate Risk The potential for losses or reduced income arising from adverse moves in interest rates.

Interest Rate Swap ▶ *See* Swap.

Interim Dividend A dividend (distribution of company earnings to shareholders) paid in an interim trading period, usually half-yearly but can be quarterly. Authorized solely by the board of directors subject to shareholder approval.
   ▶ *See also* Dividend.

Internal Rate of Return ▶ *See* IRR.

International Accounting Standards Board An international organization that formulates and publishes accounting standards. Members comprise over 100 national accounting bodies. ▪ **www.iasc.org.uk** ▪

International Bank for Reconstruction and Development ▶ *See* World Bank.

International Chamber of Commerce ▶ *See* ICC.

International Cocoa Organization ▶ *See* ICCO.

International Coffee Organization ▶ *See* ICO.

International Development Association ▶ *See* IDA.

International Energy Agency ▶ *See* IEA.

International Finance Corporation ▶ *See* IFC.

International Labour Organization ▶ *See* ILO.

International Monetary Fund ▶ *See* IMF.

International Monetary Market ▶ *See* IMM.

International Organization of Securities Commissions ▶ *See* IOSCO.

International Petroleum Exchange ▶ *See* IPE.

International Securities Market Association ▶ *See* ISMA.

International Share Offering This occurs when shares of a domestic company are sold internationally via a syndicate of underwriters. They can be either new shares or a secondary offering.

International Sugar Organization A group that brings together sugar-importing and exporting countries. ▪ **www.sugaronline.com** ▪

International Swap and Derivatives Association ▶ *See* ISDA.

International Wheat Council A group that brings together wheat-producing and consuming countries.

Internet Service Provider ▶ *See* ISP.

Interpolation The process of determining a rate (or other variable) that lies between a series of known rates. Interpolation works on the assumption that a certain percentage change that applies generally can be applied to calculate a specific variable. It is a generalization, but can be used to estimate bond prices and yields. Three types of interpolation exist: linear, logarithmic and cubic.
▶ *See also* Extrapolation.

Intervention Trading by a central bank in the open market in order to influence exchange rates or stabilize market conditions.

Intervention Band Formal exchange rate limits within which a government or central bank allows its currency to trade without intervention. Also known as a trading band. It is sometimes coupled with a crawling peg system of gradual appreciation or depreciation.
▶ *See also* Crawling Peg, Concerted Intervention.

In the Money An option is described as being in the money when the current price of the underlying instrument is above the strike or exercise price for a call, and below the strike price for a put. For example, the shares of Company A are trading at £2.20 each. A trader decides to write an option on the shares, giving the buyer the right to buy the shares of Company A at £2.40 each. That is a call option, because the buyer has the right to 'call' or buy the shares at £2.40 each. The exercise, or 'strike' price, for the option is £2.40. If the price of the underlying shares rises to £2.50 then the option is 'in the money' and the holder will exercise the option because the strike price is below the market price of the shares. A put option is when a trader writes an option giving the buyer

the right to sell the shares to him at a given price. The buyer has the right to sell or 'put' the shares to the option writer. If the strike price of the option is £2.20 and the price of the underlying shares falls to £2.00 in the open marketplace then the put option is 'in the money' or valuable because the holder can make more money by exercising the option and selling at £2.20 then he can by selling in the market at £2.00. In both examples the buyer of the options has to make allowance for the cost of the options themselves before calculating whether it is worthwhile to exercise them. Options can also be described as being deep in the money when they are likely to expire in the money.
▶ *See also* Out of the Money, At the Money.

Intraday A term that means 'within the day' and usually refers to prices in financial markets. An intraday price can be any price between the opening and the close. Common intraday intervals used to record price changes include tick (the minimum movement possible in the price of a financial instrument) or five-minute, half-hourly and hourly.
▶ *See also* Tick.

Intraday Limit The limit allowed on a dealer's position in each and all currencies during the course of the trading day.

Intrinsic Value When an option is 'in the money' it is said to have intrinsic value. It is calculated by taking the difference between the forward market value of the underlying instrument and the strike price of the option.
▶ *See also* In the Money, Option.

Introduction An introduction involves the listing of existing shares on a stock exchange. No new capital is raised and there is no transfer of ownership.

Inventory A company's stock of raw materials, semi-finished and finished goods. Also known simply as stock.

Inverse Yield Curve ▶ *See* Yield Curve.

Inverted Yield Curve A chart pattern that shows yields on short-term securities above those on long-term securities. This is a reversal of a normal yield curve, where long-term rates are higher to reflect the risk of holding securities for a longer time. An inverted yield curve may reflect fears of a glut of short-term paper, which pushes down prices and pushes up yields, or of a shortage of long-term securities, which pushes up prices and pushes down yields. It may also reflect expectations that inflation will be lower in the long term than in the short term, producing an eventual drop in yields. An inverted yield curve is also known as a negative yield curve.

Investment Bank A US term used to describe banks that specialize in financial market activities, raising funds for companies through the issue of
bonds and equities, rather than concentrating on lending and the
mechanics of money transmission. In Europe they are also known as
merchant banks.

Investment Fund An investment fund is any that manages portfolios of
money. There are basically two types of investment funds – open-
ended mutual funds, which are also known as unit trusts, and
closed-end publicly quoted funds, which are known as investment
trusts. Both are means of pooling funds to allow investors to diversify
their investment assets. Open-ended funds sell shares to the public,
with each share representing proportionate ownership of the underlying assets of the fund. The fund managers can create more shares, or
reduce the total, according to demand from the public. A closed-end
fund has a predefined and fixed number of shares available to the
public. The number of shares cannot be increased. Fresh demand for
investment in the fund will push up the price of existing shares,
allowing the fund manager to issue more shares.
 ▶ See also Mutual Fund/Unit Trust, Investment Trust.

Investment Grade Bonds considered to be safe investments. They carry
credit ratings of BBB/Baa or above from the credit rating agencies,
who do not consider the issuers likely to default.
 ▶ See also Junk Bonds.

Investment Trusts Companies which issue shares and then use those funds
to invest in other companies. There is a fixed amount of authorized
share capital and new shares may not be created on demand. They are
known as closed-end publicly quoted funds in the US and investment
trusts in the UK. Investment trusts contrast with unit trusts and
mutual funds, which both sell and redeem shares on a continuing
basis according to investor demand.

Invisibles International transactions in services as opposed to trade in
physical goods or merchandise. They form part of the current account
balance of payments and include funds arising from shipping,
tourism, insurance, banking and commodity services.

Invisible Supply Stocks, notably commodities, which are outside commercial channels. Their exact quantity cannot be identified but they are in
theory available to the market. For example, cocoa beans smuggled out
of a country and sold on the black market, or stocks of palm oil from
plantations owned by manufacturers and used in their own factories.

IOI Indications of Interest. An IOI represents an investor's interest in purchasing securities that have not yet been issued.

IOSCO International Organization of Securities Commissions. An organization comprising the securities market regulators from more than 90 countries, which seeks to develop securities markets and enforce market regulation. ■ **www.iosco.org** ■

IPE The International Petroleum Exchange. Europe's leading market for energy derivatives and the home of the Brent futures contract.
■ **www.ipe.uk.com** ■
▶ *See also* Brent.

IPO Initial Public Offering. The first offering of shares to the public by a privately owned company. IPOs are used by companies to raise new funds, or achieve a listing on an exchange. The issuer normally offers the shares to the public through an underwriter who sets the price, promotes the offering and usually guarantees to take the shares at a certain price, to protect the issuer against adverse market movements. Also known as a flotation or going public.
▶ *See also* Flotation, Going Public.

IRR Internal Rate of Return. A measure of return on an investment that takes both the size and timing of cash flows into account. The formula is identical in structure to that which is used to calculate the yield to maturity of a bond because it shows not only the total return, but takes into account how quickly that return was earned. Sometimes known as annualized rate of return.

IRS Inland Revenue Service. The US federal agency responsible for the collection of taxes. ■ **www.irs.gov** ■

I/S Danish and Norwegian company title: abbreviation of Interessentskab.

ISDA The International Swap and Derivatives Association. An international trade organization for the over-the-counter, or privately negotiated, derivatives markets. It acts as a forum to discuss industry issues and promotes best practices within the derivatives business.
■ **www.isda.org** ■
▶ *See also* OTC.

ISDN Integrated Services Digital Network. A high-technology telecommunications network that allows data to be transferred over phone lines as digital signals, allowing much higher transfer rates.

Islamic Development Bank An international bank that encourages economic and social development in its 54 member nations and of Muslim communities following Islamic law in non-member countries.
■ **www.isdb.org** ■

ISM Institute of Supply Management. A US institute, formerly known as the National Association of Purchasing Management (NAPM), that produces a monthly index on business activity that is widely watched by financial markets.

ISMA International Securities Market Association. A self-regulatory body and trade association for the securities industry. ■ **www.isam.org** ■

Issue Date The date of issue of a new security. Often used as the date on which interest begins to accrue.

Issued Capital/Share Capital Share capital that has actually been issued, or allotted, to shareholders. The opposite of authorized share capital, which is the maximum amount of share capital that a company is allowed to issue by its constitution or charter.

Issue Price The price at which securities are sold on issue. This can be at par or face value, or at a discount or premium.

J

JBIC Japan Bank for International Co-operation. The JBIC provides finance to promote Japanese exports and economic activities overseas and to support international financial stability.
■ www.jbic.go.jp/english/index.php ■

J Curve An economic concept that says a variable may sometimes continue to change in the same direction in response to a stimulus, before it changes markedly in the opposite direction. For example, the balance of trade may continue to deteriorate following a devaluation because import costs rise. It then recovers to surplus as exports expand in volume due to cheaper exchange costs.

JD Slovenian company title: abbreviation of Javna Druzba.

JGB Japanese Government Bonds.

Junk Bonds High-risk high-yield bonds, which are rated below investment grade by credit agencies. Also known as speculative grade bonds.
▶ *See also* Investment Grade.

Kairi In technical analysis, this indicator charts the percentage difference between the current closing value and its simple moving average. It can be used either as a trend indicator or as an overbought/oversold signal.
▶ *See also* Overbought, Oversold, Technical Analysis.

Kampo The Postal Insurance Bureau of the Japanese Posts and Telecommunications Ministry. Kampo is one of the major Japanese institutional investors in foreign bonds and foreign exchange markets.

Kassenverein The Central Depository Bank for Securities. Germany's central securities depository and clearing agent.

Keidanren A forum of Japan's leading industry and business figures.
■ www.keidanren.or.jp ■

Kerb Market In financial markets the term kerb is used to describe trading outside official market hours. The expression comes from trading literally taking place on the kerb outside the stock exchange.

Keynesian Economics Economic theories developed by John Maynard Keynes (1883–1946), notably the use of government spending and low interest rates to stimulate demand during a recession. These theories opposed the free market philosophy and argued that economic performance could be improved by government intervention.

Kft Hungarian company title: abbreviation of Korlatolt felelossegu tarsasag.

KG German and Swiss company title: abbreviation of Kommanditgessellschaft and Kollectivgessellschaft respectively.

Kicker An added feature of a debt obligation designed to enhance marketability, such as a warrant which allows it to be converted into shares.

KK Japanese company title: abbreviation of Kabushiki Kaisha.

Kkt Hungarian company title: abbreviation of Kozkereseti tarasag.

KmG Swiss company title: abbreviation of Kommanditgessellschaft.

Knockout Option An option that is knocked out, or nullified, when the underlying instrument reaches a certain price. The option writer sets the limit, with the aim of restricting his losses if the price of the underlying financial instrument moves very sharply. In exchange the buyer pays less for an option which offers only limited opportunities for profit. For example, an option writer might sell an option on a share now trading at $95 giving the option buyer the right to buy or 'call' the share at $100, but with a knockout limit of $109. If the share price rises above $100 the buyer will exercise the option. If the price rises sharply above $109 then the option is nullified and the option writer has removed his exposure to large losses.

▶ *See also* Barrier Option.

K/S Danish company title: abbreviation of Kommanditselskab.

L

Labour Market The market for jobs – workers searching for work and employers offering work.

Laddering The allocation of shares in an initial public offering to subscribers who agree to buy more of the issue at a higher price once the issue is public. The underwriter thus helps to ensure that the price will rise after the issue, and the subscribers get access to shares in a desirable issue which is likely to rise in price.

Ladder Option An option on which the strike price can be moved to a more favourable level when the original strike price is reached or overtaken by the spot rate.
▶ *See also* Option.

Laffer Curve A description of the theoretical effect of different tax rates on total tax income. Total government income rises as tax rates rise from low levels, but from a certain rate upwards the total income starts to fall because taxpayers do not have an incentive to work hard and increase their incomes. Named after Professor Arthur Laffer, an advisor to President Ronald Reagan in the 1980s, this theory is a building block in supply-side economics.
▶ *See also* Supply-side Economics.

Lagging Indicators Lagging indicators are economic indicators that follow a change in the economic cycle, reflecting what has already happened in the overall economy. They include such things as labour costs and interest rates. They contrast with leading indicators, which measure economic factors that alter ahead of changes in the overall economic cycle, and coincident indicators, which change at the same time as the overall economic cycle.
▶ *See also* Economic Indicators.

Lambda The measurement of the leverage of an option, showing the relationship between a percentage change in the price of the underlying instrument and a percentage change in the option premium.
▶ *See also* Option, Gearing.

Landesbank Baden-Württemberg (LBBW) LBBW was formed in 1999 and is the largest bank in the southwest of Germany. It numbers among the 50 largest credit institutions worldwide. LBBW serves as clearing bank for its catchment area, provides commercial banking services in competition with private sector banks, and acts as a savings bank in the territory of the state capital of Stuttgart. ▨ **www.lbbw.de** ▨

Last Notice Day The final day for the issuing of notices of intent to deliver against a futures contract.
> ▶ *See also* Futures.

Last Trading Day The last day for trading in the current delivery month. Futures contracts outstanding at the end of the last trading day must be settled by delivery of the underlying asset or by cash settlement.
> ▶ *See also* Cash Settlement, Futures.

Laundering The covert action of passing money through secret channels or via a chain of financial transactions, to evade detection – often using offshore facilities. Laundering is often used to avoid sanctions or to mask an illegal source of funds, such as drugs and gambling.

LBMA London Bullion Market Association. A trade association for precious metals traders and associated banks, brokers, refiners and fabricators. ▨ **www.lbma.org.uk** ▨

LBO ▶ *See* Leveraged Buyout.

L/C Letter of Credit. A letter of credit is a guarantee by a bank on behalf of its corporate customer that a payment will be made if contractual obligations are met. Letters of credit can be traded on the secondary market.
> ▶ *See also* Secondary Market.

Lda Portuguese, Brazilian and Spanish company title: abbreviation of Limitada.

LDC Lesser (or less) developed country. A term that was used to describe developing countries where the economy was primarily based on agriculture and industry contributed less than 10 percent of GDP. LDC has been replaced by the more widely defined term emerging markets.
> ▶ *See also* Emerging Markets.

Lead Manager/Underwriter The institution awarded the mandate by a borrower to raise money via a bond or loan or share issue. The lead manager guarantees the liquidity of the deal, arranges the syndication of the issue and undertakes a major underwriting and distribution commitment. For bonds or loans, the lead manager forms a syndicate of co-lead managers, co-managers and underwriters. For share issues the underwriters guarantee to sell a certain number of shares at a certain price.
> ▶ *See also* Mandate.

Leads and Lags Accelerated and decelerated foreign trade payments and receipts, usually associated with exchange rate speculation. In anticipation of a devaluation, exporters will try to delay receipt of foreign currency while importers will accelerate payments for imports.

Leading Indicators Leading indicators are measurements of economic factors that change ahead of changes in the overall economic cycle. They are used to predict changes in overall output and activity in an economy and include such things as share prices, new orders for investment goods, housing construction orders and the index of consumer confidence. Lagging indicators are economic indicators that follow a change in the economic cycle and coincident indicators change at the same time as the overall economic cycle.

LEAPS Long-term Equity Anticipation Securities. Long-term options on individual stocks with an expiry date of up to two years.

Lender of Last Resort One of the main functions of a central bank is to step in to lend money to troubled financial institutions if they cannot find any other means of raising funds. Acting as lender of last resort, the central bank smoothes over temporary cash-flow shortages and maintains confidence in the financial system.
▶ *See also* Central Bank.

Lending Margin The fixed spread that borrowers agree to pay above an agreed base rate for calculating interest. The base, or reference rate, may be a rate such as London Interbank Offered Rate.
▶ *See* Libor.

Letter of Credit ▶ *See* L/C.

Letter Stock A US privately issued security, which is not registered with the SEC and is thus not easy to transfer. Also known as letter securities, a term which covers letter bonds as well as letter stocks or shares. A SEC rule requires the purchaser to lodge an 'investment letter' saying the purchase is for investment and not for resale.
▶ *See also* SEC.

Leverage ▶ *See* Gearing.

Leveraged Buyout (LBO) The purchase of a company using borrowed funds, with the company's assets used as collateral (or as leverage) for the borrowing. The purchaser then repays the loans out of the acquired company's cash flow, or by selling its assets.

Liabilities Liabilities are debts arising from borrowing and credits used to finance assets.
▶ *See also* Assets.

Liability Management ▶ *See* Asset Management.

Libid The London Interbank Bid Rate. The rate at which banks take deposits from each other.

Libor The London Interbank Offered Rate. The rate at which banks are prepared to lend money market funds to each other. Libor is a key interest rate level used for setting rates on loans and floating rate notes. The coupon on floating rate notes is often a fixed number of basis points above three-month dollar Libor.

Licensed Warehouse A warehouse approved by an exchange from which a commodity may be delivered under a futures contract.
▶ *See also* Futures.

Lien The right to take assets to cover an unpaid debt.

LIFFE The London International Financial Futures and Options Exchange, which trades futures and options contracts on currencies, bonds, short-term interest rates, equities and commodities. ▣ **www.liffe.com** ▣

LIFO Last In First Out. A method of valuing stocks, or inventory, where the newest stock is sold first.
▶ *See also* FIFO.

Limean The London interbank mean price – the mean of Libid and Libor.
▶ *See also* Libid, Libor.

Limited Liability A restriction of the owners' loss in a business to the amount of capital they have invested.

Limit Order An order that stipulates the price at which a market transaction can be executed. The maximum price is stipulated for a buy order and the minimum for a sell. Limit orders are normally valid until a certain time specified by the client. They can also be Good Till Cancelled (GTC), remaining valid until the limit is reached and the order is executed, or until the order is cancelled.

Limit Up/Down The maximum advance or decline from a previous day's settlement price that is allowed in one trading session. Some markets do not trade again during the session after a limit up/down move unless prices retreat from that limit. Other markets suspend trading temporarily when limits are hit and then reopen with expanded limit levels.
▶ *See also* Circuit Breakers.

Line Chart Used in technical analysis, a line chart is the simplest form of chart. It is a plain record of a price charted against time, with the changes marked as dots and joined together by a line. (Figure 11.)
▶ *See also* Technical Analysis.

Liquidate To close or offset a long or short trading position to realize a gain or loss.

Liquidation The sale of assets of a bankrupt company to pay creditors. Any remaining surplus is distributed to shareholders.

Liquidity The ease with which financial instruments can be traded on a market and turned into cash. Markets or instruments are described as being liquid, and having depth or liquidity, if there are enough buyers and sellers to absorb sudden shifts in supply and demand without price distortions. The opposite of illiquid. The term can also be used loosely to describe cash flow in a business, so a company that has fallen into a liquidity trap may have growing orders and production but has run out of cash.
▶ *See also* Illiquid.

Liquidity Margin A liquidity margin is a performance guarantee in a financial transaction. In repurchase agreements (repos), lenders often seek such a margin from borrowers, perhaps by receiving securities that are worth more than the money borrowed.
▶ *See also* Repurchase Agreement.

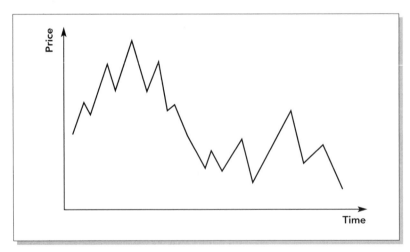

FIGURE 11 Line chart

Liquidity Risk The risk a dealer has of not being able to unwind a position or enter into a position at a desired point of time because there is not enough market volume or a lack of willing counter parties.

Listed Stock A security that is listed on a stock exchange and can therefore be traded in the market.

Listing Particulars The details a company must publish before it qualifies for listing on a public stock exchange. Usually contained in a prospectus.
▶ *See also* Prospectus.

Listing Requirements Each stock exchange sets its own listing requirements that must be fulfilled before a stock is listed and ready to trade. Criteria include considerations such as the number of publicly-held shares, the number of shareholders and published accounts for a minimum number of years.

LLC US company title: abbreviation of limited liability company.

Lloyd's An insurance underwriting market based in London, which covers risks such as marine, aviation, catastrophe cover and professional indemnity. ▥ **www.lloydsoflondon.co.uk** ▥

LLP US company title: abbreviation of limited liability partnership.

LME London Metal Exchange. Europe's leading market for trading in metals futures and options. The LME acts as an international barometer of supply and demand for metals worldwide and its official prices are used by producers and consumers for their long-term contacts. ▥ **www.lme.co.uk** ▥

Load A premium charged by some investment funds at either purchase or sale, to cover the fund's expenses.

Loan Loss Provisions Funds set aside to cover anticipated loan losses. They appear on a bank's income statement as an operating expense.

Locals Individual traders operating on futures or options exchanges purely for their own account.

Lock-up Period A period when shareholders are not allowed to trade in a share. It applies particularly to employees of a company who are granted shares on concessionary terms and are then required to hold them for a minimum period.

Loco The cost of goods where they lie. In gold trading the price is quoted for delivery to a certain location.

London Bullion Market Association ▶ *See* LBMA.

London Clearing House A central counter party and clearing house, particularly used for European government bonds. It acts on behalf of the International Petroleum Exchange and the London Metal Exchange, among others. ■ **www.lch.co.uk** ■

London Club An informal group of commercial bank creditors, the London Club negotiates with debtor governments that have loan problems and need to reschedule debt.
▶ *See also* Paris Club.

London Commodity Exchange ▶ *See* LCE.

London International Financial Futures and Options Exchange
▶ *See* LIFFE.

London Metal Exchange ▶ *See* LME.

London Stock Exchange ▶ *See* LSE.

Long Investors are 'long' when they have bought assets in the hope that prices will rise and that they can sell them when prices have peaked. A long position can be closed out through the sale of an equivalent amount. The opposite of short.
▶ *See also* Short.

Long Dated Forwards Forward foreign exchange contracts with value dates beyond 12 months.
▶ *See also* Forwards.

Long Hedge The purchase of a futures or option position to protect against a price rise in the corresponding cash market. Increased costs from the need to buy a cash commodity which has risen in price will be offset by the profits from a future or option which has also risen in price. The opposite to short hedge.
▶ *See also* Hedging.

Long Ton A ton of 2,240 pounds weight – equal to 1.016 metric tonnes.

Lookback/Forward Option An option that grants the holder the retroactive right to set the strike at the lowest price (on a call) or at the highest price (on a put) reached by the underlying instrument within the lookback period.
▶ *See also* Option.

Loss Limit The maximum loss permitted on a position before the dealer is required to cut his losses and square or reduce the position.

LP US company title: abbreviation of limited partnership.

LSE London Stock Exchange. ▨ **www.londonstockexchange.com** ▨

Ltd UK company title: abbreviation of limited. Generally replaced by public limited company or plc. Also used for quoted companies in Australia, Canada and New Zealand.

Ltée French Canadian company title: abbreviation of Limitée.

Maastricht Criteria The criteria, set out in the Treaty of Maastricht, that need to be met by European countries if they wish to become full members of the Economic and Monetary Union. They include:

- inflation of no more than 1.5 percentage points above the average rate of the three member states with the lowest inflation
- a national budget deficit close to or below 3 percent of gross national product
- public debt not exceeding 60 percent of gross national product.

▶ *See also* EMU, EU, Maastricht Treaty.

Maastricht Treaty An agreement signed in 1991 by the 12 member nations of the then European Community, that set the timetable and criteria for Economic and Monetary Union within the bloc. The treaty also created the European Union, with new political and social responsibilities, to replace the European Community. The Maastricht Treaty is also known as the Treaty on European Union.

▶ *See also* EMU, EU.

Macauley duration ▶ *See* Duration.

MACD Moving Average Convergence/Divergence. This technical analysis tool shows the relationship between two exponential moving averages of a share price for different periods. The two exponential moving averages are plotted on a chart, producing two lines that oscillate above and below a zero line. Sell and buy signals are generated when the two lines derived from moving averages of different periods cross. Overbought and oversold signals can be indicated when both lines are significantly above or below the zero line respectively. The exponential moving average is worked out by applying a percentage of the closing price today to the moving average calculated yesterday. This gives more weight to the most recent price changes compared with a simple moving average.

▶ *See also* Technical Analysis.

Macro-economics Study of aggregate economic behaviour such as total output, economic growth, inflation and unemployment.

▶ *See also* Economic Indicators.

Maintenance Call ▶ *See* Margin Call.

Maintenance Margin The lowest balance of funds that a clearing house or brokerage firm will allow a counterparty, or the person on the other side of a deal, when trading on margin.
▶ *See also* Margin, Margin Trading.

Majority Interest A major equity interest of more than half the shares in a company.

Majority Rule In technical analysis, this indicator calculates the percentage of the last specified periods during which an instrument had rising values. This analysis may be used either as a trend-following device or as an overbought/oversold indicator.
▶ *See also* Technical Analysis.

Majors Multinational oil companies, which by virtue of size, age and/or degree of integration, are among the pre-eminent firms in the international petroleum industry.

Managed Currency A currency is described as managed if the government exerts some influence over the exchange rate, rather than allowing the rate to be determined purely by free market forces.

Managed Float ▶ *See* Dirty Float.

Management Buyout ▶ *See* MBO.

Management Group Group of financial institutions that co-ordinates closely with the lead manager in the distribution and pricing of a securities issue.

M&A Mergers and Acquisitions ▶ *See* Acquisition, Merger, Takeover.

Mandate The authority from a borrower to the lead manager to proceed with a loan or bond issue on the terms agreed.

Margin Margin allows trading without having the full amount of funds available. It is a part-payment of collateral to cover contractual obligations and to insure against potential unlimited loss. Clearing houses in futures markets demand an initial margin from both the buyer and the seller of a futures contract to ensure they will be able to meet their contractual obligations. To ensure that margin requirements keep pace with subsequent market movements, variation margin is also called for. This is calculated by revaluing all positions with reference to the closing prices each day.
▶ *See also* Initial Margin, Mark to Market, Margin Trading, Variation Margin.

Marginal Cost The additional cost of one extra unit of production, e.g. the leather and labour needed to produce an extra pair of shoes. In contrast with fixed costs such as buildings and machinery that do not change no matter how much is produced. Also known as Incremental Cost.

Margin Account An account enabling an investor to trade without having the full amount of funds available.
▶ *See also* Margin, Margin Trading.

Margin Call A call made by the clearing house or broker to a counterparty whose margin account has fallen below the minimum requirement or the maintenance margin. Also referred to as a maintenance call.
▶ *See also* Maintenance Margin.

Margin Trading An investor pays a certain amount of cash to fund a transaction and borrows the remainder from a broker at a rate of interest. Margin trading provides gearing to investors since their small amount of funds goes a lot further when combined with additional borrowed funds. But added gearing means increased risk if the market moves against the investor.

Markdown The amount or percentage deducted from the bid price when a customer sells to a broker or market maker in the over-the-counter market, which is regarded as a type of commission. Markdown is also used to describe market makers adjusting their prices down to reflect changing market conditions. Opposite of markup.
▶ *See also* Markup, OTC.

MARKET

The **words in bold** are explained more fully under their individual entries.

MEASURING A MARKET

Equities

The simplest, crudest and most effective measure of a share is its **price**. How much does a share cost and has the price gone up or down? But that movement needs to be measured against price changes in the market as a whole, and more particularly against the sector in which the company operates. A 10 percent rise in the share price may look good in isolation but will compare unfavourably to a rise of 15 percent in the index representing the overall market or a rise of 20 percent in the sector index.

Analysts therefore need to know the main benchmark index or indices for a market and also the sector in which a company is placed within that market in order to compare **relative price movements**. Indices are constructed either by taking a simple basket of stocks, or a basket weighted for **market capitalization**. If a particular share is a member of the benchmark index it is likely to be frequently traded and widely followed by analysts. It will also be sought by **tracker funds**.

It also helps to know the **volume** of share trading on which a share price move is based. Large price changes on small trading volumes may be less significant than small price movements on very large volumes. You need to be aware of how busy the market and the sector are overall and whether the volume of a particular stock is unusually high or low.

How **volatile** are the share price movements? Increased volatility may be a sign of increased uncertainty. Again, the volatility of the share needs to be compared with the volatility of the market as a whole and whether increased volatility has been coupled with increased volume.

What is the relative status of the share? Is it a **blue chip** with a large market capitalization, or a **penny stock** with relatively low market size?

What is the size of the company's **free float**? Are the shares relatively easy to trade and in large volumes, or is the float so restricted that it is difficult to trade without **moving the market**?

Is there a large **spread** between the **bid** and **offer** prices? A narrow spread is a sign of higher volumes and greater **liquidity** in a share.

Does a particular share have traded **futures** or **options**? The additional instruments can improve the liquidity and ease of trading but may also add to volatility, especially at or near the time when futures or options expire.

Where is the share traded? Is it on an **exchange** or an **over-the-counter** market? Is it listed on one or more electronic communications networks (ECN)? Is it **dual-listed** on more than one exchange, and does it have American Depository Receipts (ADR)? The greater the number of exchanges or means of trading for a particular share then the higher the chances that trading will be liquid and high volume.

Can the share be bought by pensions and insurance companies? That usually means meeting a number of criteria such as consistent dividend payments and a minimum market capitalization.

Price alone will not tell you enough about the value of a share, although price movements, especially compared with the whole market, will give some indication of whether the company is in or out of favour.

How does the company's price compare with its earnings? What is its **price/earnings ratio** and how does that compare to the average p/e ratio of the sector and of the market as a whole?

Does the company pay a dividend and if so, for how many years has it done so? Does it increase its dividend regularly? Did it ever miss paying a dividend? Can it afford to pay its dividends? What is its **dividend cover**? How many times do net earnings cover dividend payments? What is its **dividend yield** (its dividends per share expressed as a percentage of the share price)?

How much debt does the company have? What is its **debt-to-equity ratio**, or how highly **geared** is it? Are its interest payments covered by its earnings? What is its **interest cover**?

Have its **net profits** been growing consistently? What is its **profit margin**?

What sort of sector is the company in? How does its profit margin, p/e ratio and dividend yield compare with companies in the same business? Is it a cyclical stock likely to suffer in a general economic downturn or a counter-cyclical stock that would be relatively immune to a downturn?

Bonds

The best measure of what is happening in the bond market is to look at the **yield**. This is much more meaningful than **price**, which cannot be compared for different bonds because of the differing original **coupons**.

Yields can be compared between different bonds of the same **maturity**, but they cannot be compared between bonds with different ratings. A **junk** bond would naturally pay a higher yield than an investment grade bond because of the higher risk involved, just as a government of a **G7** country would pay less to borrow than that of an **emerging market** country.

The opinion of **credit rating** agencies is very important to the bond market and the **downgrading** of a credit rating can have a major influence on the market.

Differences in the risk assessment of the borrower are reflected in the yield **spread** between bonds of the same maturity and coupon. Yields on long-term bonds are usually higher than yields on short-term debt, reflecting a payment for the higher risk of holding the debt for a longer period. The pattern of yields for varying maturities of debt is depicted in the **yield curve**, which plots yield on one axis of a graph and years to maturity on the other axis. The curve normally slopes upwards, with yields rising as maturities lengthen. Sometimes the pattern is disrupted and there is an **inverse yield curve**, with yields on short-term debt higher than those on long-term debt.

Most bonds are traded on an **over-the-counter** market rather than on an **exchange**. But the interest-rate risk of an underlying bond portfolio can be hedged by trading interest rate **futures** on an exchange.

Bond prices can be affected by the **liquidity** and **volatility** in the market. Government bonds are the most easily traded, but other issues may be more difficult to trade. Bond issues, however, are to a certain extent **fungible**. They may not have exactly the same characteristics but can be seen as broadly comparable in risk and maturity, with small differences expressed in the small differences in yield.

Commodities

When you look at a commodity market you need to distinguish between the physical or **spot** market and the **futures** markets.

The most important feature in tracking prices is whether the commodity is traded on an **exchange** or whether it is restricted to **over-the-counter** trading (long-term contract deals between supplier and end-user). If a commodity is traded on an exchange it is important to know which is the principal trading centre, because that contract tends to be a benchmark for prices throughout the world.

Market watchers need to know the currency of the contract and the specified quality, quantity and delivery points of the contract. They also need to know who acts as the **clearing house** for the contract, how much **hedging** and how much **speculation** there is, and what is the most actively traded contract in **futures** and **options**.

Market Capitalization The total value of a company's securities at current prices as quoted on a stock exchange. Market capitalization is calculated by multiplying the total number of shares by the market price. It can also denote the total value of all the securities listed on a stock exchange, or the total value of one sector of a market's listed securities.

Market Economy An economy where supply and demand in free markets determine the allocation of resources. However, most countries impose some limitations within this economic system.

Market If Touched ▶ See MIT.

Market Maker An individual or firm that stands ready to trade in one or more securities at quoted bid and ask prices. Market makers usually hold an inventory of the securities in which they make markets.

Market Order An order that should be executed immediately whatever the current price.

Market Risk ▶ See Systematic Risk.

Market Sector Listed securities from a particular industry. Stock exchanges have sector indices which track the performance of listed companies by industry, e.g. banks, chemicals or forestry and paper.

Market Trend The general direction of overall price movements in a market, ignoring short-term fluctuations.

Market-value Weighted Index An index in which greater weight is given to shares that have a larger market capitalization, so that they have more influence than shares with a lower market capitalization.
▶ See also Market Capitalization.

Mark to Market The process by which a position or portfolio is revalued based on the current day's closing price. Instead of being valued at the original purchase price the portfolio is valued at its current worth, reflecting any profit or loss which is not yet realized but which would be taken into account if the position were sold immediately.

Markup The amount or percentage added to the offer price when a customer buys from a broker or market maker in the OTC market, which is regarded as a type of commission. Also used to describe market makers adjusting their prices upwards to reflect changing market conditions. Opposite of markdown.
▶ See also Markdown.

Master Agreement The initial agreement signed between two parties proposing to enter into a swap, which defines all criteria such as references for fixing rates and the status of counterparties.
▶ *See also* Swap.

Matched Book A book where the maturity dates for a bank or trader's liabilities match those of the assets. Also, where borrowing costs equal the interest earned on investments.
▶ *See also* Book.

MATIF Marché à Terme International de France. France's financial futures exchange. ■ **www.matif.frindexE4.htm** ■

Maturity The length of time between the issue of a security and the date on which it becomes payable in full. Most bonds are issued with a fixed maturity date. Those without one are known as perpetuals.

Maturity Value The amount to be paid back at maturity. Also called principal in bond trading.

MBO Management Buyout. A purchase of part or all of a company's shares by the managers of that company in order to set it up as an independent concern. The managers act as principals and do not usually provide all the financing.

MBS Mortgage-backed Security. A security backed by, or secured by, a pool or package of mortgage loans. Monthly payments of principal and interest from the underlying pool of mortgages are passed along to the holder of the security.
▶ *See also* Securitization.

Mean Calculated by taking the sum of a set of values and then dividing that figure by the total number of values. Also known as the average.

Median The middle-ranking value of a set of values laid out in numerical order.
▶ *See also* Mode.

Medium-term Notes ▶ *See* MTN.

Merchant Bank ▶ *See* Investment Bank.

MERCOSUR Mercado Común del Sur (Southern Common Market). A Latin American trade bloc that aims to promote free trade and co-operation between its members. Argentina, Brazil, Paraguay and Uruguay were founding members, Chile and Bolivia are associate members.
■ **www.mercosur.org.uy** ■

Merger A fusion of two or more companies. Can also represent an acquisition or takeover.

Merger Arbitrage A trading strategy which takes advantage of share price anomalies arising from an announced or expected merger between two companies. It usually involves going long in the takeover target's shares, which are expected to gain in value during the merger, and going short in the bidding company's shares, which are expected to fall because of the risk and expense of acquiring another company.
  ▶ *See also* Arbitrage, Long, Merger, Short.

Mezzanine Finance A type of funding capital midway between debt and equity in that it offers a higher interest rate than senior debt, but provides a lower longer-term return than equity. This allows large deals to be structured in the most suitable method for investors and lenders. Often used in management buyouts.

Mibtel The Mibtel index is the benchmark all-share index for the Italian stock market. The MIB 30 is the Milan blue-chip index.
  ■ **www.borsaitalia.it/eng/home** ■ **www.mibtel.it** ■

Micro-economics The study of the economic action of individual firms and small well-defined groupings of individuals and sectors.
  ▶ *See also* Macro-economics.

Middleware Software that links big databases to consumer products. For example, a website.

Middle Office The part of a financial institution's settlement process that most closely liaises with the front office, recording trades and trading positions.
  ▶ *See also* Front Office, Back Office.

MIF The Mercato Italiano Dei Futures. Italy's financial futures market, which is part of the Borsa Italiana. ■ **www.borsaitalia.it/eng/home** ■
  ▶ *See also* Futures.

MIGA The Multilateral Investment Guarantee Agency. An affiliate of the World Bank, the agency was created in 1988 to offer political risk insurance guarantees in emerging economies in order to help them attract and retain private investment. ■ **www.miga.org** ■

Mine Dealers' language. The dealer takes the offer that has been quoted by his counterparty. It has to be qualified by the amount and confirms the act of purchasing.

Minimum Price Movement The smallest unit of change possible in the price of a contract.
▶ *See also* Tick, Basis Point.

Minority Interest An important but non-controlling outside ownership stake in a company or subsidiary. Also used to describe the share of a parent company's net profits or net assets that are attributable to those minority shareholders in partially-owned subsidiaries.

Minor Metals Metals such as cobalt, tantalum, tungsten, antimony, zirconium and molybdenum. ■ **www.mmta.co.uk** ■
▶ *See also* Base Metals, Precious Metals.

Mismatch
1 A difference between the length of time for which money is borrowed and the length of time for which it is invested, or the difference between the maturities of borrowing and investments. One example is when a bank borrows money for a short time but lends it for a longer period, so there is a mismatch between its source and use of funds.
2 A mismatched book, or a mismatch in an overall trading position, occurs when short and long positions do not complement each other.
▶ *See also* Matched Book, Long, Short.

Mismatch Note A variable rate note on which the changes in coupon, or refixes, are based on a mismatched reference rate in terms of maturity, a note refixing on a monthly basis against six-month Libor.
▶ *See also* Libor.

MIT Market If Touched. Written as MIT. An order to sell or buy at a specific price if the market reaches that price.

Mixed Economy Midway between a planned economy and a market economy. Thus the state runs one or more sectors or parts of the economy alongside generally free market activities.
▶ *See also* State Planning.

Mode The more frequently occurring value within a set of values.

MOFs Multi-option facilities that allow a borrower to obtain funds from various short- or long-term instruments. These may include bank advances, commercial paper and euronotes. A variety of currencies may also be available.

Momentum In technical analysis momentum is a type of oscillator that is used to measure the rate of change – as opposed to the actual price level. The momentum indicator is the difference between the price of the instrument today and the price in the previous determined periods. It is used to signal overbought or oversold conditions as well as entry and exit points.

▶ *See also* Technical Analysis.

MONEP Marché des Options Négociables de Paris. The Paris traded options market specializing in stock and index options. ■ **www.monep.fr** ■

Monetarism Theory that advocates strict control of money supply as the major weapon of monetary policy, especially against inflation.

Monetary Policy Government policy that deals with total money supply and the general level of interest rates. It has a direct effect on the overall level of economic activity and inflation. Governments often delegate monetary policy implementation to central banks.

▶ *See also* Central Banks, Fiscal Policy, Money Supply.

Monetary Policy Committee ▶ *See* MPC.

Money Money is a financial asset, a store of wealth and a recognized medium of exchange. Definitions of money and money supply vary from country to country but fall into two categories – broad and narrow. Narrow money is money that can be used in everyday transactions, including coins, notes, current accounts and travellers' cheques. Broad money is less easily accessible and includes savings accounts, time deposits and institutional funds in the money market.

▶ *See also* Money Supply.

Money Centre Bank A large bank that lends to and borrows from governments, organizations and other banks, as opposed to consumers.

Money Flow Index A technical analysis indicator. A volume-weighted relative strength index which attempts to measure the strength of money entering and leaving the market.

▶ *See also* Technical Analysis, Relative Strength Index.

Money Market A wholesale market for the buying and selling of money. Money markets trade in debt instruments with residual maturities of 12 months or less.

Money Market Yield The yield of a security expressed under the money market daycount convention (which calculates annual yield based on the number of days before the security matures). It is normally expressed in basis points, or one-hundredths of a percentage point.

Money Supply The total stock of money in an economy, including notes and coins, loans, credit and other liquid instruments. There are various definitions of money supply in each country, but in all economies the definitions gradually range from narrow, which usually includes just cash in circulation and demand deposits at commercial banks, through to the broadest measure which includes money market funds.

Monopoly When a single person or organization controls the market for a given product or service.
> ▶ *See also* Oligopoly.

Moody's A leading credit rating agency that assesses the creditworthiness of borrowers. Changes in its credit ratings are widely watched in the capital markets and can affect the price of an institution's bonds and the cost of its borrowing. ▪ **www.moodys.com** ▪

Moral Suasion The use of persuasion rather than coercion by central banks and governments to influence market participants.

Moratorium The suspension or delay by a borrower of repayments of principal, and sometimes of due interest, on a loan. If it is determined that interest will in fact be paid, then banks can continue to classify the loan as a performing asset. If neither principal nor interest is being paid it is a non-performing loan.

Most Favoured Nation Undertaking by two countries to give each other the maximum tariff concessions on their mutual trade that they already grant to other countries.

Mortgage-backed Security ▶ *See* MBS.

Mortgage Pool Mortgages are packaged, or pooled, and securities are issued representing shares in the pool. The mortgages in a pool bear the same maturity date and same interest rate on the same class of property.
> ▶ *See also* Securitization.

Moving Average A technical analysis indicator that provides a way of smoothing data and is used to confirm price trends. It reduces the effects of isolated sharp price movements and shows the underlying trend more clearly. A moving average is usually calculated by adding a series of closing prices and then averaging the data on a period-by-period basis. As the period moves on, the oldest price in the sequence is dropped and replaced by the current price. (Figure 12.)
> ▶ *See also* Technical Analysis.

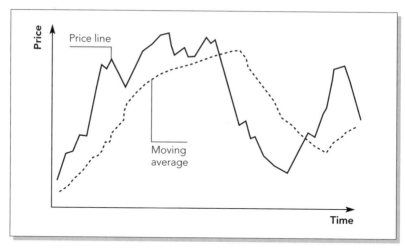

FIGURE 12 Moving average

Moving Average Convergence/Divergence ▶ *See* MACD.

Moving Average Crossover   Technical analysts interpret crossovers between two moving averages – one using a short interval and the other a longer interval – as significant buy or sell signals.
▶ *See also* Moving Average, Technical Analysis.

Moving Strike Option   An option on which a single strike price is not determined for the life of the option, but will vary over time.
▶ *See also* Strike Price.

MPC   Central banks, such as the Bank of England, often have a Monetary Policy Committee, which sets interest rates.

MSCI Indices   The Morgan Stanley Capital International indices. A group of regional, national and industry performance benchmarks designed to help compare world equity markets. The indices are widely used by portfolio managers to compare the performance of their funds against those of the underlying markets. The MSCI indices are calculated using weighted arithmetic averages. ■ **www.msci.com** ■
▶ *See also* Arithmetic Average, Weighted Index.

MTN   Medium-term Notes. Borrowings out to about five years typically issued under a similar borrowing facility as for commercial paper. MTNs issued in the Euromarkets are known as EMTNs.

MTS   Mercato Telematico Secondario. A screen-based system, owned by Italian and foreign banks, showing both bid and offer prices by market makers for Italian government debt issues.

Multinational A publicly-owned company that operates commercially in a number of countries outside its own base. Usually its activities in each country encompass all aspects of production of its goods or services. Such companies are often listed on more than one stock exchange or have shares available via depositary receipts.
▶ *See also* ADR.

Multiples ▶ *See* P/E Ratio.

Multiplier Bond A bond that allows the investor to convert coupons into identical bonds, and to reinvest coupons on these subsequent bonds. The borrower gains a cash flow benefit because the payouts are being converted into extra debt. Also known as a bunny bond.

Municipal Notes Short-term US securities, typically out to three years maximum, issued by state and local governments and agencies. Commonly known as Munis. Types of municipal note include tax anticipation notes (TANs); revenue anticipation notes (RANs); grant anticipation notes (GANs); bond anticipation notes (BANs) and tax-exempt commercial paper.

Mutual Fund/Unit Trust An open-ended investment trust or unit trust, which pools together funds from many investors to establish a diversified portfolio of investments. After the initial public offering, the fund continues to both sell and redeem its shares, according to demand from the public. It invests contributions from the public in various securities and pays dividends in proportion to the investors' holdings.
▶ *See also* Investment Fund.

N

NAB New Arrangements to Borrow. A credit line to the IMF arranged by 25 members and institutions following the Mexican financial crisis in 1994, to provide supplementary resources to protect the international monetary system. The NAB will be called on first before resorting to the General Arrangements to Borrow (a credit line with the G10 group of countries).
▶ *See also* GAB.

NAFTA North American Free Trade Agreement. A three-member free trade zone between the US, Canada and Mexico.
■ **www.nafta-sec-alena.org** ■

Naked Position A long or short position that has not been hedged.
▶ *See also* Hedging.

Naked Warrant Issued as a stand-alone warrant instead of being attached to a bond. Issuers save costs because the warrant exercise period corresponds to the call feature of a previous bond issue, so a call premium need not be paid. If holders exercise their warrants, resulting in new securities being issued, then the issuer can match that exposure by exercising previous existing calls.
▶ *See also* Warrants.

NAPM National Association of Purchasing Management. Now known as the Institute of Supply Management. ■ **www.ism.ws** ■
▶ *See* Institute of Supply Management

NASD National Association of Securities Dealers. A US regulatory organization for brokers and dealers that enforces legal and ethical standards.
■ **www.nasd.com** ■

NASDAQ The National Association of Securities Dealers' Automated Quotations System, formerly owned and operated by the National Association of Securities Dealers (NASD). NASDAQ is an electronic stock market based in New York listing many leading high-tech companies. The exchange's index – the NASDAQ Composite – has become an alternative benchmark to the DJIA. ■ **www.Nasdaq.com** ■
▶ *See also* High Tech Stock, DJIA.

NASDAQ Composite An index of all NASDAQ-listed shares, both domestic and foreign, weighted by market capitalization. A broad-based index of more than 5,000 companies, which is widely followed.
▶ *See also* NASDAQ.

NASDAQ Europe NASDAQ's European operation.
■ **www.nasdaqeurope.com** ■

National Accounts The national accounts are the official income account, cash flow statement and balance sheet for the economy of a country. These accounts give a comprehensive analysis of gross domestic product and its components, and include detailed financial accounts related to the government, company, household and foreign trade sectors.

National Association of Purchasing Management ▶ *See* ISM.

National Association of Securities Dealers ▶ *See* NASD.

National Association of Securities Dealers' Automated Quotations System ▶ *See* NASDAQ.

National Debt The total indebtedness of a government resulting from cumulative net budget deficits. National debt is normally financed by the sale of government securities and debt instruments.

Nationalization The compulsory purchase of a company and its assets by a state, sometimes without compensation, in order to bring them under public ownership and control.

Native Yield The convention used in a particular country or market for the calculation of a bond's yield if it is held to maturity. A widely used convention is the ISMA (International Securities Market Association) yield to maturity which makes all future cash flows equal to the price of the bond plus accrued interest.

NAV ▶ *See* Net Asset Value.

Nearbys The nearest delivery months of a futures contract.

Near Money Assets, such as money market fund shares, bank time deposits and government securities, which are readily convertible into cash. This also applies to bonds near their redemption date.

Negative Carry A term used to describe a situation where the financing cost of a position is greater than the return. It is the opposite of 'positive carry', where the financing cost is less than the return.

Negative Goodwill The gain for a company when it makes an acquisition and pays less than the market value of the assets acquired.
▶ *See* Goodwill.

Negative Pledge A clause in a bond agreement which prevents the borrower from pledging greater security or collateral to other lenders.

Negative Stock Split ▶ *See* Reverse Stock Split.

Negotiable An item that can be traded or transferred freely. Also refers to any part of a transaction where a fee, commission or interest rate, for example, can be negotiable (i.e. agreed to the satisfaction of one or more parties).

NEPAD New Partnership for Africa's Development. An intergovernmental programme to combat poverty and promote development in Africa.
■ **www.nepad.org** ■

Net Any figure from which some liability, such as tax, has been deducted.

Net Assets A company's total assets minus its liabilities. Also known as net worth.

Net Asset Value (NAV) The valuation of a company or fund based on its assets. This can lead to differences of perception depending on how assets are valued. For mutual funds and unit trusts, the NAV is calculated daily by dividing the net value by the number of outstanding shares. This is the price at which investors can redeem their mutual fund shares.
▶ *See also* Mutual Fund.

Net Cash Flow Retained earnings plus depreciation.
▶ *See also* Retained Earnings, Depreciation.

Net Earnings The company's profit that remains once all coupons on outstanding bonds, taxes and dividends on outstanding preferred shares have been settled. Effectively the earnings that belong to the holders of common stock, or ordinary shares, in the company.

Net Position The difference between long and short positions held by a dealer in a given market. If a dealer has sold 100 contracts and bought 80 contracts he has a net short position of 20 contracts. Conversely if he has sold 120 contracts and bought 150 contracts he has a net long position of 30 contracts.

Net Present Value ▶ *See* Present Value.

Net Profit Trading profits after deducting the charges detailed in the profit and loss account such as tax, depreciation, auditors' fees and directors' fees.

Net Transaction A transaction whereby the investor is not charged a commission. If a company sells new issues, the underwriter's commission is incorporated in the issue price. A commission will only be charged in secondary market trading.

Net Worth A measure of the difference between the total value of assets and possessions and total indebtedness. Also known as net assets.

Netting A system whereby outstanding financial contracts can be settled at a net figure. Receivables are offset against payables to reduce the credit exposure to a counterparty and to minimize settlement risk.

Neutral A market that displays neither bullish or bearish tendencies.
> ▶ *See also* Bear, Bull.

New Economy A term used to describe the fast-growing technology-oriented industries with global reach, mainly selling computers and software and involved in the internet, electronic commerce and telecommunications. A key example of the shift to the 'new economy' was the listing of high-tech companies Microsoft and Intel in the blue-chip Dow Jones 30 industrial index in 1999, replacing such labour-intensive 'old economy' institutions as tyre-maker Goodyear and retailer Sears.

New Issue A security that is being offered for sale in the primary market.
> ▶ *See also* IPO, Primary Market.

New York Mercantile Exchange ▶ *See* NYMEX.

New York Stock Exchange ▶ *See* NYSE.

NIF Note Issuance Facility. An NIF allows borrowers to offer short-term paper (usually three or six months) in their own names. Fund availability is guaranteed to the borrower by underwriting banks who buy any unsold notes at successive rollover dates or who provide a standby credit.

Nikkei 225 The Nikkei 225 index is the benchmark index for equity prices on the Tokyo Stock Exchange. Like the Dow Jones it is a simple arithmetic average of the 225 largest stocks on the first section of the Tokyo Exchange. Futures on the Nikkei are traded in Osaka, Singapore and Chicago. ■ **www.nni.nikkei.co.jp** ■

Nil Paid Rights Rights issues are typically offered at a discount to the prevailing market price of the existing securities, so the allotment letters have a market value and may be traded as 'nil paid rights' before payment for the new shares is due.
> ▶ *See also* Rights Issue.

N/O A normal order to buy or sell at a certain level, i.e. to sell at higher, or to buy at lower levels than prevailing market rates.

No-load Indicates that no commission is charged on a mutual fund.
> ▶ *See also* Mutual Fund/Unit Trust.

Nominal Unadjusted for inflation. A calculation of nominal economic growth simply adds up the total of goods and services in current cash terms and makes no adjustment for inflation, which may lead to great overstatement of the real, underlying position.

▶ *See also* Real.

Nominal Interest Rates The interest rate expressed in money terms, with no allowance made for the effects of inflation. In contrast with real interest rates, which are nominal rates minus inflation.

Nominal Value Apparent worth. The nominal value that appears on the face of the document recording an entitlement, generally a certificate or a bond. For debt instruments, the amount to be repaid at maturity. Also known as face value or par value.

Nominee Account Securities owned by an investor but registered in the name of the brokerage firm are held in nominee account. The certificate bears the name of, and is held in safekeeping by, the brokerage firm. Records of the issuing company show the brokerage firm as the holder of the record. The brokerage firm records the investor as the beneficial owner. Also known as 'street name'.

Non-competitive Bid Auction An auction which allows bids for quantity rather than price, particularly for government securities. The non-competitive bidder pays the average price determined by the competitive bidders. These bids allow small investors to participate in the auction. Non-competitive bids are given priority and are awarded in full, so they can reduce the amounts available to competitive bidders.

Non-negotiable A transaction where the terms of the contract are fixed. Also, an instrument that can only be held by the original holder and cannot be traded or transferred or used as collateral.

Non-performing Loan A loan on which neither interest payment nor principal repayment is being made. When a bank has such a loan on its books, it can either write it off against profits immediately or make loan loss provisions ready to make such a write-off in the future.

Non-voting Stock Securities that do not allow the holder to vote on company resolutions.

No Par Value Shares with no par value assigned at the time the stock is authorized. Shares are authorized for issue as part of the legal process of setting up a company. Par value is the nominal face value of the shares and bears no relationship to the actual traded value of the shares or to the underlying assets which they represent. The advantage of issuing no par value is to avoid the situation of creating a liability to shareholders in the unlikely event of the traded share price falling below the par value of the shares.

▶ *See also* Par Value.

Normal Market Size The number of stocks that can be purchased without moving the market price.

Normal Yield Curve A chart illustrating that yields on long-term securities are at higher rates than the rates on short-term securities, to reflect the extra risk of holding them for a longer period. Also known as a positive yield curve. The opposite of an inverted yield curve, when short-term yields are above longer-term yields.

▶ *See also* Inverted Yield Curve.

North American Free Trade Agreement ▶ *See* NAFTA.

Note Issuance Facility ▶ *See* NIF.

Notes Medium-term government debt instruments, equivalent to bonds, usually with a maturity from two to five years, although usage varies according to market. For commercial borrowers notes usually have a much shorter term and can be comparable to Treasury bills, with maturities as short as three months.

Notional Bonds A standardized bond with hypothetical terms (coupon and maturity), which represents the basis for a bond futures contract.

Notional Principal The hypothetical amount on which interest payments are based in products such as interest rate swaps, forward rate agreements, caps and floors.

▶ *See also* Cap, FRA, Floor, Swap.

NPV ▶ *See* Present Value.

NV Dutch company title: abbreviation of Naamloze Vennootschap.

NYBOT The New York Board of Trade. Parent company of the Coffee, Sugar and Cocoa Exchange and of the New York Cotton Exchange.
■ **www.nybot.com** ■

NYMEX The New York Mercantile Exchange. Trades futures and options on precious metals and crude oil. ■ **www.nymex.com** ■

NYSE The New York Stock Exchange. ■ **www.nyse.com** ■

OAPEC Organization of Arab Petroleum Exporting Countries. OAPEC aims to improve economic co-operation in the petroleum industry. Its members are Algeria, Bahrain, Egypt, Iraq, Kuwait, Libya, Qatar, Saudi Arabia, Syria and the United Arab Emirates. The group does not make decisions on oil output or pricing. ■ **www.oapecorg.org** ■

OAT Obligations Assimilables du Trésor. Fungible Treasury bonds issued in France with maturities ranging from 7 to 30 years at fixed or floating interest.
▶ *See* Fungible.

OCO One cancels the other. A limit order that consists of two buy orders (or two sell orders) at different levels either side of the current market level. The execution of one order automatically cancels the other.

Odd Coupon This occurs when the first or last coupon period is longer or shorter than the normal coupon period.

Odd Date ▶ *See* Broken Date.

Odd Lot Trade A block of securities or commodities that is smaller or larger than the standard lot size traded in that market. The price can vary from the current market value.

ODR Ordinary Drawing Rights. Similar to special drawing rights (SDRs) and also allocated to members of the IMF. However, ODRs are credits as opposed to SDRs, which are used as currency reserves in addition to a member nation's existing gold and dollar reserves.
▶ *See also* SDR.

OECD Organization for Economic Co-operation and Development. A group of 30 countries which promote democratic government and the market economy. They discuss and define economic and social policies and also work with non-member countries and less developed nations. ■ **www.oecd.org** ■

Off Balance Sheet An obligation entered into by a company that does not have to show on the balance sheet, such as leases and project finance. With banks, where money earned is fee-based, examples include trading of swaps, options and letters of credit.
▶ *See also* Letter of Credit, Option, Swap.

Offer A market maker's price to sell a security, currency or any financial instrument. Also known as ask. A two-way price comprises the bid and ask. The difference between the two quotations is the spread. For example, a dealer may bid for (or offer to buy) shares at $5 and offer to sell them at $5.50 so the bid/offer is $5/$5.50 and the dealer's spread is 50 cents.
▶ *See* Bid-Ask Quote.

Offer Document An official document from a bidder in a takeover battle that is sent to shareholders in the target company. In the US, an offer document can be synonymous with a prospectus.
▶ *See also* Prospectus.

Offer for Sale/Subscription There are two main ways to list new securities: an offer for sale is a public invitation by a sponsoring intermediary, such as an investment or merchant bank, of new or existing securities; and an offer for subscription or 'direct offer' is a direct invitation to the public by the issuer to subscribe for new securities.
▶ *See also* New Issue.

Offer Market A market in which there is more interest from sellers than buyers. The opposite of a bid market.
▶ *See also* Bid Market.

Offshore Fund Funds based outside the tax system of the country in which prospective investors reside.

Off-the-Run Issue Benchmark securities issues that are no longer the most recently issued in that maturity. They tend to trade with a wider spread than the on-the-run issues.
▶ *See also* On-the-Run Issue.

Oils Key products in international commodity and agricultural trade. The major oils are palm and soy.

Old Lady of Threadneedle Street An affectionate name for the Bank of England, Britain's central bank, derived from the street where it is situated.

Oligopoly A situation where a few firms selling an item control its supply and hence influence its price.
▶ *See also* Monopoly.

OMLX The London Securities and Derivatives Exchange was set up in 1990 to trade options and futures on Swedish equities.
■ **www.omgroup.com** ■

Omega The currency risk involved in an options deal when the option writer or holder accounts for the transaction in a different currency.
▶ *See also* Option.

OM Stockholm The Swedish futures and options market which trades options on Swedish stocks as well as index and interest rate derivatives. ■ **www.stockholmsborsen.se/index.asp?lang=eng** ■

O/N Abbreviation for overnight that is used in swap and deposit transactions when the first value date is today and maturity falls tomorrow. The overnight swap price is adjusted by the interest rate differential for that short period.

On Balance Volume A technical analysis indicator that is based on the trend in the volume, or the number of shares traded, in a particular share compared with the trend in its price. The assumption is that changes in volume precede changes in prices. For example, a rise in traded volume coupled with a gradually weakening price may signal a sharper price fall
▶ *See also* Technical Analysis.

O/N Funds Funds traded overnight on the interbank market to satisfy commercial banks' reserve requirements at the central bank.

O/N Limit Limits authorizing dealers to carry positions overnight, removing the obligation to square the position at the end of the day.
▶ *See also* Flat.

On-the-Run Issue The most recent issue of a security. As an issue ages its liquidity decreases and the spread tends to widen.
▶ *See Also* Off-the-Run, Spread.

OPEC Organization of Petroleum Exporting Countries. An association of the world's leading oil producing and exporting nations. OPEC's production quotas have a major bearing on oil prices and the 11 members are Algeria, Indonesia, Iran, Iraq, Kuwait, Libya, Nigeria, Qatar, Saudi Arabia, the United Arab Emirates and Venezuela.
■ **www.opec.org** ■

Open-end Management Company The legal name for a mutual fund.
▶ *See also* Investment Fund, Mutual Fund.

Open Interest A figure for the number of outstanding contracts on a futures contract which are not offset by an opposing futures transaction or fulfilled by delivery. In most cases, the open interest is measured on a daily basis. The figure reflects the degree of liquidity in that contract.
▶ *See also* Futures.

Open Market Operations Routine interventions by central banks in financial markets, usually by means of sale or purchase of securities in the domestic money market, in order to influence the volume of money and credit in the economy. The intervention usually involves short-term government securities and purchases of such paper from commercial banks, which puts cash in their hands, injecting reserves into the system to expand credit. However, sales of government securities by a central bank drains cash from the commercial banks, reduces reserves and limits credit expansion.

Open Outcry An open-outcry market is one where buyers and sellers are brought together on a trading floor and cry out bids and offers to each other. In theory all buyers and sellers should be able to hear all the current bids and offers at all times.

Open Position A position that has not yet been offset or closed, i.e. the holder has a commitment to buy or sell something which has not yet been fulfilled, or for which there is no matching contract in the opposite direction.

Operating Cash Flow The change in a company's net cash position during a given trading period.

Operating Costs A company's direct costs in producing goods and services for sale, including raw materials, labour, sales and administration costs. Also known as cost of sales.

Operating Margin The ratio of operating profit to turnover over a given period, expressed as a percentage and used to indicate a company's ability to control its variable costs.

Operating Profit Profits from a company's ordinary revenue-producing activities, calculated before taxes and interest costs. Exact definitions vary from country to country. Also known as PBIT (profit before interest and tax) or trading profit.

Operational Balances Commercial bank funds held on deposit at the central bank to settle the final position at the end of the day between the banking system and the central bank.

Opportunity Cost The cost of using a resource, i.e. its actual cost plus the profit forgone by not putting it to another use. For example, the purchase price of a city-centre garden might be $100,000 and the profit forgone by not building an office block on it might be $1.0 million, making its total opportunity cost $1.1 million.

Option An option gives the buyer or holder the right, but not the obligation, to buy or sell an underlying financial asset or commodity. Unlike futures, where the buyer has to fulfil the contract, an option gives the choice of whether to exercise or not. An option contract specifies a future date on or before which it can be exercised. This date is known as the expiry date. The price of an option – the 'strike' or 'exercise' price – is the price at which it can be exercised. Options are very flexible instruments. They allow investors to benefit from favourable price movements while limiting the consequence of unfavourable price movements. Options holders have to pay a 'premium' for this protection as with any insurance contract. There are two kinds of option: a call, which gives the holder the right to buy the underlying instrument at a set exercise price; and a put, which gives the holder the right to sell the underlying instrument at a set strike price. More than one option transaction can be combined to create a spread. These strategies usually involve the simultaneous purchase and sale of options with different prices, or expiry dates, within the same class. American style options can be exercised at any time before the expiry date, whereas European style options can be exercised only at the specific expiry date and not before. Options can be traded on a recognized exchange such as the Chicago Board of Trade or over-the-counter (OTC).
▶ *See also* Derivatives, Futures, OTC, Spread.

Optional Dividend A dividend that is payable either in cash or stock form. The shareholder is allowed to choose which method of payment to take.

Option Holder An individual who pays a premium for the right to buy or sell the underlying instrument under an option contract.

Option Premium The price paid for an option. The premium comprises the intrinsic value of the instrument plus time value of controlling that instrument for a set period. It is paid by the holder to the writer of the option.

Option Series Option contracts on the same underlying instrument, all having the same expiry date and strike price.

Option Strategies Combinations of calls and puts to create strategies for hedging and speculation. Examples are butterfly spread, straddle and strangle.

▶ *See* Call, Put, Hedging, Butterfly Spread, Strangle, Straddle.

Option Writer An institution or individual that sells an option and thereby commits to buy or sell the underlying at a predetermined strike price in exchange for the premium paid by the option holder.

Order Driven A market is described as being order driven when investors submit, buy and sell orders to a central location where they are then matched. Such markets are continuous auction markets, such as the NYSE.

▶ *See also* NYSE, Quote Driven.

Ordinary Capital The capital invested by shareholders who are then entitled to the remaning profits and assets after creditors and holders of the company's senior debt have been repaid.

Ordinary Drawing Rights ▶ *See* ODR.

Ordinary Share Capital Ordinary shares represent ownership in a limited liability company. Shareholders are entitled to dividends when they are declared by the company board of directors. Shareholders also have the last claim on the assets and income, after other creditors and holders of senior debt have been paid. They appoint and approve the company directors and usually have one vote for each share they hold. Ordinary shares are the most widely traded of all securities because of continuing market liquidity and the ease of ownership transfer from one investor to another. Ordinary shares are known as common stock in the US.

▶ *See also* Preference Share.

Organization of Arab Petroleum Exporting Countries ▶ *See* OAPEC.

Organization for Economic Co-operation and Development ▶ *See* OECD.

Organization of Petroleum Exporting Countries ▶ *See* OPEC.

Oscillator Used in technical analysis, the oscillator is an indicator which moves back and forth between an upper and lower boundary. The oscillator attempts to indicate buy and sell signals by graphing the difference between a short- and long-term simple moving average.

▶ *See also* Moving Average, Technical Analysis.

OSE Osaka Securities Exchange. ■ **www.ose.or.jp** ■

OTC Over the counter A market conducted directly between dealers and principals via a telephone and computer network rather than via an exchange trading floor. Unlike an exchange there is no automatic disclosure of the price of deals to other market participants, and the deals and traded instruments are not standardized.

Out of the Money An option is described as being out of the money when the current price of the underlying instrument is below the strike or exercise price for a call (an option to buy), and above the strike price for a put (an option to sell). Options can also be described as being deep out of the money when they are likely to expire out of the money.
▶ *See also* In the Money, At the Money, Option.

Outright Purchases Government securities purchased outright by the authorities, with no agreement to subsequently sell them through a repurchase pact or reverse repo.
▶ *See* Repurchase Pact, Reverse Repo.

Over-allotment Option ▶ *See* Greenshoe Option.

Overbought When prices have risen more than they should according to fundamental factors. This could mean the market is liable to a downward correction. In technical analysis, an instrument is overbought when it registers more than 75 percent on its RSI. The opposite of oversold.
▶ *See also* Oversold, RSI, Technical Analysis.

Overdraft A short-term borrowing facility offered by banks. Overdrafts are usually repayable on demand and are more expensive than longer-term borrowing.

Overnight ▶ *See* O/N.

Oversold When prices have dropped more than they should according to fundamental factors. This could mean the market is liable to an upward correction. In technical analysis, an instrument is oversold when it registers less than 25 percent on its RSI.
▶ *See also* Overbought, RSI, Technical Analysis.

Oversubscribed When an issuing house receives more subscriptions for a new issue than are available. Applications cannot be met in full and the issue will then be shared out, typically on a pro rata basis. The issue will tend to open at a premium to represent the over-demand.

Overvalued A term implying that a security or currency is trading at a price higher than it should be relative to fundamental factors. The opposite of undervalued.
▶ *See also* Undervalued.

Oy Finnish company title: abbreviation of Osakeyhito.

P

Paid-up Capital Used to describe shares issued by a company for which the company has received full nominal value in payment, whereas callable capital is that part of a share for which the company has not received payment.

Paper Colloquially used, paper refers to any securities.

Paper Barrel A cargo of oil traded for short-term hedging or speculative purposes, but not usually physically delivered.
> *See also* Hedging.

Paper Chain ▶ *See* Daisy Chain.

Paper Profit Apparent, and as yet unrealized, profit arising out of an increase in the value of an asset.

Parallel Loans ▶ *See* Back-to-back Loans.

Par Bond A bond issued at par or face value. Alternatively, to provide debt service reduction, old debt can be swapped at par for new 'par bonds' which may have lower interest rates or longer repayment periods.

Pari Passu Securities issued with a pari passu clause rank equally with existing securities of the same class. Pari passu means 'with equal step' in Latin.

Paris Club An ad hoc forum for Western creditor governments to discuss the renegotiation of debt owed to them, or guaranteed by them. The Paris Club groups government creditors while the London Club groups commercial creditors.
> *See also* London Club.

Parity Used loosely in the foreign exchange market to denote an exchange rate, e.g. the euro's parity against the dollar. Currencies are described as being at parity when their exchange rate is exactly one-to-one.

Participation Part ownership of an oil venture or operation, by a company or government. It can also refer to a mortgage loan made jointly by two or more lenders.

Participation Certificate These US certificates represent an interest in mortgage loans. The buyer receives the cash flows and is the owner, but the seller remains the mortgagee of record. In Switzerland, a participation certificate is a non-voting form of equity issued by Swiss companies.

Partly Paid A system of payment that allows shareholders or bondholders to pay only part of the determined price for a new issue, with the rest being settled on a fixed future date.

Par Value The value that appears on the face of a document recording an entitlement, generally a share certificate or a bond. The par value of a share is a fairly arbitrary amount and shares usually trade in the market above that value. For debt instrument such as bonds, however, par is far more important because it represents the amount to be repaid at maturity. Also known as face value or nominal value.

Passing the Dividend A term used to describe a company's failure to pay a dividend that is already announced or expected. The company may lack funds, or it may be in a recovery phase and prefer to invest the cash directly in its underlying activities.

Passive Management An investment strategy that focuses on mirroring the composition of a given market or sector to match its return and risk characteristics.
▶ *See also* Active Fund Management.

Pass-through Certificate This represents an interest in a pool of mortgages in the United States. Payments received on the underlying pool are passed through to the investor by the firm servicing the mortgage payments.

Patterns Shapes created by price movements on a chart. Patterns are used by technical analysts to identify market trends, then to decide on the strength of the trend and whether it will continue or be reversed.
▶ *See also* Technical Analysis.

Payables A US term for creditor.

Payback The number of years needed for an investment project to recover its cost.

Pay Date The date when a dividend is due to a shareholder.

Paydown A paydown is when the amount of debt being redeemed by a government or a company exceeds the amount of new debt being issued. The government or company is repaying more debt than it is borrowing. The total net reduction is called the paydown.

Payer of Fixed In the interest rate swap market this refers to a party who pays the fixed interest rate and receives the floating rate. The opposite of receiver of fixed.

▶ *See also* Swap.

Paying Agent An institution appointed to supervise the payment of dividends to shareholders and the payment of principal and interest to bond holders, on behalf of the issuers of those shares or bonds. For floating rate notes the paying agency also sets the level of the coupon each quarter, based on a reference interest rate on a predetermined day.

▶ *See also* FRN.

Payment Date The date on which a coupon payment, dividend or fund distribution is due to be made.

Payout Ratio The proportion of a company's net profits that is paid out to shareholders in cash dividends. The ratio is calculated by dividing the total cash dividends by the company's earnings in the same period.

Payrolls The colloquial term for the statistic issued by the Department of Labor for US Non-farm Payrolls, or the number of people in work. It is more generally used to describe an employer's financial record of employees' salaries.

PBIT Calculated as sales minus operating costs, it is also known as operating profit or trading profit.

P/E RATIO

Price/earnings ratio (PER) is the latest closing share price divided by the net profit for the latest reported 12-month period. If a company has an EPS of 10 and a share price of 150, its P/E is 15. In other words, it would take fifteen years for the stock investment to pay for itself. The reverse of the P/E ratio is the 'earnings yield', or 1/PER. A company with a P/E of 15 has an earnings yield of 6.66 percent (1 divided by 15).

The ratio is one of the most important tests of investment value and is widely used by the media as an indicator of whether a stock is expensive or cheap. The higher the PER, the higher the market values the company's earnings. A high PER may be a sign that the market expects the company's earnings to grow rapidly,

▶

or it may be a sign that earnings have slumped and the share price does not yet fully reflect that fall. A relatively low P/E means that investors' outlook for the company is gloomy, and that they do not want to buy the share even at that low multiple.

Average P/E ratios for stock market indices historically range between 10 and 20, but for some individual companies the ratio might swing wildly, from less than three to 1,000 or more, depending on investors' outlook for the share. Sometimes even stock market indices have average P/Es of 50 or more, as was the case in Japan in the late 1980s and the US NASDAQ market at the start of this century.

An historic PER is calculated using earnings figures already released and a prospective PER is calculated by using consensus estimates of figures yet to be released. If investors expect a company's earnings to triple every year in the next five years, they will have no problem paying a historical (or 'trailing') P/E of 1,000, because the P/E for Forecast Year 1 would be 333; for FY2 the P/E would fall to 111; and so on.

P/E ratios cannot be considered in isolation and should be compared against industry and national averages. Low-growth companies such as steel makers, shipyards and construction companies often trade at relatively low P/Es (10 or less) while high-tech firms often command P/E multiples of 40 or more.

The P/E ratio is the most widely used measure of corporate valuation, because it is easy to understand and widely available in financial newspapers, but it also has many flaws. The divider – net profit – is subject to the vagaries of accounting standards, depreciation regimes, interest rate levels and corporate tax rates. Two companies having the same cash flow may have very different bottom-line net profits. That is why analysts increasingly use price/EBITDA (earnings before interest, taxation, depreciation and amortization). If a company has no earnings, which is often the case with high-tech start-ups, investors will look higher up on the profit and loss account and relate the stock price to sales in order to work out the price/sales ratio (stock price divided by sales per share).

The divider of the P/E ratio – market capitalization – is not a perfect measure of the total cost of the company either. Two companies with a market capitalization of $1 billion and net profit would each have a P/E of 10. But if company A has debt of $1 billion, while company B is debt-free, the P/E ratio would not highlight this. Therefore, analysts replace market cap by 'enterprise value', which is the sum of market cap, plus debt, minus cash and gives a much better perspective on the true value of a listed company.

The enterprise value/EBITDA ratio measures both value and risk and eliminates the distortion of national depreciation rates, interest rates and tax regimes. Its drawback is that it requires a lot of homework.

Formula: Share Price/EPS

Example

The Old Rope Corporation's share price is now £1.50 or 150 pence. The company's earnings per share (EPS) were 18.3 pence in the last complete financial year. They are forecast to be 20.5 pence in the current financial year and 24.3 pence in the following year.

Old Rope's P/E
Last financial year = 150 / 18.3 = 8.19
This financial year = 150 / 20.5 = 7.31
Next financial year = 150 / 24.3 = 6.17

The comparative trailing P/Es for Old Rope, its main country index and its sector index are:

Old Rope	8.19
All Share Index	10.12
Sector Index	9.50

▶ *See also* EPS, PEG Ratio.

Peaks/Troughs Terms used by technical analysts to describe patterns that appear on their share price charts. Peaks, or reaction highs, are resistance points and represent a price level where selling pressure overcomes buying pressure, halting a price rise. Troughs, or reaction lows, are support points and represent a price level where buying pressure overcomes selling pressure, thereby halting the price drop.
▶ *See also* Technical Analysis.

PEG Ratio The price/earnings growth ratio is calculated by dividing a stock's prospective price/earnings ratio (PER) by the rate of estimated future growth in earnings per share (EPS). The higher the PEG ratio, the more the market has already valued future earnings growth.

- A company with a PER of 15 and estimated growth rate of 15 percent would have a PEG of 1.0.
- A company with a PER of 15 and an estimated growth rate of 10 percent would have a PEG of 1.5.

The ratio was invented by 1960s markets expert Jim Slater, who used it as his main investing criterion. Consensus estimates are used to derive the PER and EPs used in the calculation.

▶ *See also* Consensus Estimates, P/E Ratio, EPS.

Pennants ▶ *See* Flags/Pennants.

Penny Stocks A type of ordinary share which is of negligible value, but may prove to be a good speculative investment. In the US these shares are priced at less than one dollar. In the UK they cost less than one pound.

▶ *See also* Ordinary Share.

PER ▶ *See* P/E Ratio.

Performing Loan A loan is performing if the borrower is paying the interest on it.

▶ *See also* Non-performing Loan.

Perpetual Note A floating-rate note that has no final maturity, and therefore has no arrangement for repayment of principal. For this privilege, the borrower pays a higher margin over a relevant base interest rate. As they will never be repaid, the notes assume the characteristics of an equity issue.

Petrodollars A term prevalent in the 1970s to describe the abundance of dollars held and invested by members of OPEC when they pushed up oil prices.

Pfandbriefe German bonds issued to refinance mortgages or public projects. They can only be issued by specially authorized banks, which are also fully liable for each issue and are secured by mortgage or public sector loans. Pfandbriefe are officially quoted on German stock exchanges, while issuers maintain a secondary market.

PHLX Philadelphia Stock Exchange. A US stock market that also lists currency derivatives. ■ **www.phlx.com** ■

Physical market ▶ *See* Spot Market.

Pibor Paris Interbank Offered Rate. The rate at which banks in Paris are prepared to lend money market funds to each other.

▶ *See also* Libor, Euribor.

Pink Sheets A weekly publication listing the prices of small over-the-counter stocks in the US.
  ▶ *See also* OTC.

Pip Price movements are expressed in terms of pips or points. Pip is usually synonymous with point, although may refer to one-tenth of a point. The size of a pip or point depends on the market and the quoted instrument.
  ▶ *See also* Point.

Pit An often self-contained section on an exchange floor for the trading of a particular type of financial instrument or commodity.
  ▶ *See also* Open Outcry.

Placing A sale of new shares directly to institutional investors, bypassing the public.
  ▶ *See also* Flotation, IPO.

Plain Vanilla Standard financial or derivative instruments without special features.
  ▶ *See also* Exotic.

Planned Economy An economy where the government fixes prices and production. A planned economy contrasts with a free market economy.

Platinum Share A platinum share confers predominant voting rights in a company, similar to a golden share. Often used to prevent a company from being taken over by predators. Alternatively used to safeguard a relatively stable subsidary if an administrator, receiver or liquidator is likely to be appointed to a parent company.

Platt's An international oil price reporting agency which specializes in data and news for the oil markets. ■ **www.platts.com** ■

Plaza Agreement An agreement in 1985 which set up the G5 group of the United States, Japan, France, Germany and Britain and promoted further depreciation of the US dollar.

Plc A UK company title: abbreviation of public limited company.

Ploughed Back Earnings that are reinvested in the company and not distributed to shareholders as dividends.

PMI Purchasing Manager's Index. A monthly survey of purchasing managers in industrial companies that records changes in items such as orders, employment, inventories and prices, compared with those of the previous month. It is expressed as a number, with 50 regarded as neutral (i.e. the same number of respondents reporting increased activity as there were reporting decreased activity). Figures above 50 indicate growth and below 50 contraction. The index is regarded as a leading indicator of economic activity, but methodology varies from country to country.

▶ *See also* Economic Indicators, Leading Indicators.

Point Price movements are expressed in terms of points.

▶ *See also* Pip.

Point and Figure Chart A price chart that captures pure price movement with no regard for time or volume. Rising prices are denoted by a column of Xs and falling prices by a column of Os. Subsequent columns are placed to the right of earlier columns. (Figure 13.)

▶ *See also* Technical Analysis.

Poison Pill Actions taken by a company to outwit a predator in a potential hostile takeover, so that swallowing the company will be like swallowing a poison pill. Examples are the issue of high yielding bonds, conditional rights to shareholders to buy shares at a large discount if the takeover succeeds or making massive long-term commitments to the company's pension funds.

Political Risk The risk associated with investing in politically unstable countries.

Ponzi Scheme A fraudulent investment scheme that promises high returns which are derived from an inflow of new investors' funds rather than from sound investments. The scheme collapses when there are not enough new investors to pay the old investors. Also known as a Pyramid Scheme.

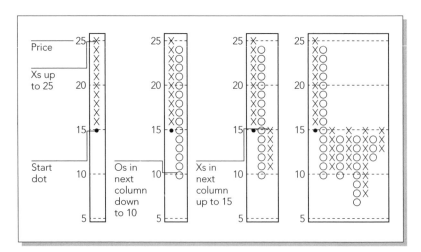

FIGURE 13 Point and figure chart

POP Public Offering Price. The issue price of a new share that is fixed by the underwriter on behalf of a company. The underwriter's commission is built into the price. Shares in a mutual fund may be purchased at the POP.

▶ *See also* Mutual Fund.

Portfolio An investor's collection, or holding, of financial instruments.

Portfolio Investment Investment through financial instruments rather than by taking a direct stake in a company and its management and development. It contrasts with foreign direct investment, which takes direct ownership in a company or builds new factories, rather than investing in shares and bonds.

▶ *See also* Foreign Direct Investment.

Portfolio Manager A designated advisor, who manages a portfolio of investments on behalf of an investor. Often the manager has full authority to take decisions, known as acting on a discretionary basis.

Position The balance of purchases and sales in a given financial instrument for a given maturity.

▶ *See also* Short, Long, Flat.

Position Keeping The monitoring of a dealer's position.

Position Limit The maximum position, either net long or short, which may be held by a dealer, a group of dealers or a dealing room. The limit can cover any financial instrument such as shares, foreign exchange and futures, and is usually expressed as a cash amount. It restricts the amount of risk that a particular dealer can be exposed to.

Positive Carry Where the financing cost of a position is less than the return. Negative carry is when it costs more to finance a position than it earns.

PPP Purchasing Power Parity. A theory which states that the rate of exchange between two currencies is in equilibrium when it exactly reflects the difference in cost of standard goods in the two countries. If the same radio costs £100 in the UK and $150 in the US, there is purchasing parity if the exchange is £1 = $1.5 and the radio costs effectively the same amount in both countries. Purchasing power parity cannot apply to immobile goods such as houses and it does not take into account distortions caused by transport costs and trade restraints, so standard goods that are widely available in both countries are used as a measure.

▶ *See also* Big Mac Index.

Praecipuum Part of a management fee, assessed on the full principal amount of a new issue, to compensate the lead manager for the responsibility of handling the issue.

Pre-market Trading Takes place before the official opening of business on the trading floor of an exchange.

Pre-marketing A meeting of investment bankers with potential investors before an initial public offering, or a secondary offering, to determine potential demand.

Precious Metals There are eight precious or noble metals – gold, silver, platinum, palladium, rhodium, iridium, osmium and ruthenium. The latter four are co-products of platinum and palladium.
▶ *See also* Base Metals, Minor Metals.

Preferential Issue A certain percentage of a share offer to the public which is set aside for subscriptions from employees.

Preference Share Preference or preferred shares entitle a holder to a prior claim on any dividend paid by the company before the payment is made on ordinary shares. The holder also has a prior claim on assets in the event of a liquidation. Typically these shares do not carry voting or pre-emptive rights.
▶ *See also* Ordinary Share.

Pre-emptive Rights The right of ordinary or common shareholders to maintain their relative ownership of a company by buying a proportional number of shares of any future issue of shares. This means that their interests in the company will not be diluted by new shares.
▶ *See also* Rights Issue.

Premium Premium is generally used to describe when something is trading above its normal price. An asset or fund is described as being at premium when its market price is above its face value. In the capital markets, it is the amount by which a bond sells above par. In foreign exchange terms, it is the margin by which the forward rate is higher than the spot. In commodity markets it is the additional price paid by a consumer when the delivered commodity is of better quality than that specified in the original contract. Premium is the opposite of discount.
▶ *See also* Discount, Par Value.

Prepay Cash paid or lent to a company in exchange for a promise that it will deliver commodities at a later date.

Prepayment In mortgages, any unscheduled principal payment made in addition to the normal amortization.
▶ *See* Amortization.

Present Value The current value of a future cash flows, discounted at an appropriate interest rate. Cash earned in the future is worth less than cash earned immediately because today's cash can be invested and earn interest.

Presold The sale of all of a new issue of securities, even before all issue details have been announced.

Price Channel Used in technical analysis, the price channel provides buy and sell signals by indicating when a value moves outside set deviation limits. The channel chart consists of two bands either side of a simple moving average. Channels can also be used on volume charts and as an overbought/oversold indicator.
▶ *See also* Moving Average, Technical Analysis.

Price Driven Trading where prices set by the market makers determine the order flow. Also known as quote driven.
▶ *See also* Order Driven.

Price Earnings Growth Ratio ▶ *See* PEG Ratio.

Price Earnings Ratio ▶ *See* P/E Ratio.

Price Indicators Measures of the level of prices and their rates of change. For example, the price of a basket of goods purchased by the average consumer or the prices of goods at the factory gate.
▶ *See also* Economic Indicators.

Price To Book ▶ *See* Net Asset Value.

Price Volume Index A technical analysis indicator that is essentially a volume-weighted RSI (relative strength index). It attempts to measure the amount of money entering and leaving the market.
▶ *See also* Moving Average, RSI, Technical Analysis.

Primary Commodities Commodities in a raw or unprocessed state, e.g. iron ore.

Primary Dealer Dealers who are authorized by the central bank to deal in the primary market for government securities. Primary dealers are normally required to play a significant part in auctions and act as market makers in the secondary market as well as keeping the central bank well informed of market conditions and developments. Primary dealers are also known as primary distributors, jobbers, SVTs (in France), underwriters and lead managers.
▶ *See also* Primary Markets.

Primary Markets Primary markets are markets where new issues of securities take place. Any subsequent resale or purchase of such securities is handled on the secondary market.
▶ *See also* Secondary Market.

Primary Metals Metals produced from smelting ore rather than refining scrap or alloys.

Primary Offer ▶ *See* IPO.

Prime Bank A prime bank is one of the highest-rated and best-funded banks.

Prime Rate The borrowing rate charged by banks to their best customers.

Principal The total amount borrowed or invested, e.g. the face amount of a bond bought by an investor. Also, the originator or prime mover in a financial deal, on whose behalf brokers act as agents.
▶ *See also* Brokers.

Printing Money A term used to describe a government increasing the money supply. This can be achieved in a number of ways including actually printing more bank notes, or issuing new government debt, which is then bought by the central bank in exchange for credits that can be spent in the real economy.

Prior Charges Charges payable on a company's senior debt such as debentures, loan stock and notes that rank ahead of ordinary share capital. Senior debt ranks first for repayment in the event of default.
▶ *See* Debenture Bond.

Private Company A company not listed on a stock exchange and which therefore cannot offer its shares to the public.

Private Placement Usually refers to a bond issue that is placed directly with investors, is not listed on a stock exchange and does not have a prospectus.
▶ *See also* Placing.

Privatization The sale of state-owned commercial and industrial businesses to the private sector by the government.

Profit Company profit is the amount left after deducting the total costs from the total sales. It is usual to define profit more precisely, such as operating profit or net profit.
▶ *See* Net Profit, Operating Profit.

Profit and Loss Account A summary of all the expenditure and income of a company over a set period of time. Also called an income statement.

Profit Margin Net profit as a percentage of sales or capital. Sometimes known as return on sales, or return on capital.

Profit-taking Realizing profits by closing out an existing position (for example, selling a share or exercising an option).

Program Trading A computer-based trading technique based on the flow of trading and price levels, rather than fundamental data. Program trading aims to exploit arbitrage possibilities between stock index futures or options and underlying equities.
▶ *See also* Arbitrage.

Promissory Note A note that represents a promise by a borrower to repay a loan. Promissory notes are not classed as securities. Failure to pay a promissory note renders the borrower immediately liable to be sued for payment.
▶ *See also* Security.

Prompt Date The date on which a commodity must be delivered to fulfil a contract.

Pro Rata Sinking Fund A sinking fund is a special account that finances the compulsory early repayment by a borrower of a certain amount of a bond issue, usually at par value, regardless of the current value of the bonds in the secondary market. A pro rata sinking fund forces each investor to give up an equal percentage of his or her bond holdings when the issuer calls for sinking fund retirements of the bonds. Typically only applied to registered securities.
▶ *See also* Purchase Fund, Sinking Fund.

Prospectus A document produced by the issuing company, which provides detailed terms and conditions of a new stock or debt offering.

Protectionism Protection of a domestic industry from cheaper competitive imports by such means as import duties, import quotas, export subsidies, health and environment regulations.

Provisions Long-term liability that appears on a balance sheet, such as an employee pension scheme. Provisions are estimates of costs which cannot yet be precisely defined.
▶ *See also* Assets/Liabilities.

Provisions for Bad Debts Charges against profits for debtors who may not pay for goods and services thay have received.

Proxy A written authorization by a shareholder for another party, or a company's board of directors, to cast votes at a shareholders' meeting. Proxy votes are often gathered by dissident shareholders who wish to force the board of directors to change policy.

Pump and Dump A type of fraud that involves publishing falsely opti-
mistic announcements about a company, often on the internet,
which push up the share price. The fraudsters then dump their shares
at a large profit before the price subsequently drops sharply. Also
known as hype and dump manipulation.

PSNBR Public Sector Net Borrowing Requirement.
▶ *See* PSNCR.

PSNCR The public sector net cash requirement is a measurement of the UK
government's borrowing requirement, i.e. the difference between
what the government spends each year and what it receives in taxes.
The market watches the PSNCR closely because it reflects actual cash
flows each month. Public sector net borrowing is the government's
preferred measure, as it is calculated on an accruals basis which
smooths out monthly fluctuations. It also excludes financial transactions such as privatization proceeds.

Pte Singapore company title: abbreviation of private.

Pty Australian company title: abbreviation of proprietary.

Public Offering Price ▶ *See* POP.

Public Placement A public bond placement is to a market in general,
rather than to selected investors. It is usually listed on a stock
exchange in relatively small denominations. The costs to the issuer
are usually more than for a private placement, but there may be benefits in obtaining a wider range of investors in terms of public
recognition and liquidity for the secondary trading of the debt.

Public–Private Partnerships (PPP) Usually a medium- to long-term relationship between the public and the private sectors, varying in scope,
legal structure and purpose, but involving the use of resources (either
financial, expertise or physical) from the private sector in the running
of public sector of government-owned entities. Where the partnerships extend to private entities owning part of a public entity, the
relationship is also known as Public–Private Ownership (PPO). The
main reasons for PPPs include realizing cost savings or other efficien-
cies, accessing specialist skills, sharing risks or tapping into private
sources of capital.

Publicly Traded Fund ▶ *See* Closed-end Fund.

Purchase Fund A borrower uses a purchase fund to buy back issued bonds in the secondary market if the price is advantageous, i.e. at par or below. This can save money on repayment of the bonds at par at maturity. Similar to a sinking fund but not mandatory.
▶ *See also* Pro Rata Sinking Fund.

Purchase Price A purchase price becomes legally enforceable on both buyer and seller once a written order to buy has been accepted by the vendor.

Purchasing Managers' Index ▶ *See* PMI.

Purchasing Power Parity ▶ *See* PPP.

Put Call Parity Put call parity is a fundamental relationship that must exist between the prices of a put option and a call option on the same underlying instrument with the same strike price and expiration date. If they are not the same then there is room for arbitrage. Put call parity applies to European-style options which can be exercised only on expiry and not before. American-style options can be exercised at any time during the life of the contract.
▶ *See also* Option, Arbitrage.

Put/Call Ratio The number of puts (options to sell) traded in relation to the number of calls (options to buy) traded in the market. This ratio is an indicator of market sentiment.
▶ *See also* Option.

Put An option giving the buyer or the holder the right but not the obligation to sell the underlying instrument at an agreed price within a specified time. The seller or writer has the obligation to buy if the holder exercises the option to sell.
▶ *See also* Call.

Put Through ▶ *See* Cross.

Puttable A bond is described as puttable, or having a put feature, when the holder has the right to sell the bond back to the issuer at a specific date before maturity. The repurchase price, which may be at par, premium or discount, is specified at the time of issue.
▶ *See also* Callable.

Pyramid Scheme ▶ *See* Ponzi Scheme.

Qualified Accounts The published balance sheet and accounts of a company, in which the auditors' report expresses any reservations as to whether a true and fair view of the company's activities has been presented.

Quantitative Analysis The statistical study of historic returns, price volatility and price correlations of different assets in order to construct optimal portfolios. QA relies heavily on mathematical models such as the capital asset pricing model (CAPM) and the dividend discount model (DDM). More generally, quantative analysis is any statistical analysis based on numerical data, as opposed to qualitative analysis, which is based on values and opinions.

▶ *See also* CAPM, DDM, Fundamental Analysis, Technical Analysis.

Quick Ratio Sometimes called the acid test, the quick ratio is an indicator of a company's ability to meet its short-term liabilities. It is the total of a company's cash plus accounts receivable plus short-term investments divided by its current liabilities. The higher the number, the healthier the position, and within an industry, high quick ratios suggest relatively high liquidity. The quick ratio is similar to the current ratio, which is a less stringent test because it adds inventory (which may not always be easy to sell quickly) to cash, accounts receivable and short-term investments before dividing by current liabilities.

▶ *See also* Current Ratio.

Quotation Current price or rate given in the market or exchange. Not necessarily the price at which a trade will be made.

Quote Driven A market is described as being quote driven when registered market makers are required to display bid and offer prices, and in some cases the maximum bargain size to which these prices relate. The London SEAQ system and NASDAQ are examples of quote driven markets. The alternative trading system, such as used on the New York Stock Exchange, is an order driven one where market prices are set by the balance of supply and demand in a continuous auction.

▶ *See also* NASDAQ, Order Driven, SEAQ.

Quoted Currency The currency quoted against the base currency, i.e. the numerator quoted in terms of the denominator. For example, the quoted currency in the US dollar/euro quotation is the euro.

▶ *See also* Base Currency.

R

Rally General trading term for when a whole market or sector reverses a previous general fall, or moves up from a narrow trading range.

RAN Revenue anticipation notes.
> ▶ *See also* Municipal Notes.

R&D Research and development.

Range Forward ▶ *See* Risk Reversal.

Ranking Denotes where a bond stands in relation to priority claims from a lender upon default by the borrower. Senior debt earns high priority if lenders have to reclaim funds, hence the bond issue terms can be less onerous for the borrower. Subordinated debt ranks a bond lower down the scale, thus a borrower has to offer a lender more advantageous terms.

Rate of Change ▶ *See* ROC.

Rate of Return The return on an investment. For a company this would be net profits expressed as a percentage of average capital employed.

Ratio Analysis Determination of the prospective future performance of a company. An analysis of a company's accounts involving examining three kinds of ratios – profitability, liquidity and balance sheet ratios.

Real Adjusted for inflation. Crude, unadjusted figures are misleading in times of high inflation, so real or inflation-adjusted figures are often used for measurements of economic growth.

Real Interest Rates The actual rate of return calculated by deducting the inflation rate from the current interest rate. Also known as real yield.
> ▶ *See also* Nominal Interest Rates.

Realized Gain The cash profit from liquidating a position.

Realized Loss The cash loss from liquidating a position.

Real-time Data Term used to describe live prices as opposed to historical data.

Real Yield ▶ *See* Real Interest Rates.

Receivables Any outstanding debts due to a company.

Receiver A receiver is appointed by creditors to take control of the assets of a bankrupt or insolvent company.
▶ *See also* Bankruptcy, Insolvency.

Recession A period of static or negative economic growth. Various nations have differing definitions but the US definition of two succeeding quarters of negative growth is widely used.

Record Date The date on which a shareholder must be the official owner of shares to be entitled to the dividend. This date is set by the board of directors.
▶ *See also* Ex, Ex-Dividend.

Rectangle A technical analysis pattern that represents a pause in a trend in which prices move sideways between two parallel trendlines. A rectangle portrays a consolidation period in the main trend and is generally resolved in the direction of that trend. Also known as a trading range or congestion area.
▶ *See* Technical Analysis.

Red Book An annual statement in the UK that accompanies the budget. It is published by the government and contains detailed information on announced measures. Named for the traditional colour of its cover.

Redemption The repurchase of a bond at maturity by the issuer.

Redemption Warrant The borrower offers the holder a guaranteed redemption price if the warrant is not exercised.
▶ *See also* Warrant.

Redemption Yield Current yield increased or decreased to take account of the capital gain or loss on redemption.

Red Herring US term for the preliminary prospectus for a new issue, which may be used to obtain an indication of the market's interest in that security. Key figures are left blank, such as issue price, profit and dividend forecast. Business is not conducted on the basis of a preliminary statement and in the US the law demands a red notice be printed to that effect on the face of the document, giving rise to the phrase 'red herring'.

Rediscount Purchase before maturity by a central bank of a government obligation or other financial instrument already discounted in the money market.

Refinancing The issuing of new debt to replace old. A borrower pays off one loan with the proceeds from another provided by other lenders. If the lenders are effectively the same then it could technically be called a rescheduling. Bankers might use the term refinancing.
▶ *See also* Restructuring.

Refinery A plant used to separate the various components present in crude oil and convert them into either end-user products or feedstock for other manufacturing processes.

Refining Processing a raw material into a pure state, in particular metals and sugar.

Refunding Rollover of government debt by replacing one issue with another whose maturity is deferred to a later date.

Refunding Operations The quarterly auction of US Treasury securities with maturities of five and 10 years in the months of February, May, August and November. ■ **www.savingsbonds.gov** ■

Registered Form A security that is registered in the books of the issuer in the name of the owner. Securities are kept in either registered or bearer form and government bonds are most commonly registered.
▶ *See also* Bearer Shares/Bearer Forms.

Registrar The body responsible for keeping a record of the company's shareholders. When securities are dealt in book entry form and no certificates are issued, it is particularly important to have an accurate list of shareholders.

Regular Way Settlement Market standard for settlement and delivery, five business days or seven calendar days from the trade date. Also known as corporate settlement.

Reinsurance The spreading of risks in the insurance market. A company will insure a risk and then pass on some of the exposure by taking out reinsurance contracts with other companies. There is a danger that risks may be passed from hand to hand and end up with unreliable companies, or even inadvertently back in the hands of the original insurer.

Reinvestment Risk The risk that future cash flows from a particular investment will be reinvested at a lower rate of return.

Relative Performance The performance of a security compared against an index.

Relative Strength Comparison between a current share price, portfolio of shares or a stock index and the price of the same instrument, portfolio or index at a given time in the past.

Relative Strength Index ▶ *See* RSI.

Replacement Cost The cost in current terms of replacing a fixed asset already in use with a new asset.

Repo ▶ *See* Repurchase Agreement.

Repo Market ▶ *See* Gensaki Market.

Repo Rate A simple interest rate calculation to determine how much interest is to be added on to the second leg of a repo transaction.
▶ *See also* Repurchase Agreement.

Reporting Dealer In the US, primary dealers first have to achieve the status of reporting dealer, whereby they report their positions and trading volumes to the Federal Reserve.
▶ *See also* Primary Dealer.

Repurchase Agreement A repurchase agreement or Repo is a transaction in which Party A sells a security to Party B and agrees to repurchase it at a specific date in the future and at a pre-agreed price. Repos allow Party B to borrow securities and sell them short in the belief that they can be bought back in the market at a cheaper price by the time they must be returned to Party A. The advantage for party A is that it earns added income by lending the securities. Through this operation trader B is effectively a borrower of funds to finance further purchases of securities, and he pays interest to the holder, trader A. The rate of interest used is known as the repo rate. A reverse repo is the reverse situation, whereby the Party A agrees to buy securities from Party B and sell them back at a pre-agreed price and date. Party B is then effectively the lender of funds. Some central banks use repos and reverse repos in government debt as part of their money market operations.

Required Return The rate of return used by investors to decide whether an investment is attractive or not.

Rescheduling A borrower delays redemption of principal under the terms of a new repayment schedule. Interest continues to be paid and the rate of interest can be raised or lowered.
▶ *See also* Refinancing, Restructuring.

Reserve Currency Internationally accepted currency, used by central banks to meet their financial commitments.

Reserve Requirements Percentage of deposits that, by law, depository institutions must set aside in their vaults or with their central bank. Lowering or raising this requirement influences the money supply. A reduction in reserve requirements enables banks to increase lending while an increase forces them to reduce lending. Sometimes known as minimum reserve requirements, registered reserves or reserve ratio.

Reserves A company's reserves are primarily profits retained in the business and accumulated over the years, rather than paid out by way of dividends. They are usually held as cash or in highly liquid assets. Shareholders have no rights over reserves so that a company can disburse them or not, as it sees fit, within the usual accounting rules. The term reserves is also used to describe the official foreign exchange reserves held by governments to ensure they can meet current and near-term claims.

▶ *See also* Dividends, Retained Earnings.

Resiliency Test The statutory solvency margins set for insurance companies, to ensure that they have sufficient assets to meet their liabilities.

▶ *See also* Solvency Margin.

Resistance Resistance is a level, usually identified on a price chart, where selling interest is strong enough to overcome buying pressure so that the price does not rise beyond the resistance level. Each time a level of resistance is penetrated it will create a new level of support.

▶ *See also* Support, Trendline.

Restructuring A process whereby a borrower arranges to replace debt of one maturity with debt of another maturity. Can also be used loosely to describe the exchange of corporate debt for shares when a company cannot meet its debt repayments.

▶ *See also* Refinancing, Rescheduling.

Retail Price Index ▶ *See* RPI.

Retained Earnings Earnings not paid out as dividends by a company. Retained Earnings are typically reinvested back into the business and are an important component of shareholders' equity.

▶ *See also* Reserves.

Retracement Percentage retracements of market price movements are used by technical analysts to determine price objectives. Markets usually retrace previous moves by predictable percentages such as 33, 50 and 67. The 33 and 67 percent retracements are the minimum and maximum in Dow theory. The 50 percent retracement is the most important according to Gann. The Fibonacci number sequence refines these numbers to produce retracements of 61.8 percent and 38 percent and 50 percent.

▶ *See also* Dow Theory, Fibonacci, Gann, Technical Analysis.

Return on Assets ▶ *See* ROA.

Return on Capital Employed ▶ *See* ROA, ROCE.

Return on Equity ▶ *See* ROA, ROE.

Return on Sales ▶ *See* Profit Margin.

Revaluation Formal upward adjustment of a currency's official par value or central exchange rate. Opposite of devaluation.

Revaluation Reserve A reserve attributable to shareholders, produced by revaluation of a company's capital assets such as its property holdings.

Revenue The amount of goods or services sold by a company in a given period. Also known as sales or turnover.

Reversal In technical analysis, a reversal is a change in trend. Many technical analysts use patterns in price charts to spot a reversal. Key reversal patterns include head and shoulders, triple top/bottom, double top/bottom and V-formation/spikes.
▶ *See also* Patterns, Technical Analysis.

Reversal Day A term used in technical analysis. A key reversal day marks an important turning point on a chart but it cannot be correctly identified until prices have moved significantly in the opposite direction to the previous trend. A top reversal day is defined as when a new high has been set in an uptrend and is followed by a lower close than the previous close. A bottom reversal day would be a new low followed by a close above the previous day's close. An island reversal occurs when an upward gap has formed, prices have traded in a narrow range for a few days and a breakaway gap to the downside then occurs. This leaves the price action looking like an island, which indicates a trend reversal.
▶ *See also* Gap, Technical Analysis.

Reverse Cash and Carry Trade ▶ *See* Cash and Carry Trade.

Reverse Stock Split A reduction of the number of outstanding shares in a company into a smaller number of stocks without cost to the shareholders who retain their proportionate holdings. This is not as common as a stock split and is usually only seen when the stock price is low. The move boosts the nominal price of each share, although it does not affect their value because each of the reduced number of shares now represents a larger share of ownership of the company. Also known as a negative stock split.
▶ *See also* Stock Split.

Reverse Takeover Where a company takes over a larger concern or when an unlisted company takes over a concern that is listed on a stock exchange.

Revolving Line of Credit A bank line of credit for which customers pay fees and can then take money according to their needs. Also known as a revolver.

Rich Cheap Analysis Rich and cheap refers to the pricing of a security relative to comparable securities in the secondary market. Rich, or overvalued bonds, have lower yields than bonds with similar terms and credit ratings. Cheap, or undervalued bonds, have higher yields than paper with similar maturity and credit risk.

Rights Issue One of the ways that a company can raise additional funds is to issue new shares. These new shares must be first offered to current shareholders and a rights issue allows a shareholder to buy an additional number of shares for each share held. For example, a two-for-three rights issue entitles shareholders to buy two additional shares for every three owned. Rights can be traded in the market.

Riksbank The central bank of Sweden.

Risk The probability that an investment or venture will make a loss or not make the returns expected. This probability can be measured. There are many different types of risk including basis risk, country or sovereign risk, credit risk, currency risk, economic risk, inflation risk, liquidity risk, market or systematic risk, political risk, settlement risk, systemic risk and translation risk.

Risk Management Risk management is a 'middle office' function that sits between the dealing room and settlement. It involves revaluing all positions at least daily to estimate the risk of possible future losses on those positions and ensure that they are within acceptable limits.
▶ *See also* Middle Office, Mark to Market.

Risk Premium The extra reward required from an investment in order to compensate for higher risks.
▶ *See also* Equity Risk Premium.

Risk–Return Relationship The relationship between risk and return. To achieve greater returns an investor must take greater risks.

Risk Reversal An option strategy involving the purchase of a put and the sale of a call, or vice versa, with different strike levels. The premium generated from the sale of an option could partly or totally finance the premium to be paid for the purchase of an option. Also known as a cylinder, a break forward or range forward.
▶ *See also* Option.

ROA

Return on Assets. A company's ability to operate profitably can be measured directly by calculating its return on assets using three ratios.

1. RETURN ON TOTAL ASSETS (ROA)

ROA is calculated as a ratio of the attributable profits for the last 12 months to total assets (fixed and current) for the same period, expressed as a percentage. It measures how effectively a company can generate earnings from its assets. It is a better measure of operating efficiency than ROE (Return on Equity), which only measures how much profit is generated on the shareholders' equity, but ignores debt funding. ROA is particularly relevant for banks, which typically have huge assets. Some analysts use earnings before interest and taxes (EBIT) rather than net profit to measure operating efficiency, arguing that management has little influence on interest rate and taxation levels.

Formula: Net profit/total assets x 100

Example

In the last financial year The Old Rope Corporation had total assets of £1,407 million and net profits of £64 million.

ROA
64/1,407 = 4.54 percent

2. RETURN ON FIXED ASSETS

This is the ratio of attributed profits to fixed assets alone, expressed as a percentage. It measures how effectively a company can generate earnings for its long-term assets such as land and machinery.

Formula: Net profit/fixed assets x 100

Example

In the last financial year The Old Rope Corporation had fixed assets of £960 million and net profits of £64 million.

Return on fixed assets: 64 / 960 x 100 = 6.66 percent

3. RETURN ON CAPITAL EMPLOYED (ROCE)

ROCE is the ratio of operating profit (earnings before interest and tax) to capital employed, expressed as a percentage. Capital employed equals shareholders' funds plus long-term liabilities – in other words, all the long-term funds used by the company. The

▶

ratio measures the return on all sources of finance used by the company (i.e. equity plus debt) and is very similar to return on assets (which includes current liabilities).

Formula: ROCE = EBIT/total capital employed x 100

Example

In the last complete financial year The Old Rope Corporation earned an operating profit of £77 million. It had shareholders' equity of £300 million and long-term debt of £267 million, making its total capital employed £567 million.

ROCE: −77 million/567 million x 100 = 13.58 percent

ROC Rate of Change. In technical analysis, the ROC is an indicator that measures the ratio of the most recent closing price to a price in a previous set period. Thus, a five-day rate of change oscillator is constructed by dividing the latest closing price by the price five days previous and multiplying by 100. The 100 line becomes the midpoint or zero line.

▶ *See also* Oscillator, Technical Analysis.

ROCE Return on Capital Employed. ROCE or ROC is the ratio of operating profit (earnings before interest and tax) to capital employed, expressed as a percentage. Capital employed equals shareholders' funds plus long-term liabilities – in other words, all the long-term funds used by the company. The ratio measures the return on all sources of finance used by the company (i.e. equity plus debt) and is very similar to return on assets (which includes current liabilities). Also known as ROI or Return on Investment.

ROE

Return on Equity. The ratio of a company's profit to its shareholders' equity, expressed as a percentage. It is the most widely used measure of how well management uses shareholders' funds.

Its main advantage is that it is a benchmark that allows investors to compare the profitability of hugely differing industries. Investors do not care whether their holdings are in low-margin retailers or high-margin technology companies, as long as they produce an above-average ROE.

Its main flaw is that it ignores the debt side of the company's funding and thus fails to measure the amount of risk involved in obtaining a given amount of earnings. A high ROE can be due to high earnings or low equity, therefore it is always wise to keep an eye on the company's leverage (as measured by its debt/equity ratio).

ROE ratios for healthy companies range between 10 and 25 percent. Most investors look for companies with double-digit ROEs, or at least higher than the return on a risk-free investment such as a government bond. Companies earning high ROEs will typically attract competition into their market segment and need to keep growing and/or cutting costs to maintain double-digit ROE levels.

Formula: Attributable Profit/Shareholders' Equity x 100

Example

In the last complete financial year The Old Rope Corporation had attributable profit of £64 million and shareholders' equity of £300 million.

ROE: 64/300 x 100 = 21.33 percent

▶ *See also* Assets, Earnings, Shareholders' Funds.

ROI Return on Investment. ▶ *See* ROCE.

Rolling Settlement Settlement of securities on a recurring cycle of a certain number of days from the trade date, rather than on fixed account days. ▶ *See also* T+1.

Rollover The periodic renewal of a loan, repriced at current market rates.

Rollover Date The date on which FRNs pay their previous coupon and from when they start to accrue interest on their next coupon. This will often be used as a flat settlement date, i.e. free of accrued interest. ▶ *See also* FRN.

RONA ▶ *See* ROA.

ROTA ▶ *See* ROA.

Round Lot Trade The size of the most common block of securities or commodities trading in a market.

Round Turn A transaction consisting of a purchase and a sale (or vice versa) of two securities or contracts in the same market, which offset each other. This is generally used when referring to commission charges.

Royalty Payment made for the use of property such as a franchise, natural resource, copyright or a patent – usually expressed as a percentage of the revenues gained by its use.

RPI Retail Price Index. The UK equivalent of US consumer price inflation (CPI).

RSI Relative Strength Index. A technical analysis tool that compares the average strength of price rises for a given instrument with the average strength of price falls over a certain number of days. It does not compare the relative strength of two securities but the internal strength of the price moves of a single instrument. It is used to identify overbought and oversold signals as well as to act as a warning when divergence exists between the direction of the index and the direction of the instrument's price. For example, the RSI may be rising when the price of the instrument is falling, which gives a buy signal.
   ▶ *See also* Momentum, Technical Analysis.

RUF Revolving underwriting facility, which allows the borrower to issue short-term notes as required. Contains an in-built underwriting agreement should the market be unable to provide funds.
   ▶ *See also* NIF.

Run Up A term for a quick rise in a share price.

Russell 3000 An index of the 3,000 largest US companies by market capitalization, compiled by the Frank Russell Company. The Russell 2000 index measures the performance of the smallest 2,000 companies within the main index. ▬ **www.russell.com** ▬

S

SA Spanish company title: abbreviation of Sociedad Anonima.

SA Italian company title: abbreviation of Societa.

SA French company title: abbreviation of Société Anonyme. The term is also used in Belgium and Switzerland.

SA de CV Mexican company title: abbreviation of Sociedad Anonima de Capital Variable.

SAE Spanish company title: abbreviation of Sociedad Anonima Español.

SAFE Synthetic agreement for forward exchange. A collective name for exchange rate agreements (ERA) and forward exchange agreements (FXA).
▶ *See also* ERA, FXA.

Safe Haven Currency A major traded currency, such as the US dollar or Swiss franc, used by investors and fund managers seeking a safe haven for their funds in times of political turmoil.

SAL Spanish company title: abbreviation of Sociedad Anonima Laboral.

Sale and Leaseback The sale of assets to another party, coupled with an agreement to lease those same assets for an agreed period of time. The seller has the benefit of an immediate inflow of funds, which can be put to use elsewhere in the business, coupled with a predicatable cost for the leased assets. The buyer has a predicatable stream of income from the leased assets.

Sales The amount of goods or services sold by a company in a given period. Also known as revenue or turnover.

Sallie Mae Student Loan Marketing Association. A publicly traded stock corporation in the US, which guarantees student loans traded on the secondary market. ■ www.salliemae.com ■

Sample Grade Usually the lowest quality of commodity acceptable for delivery under a futures contract.

Samurai Bond A bond issued in Japan by a foreign borrower denominated in yen.

S&P ▶ *See* Standard & Poor's.

S&P500 A major barometer of the US stock market. The S&P500 is an arithmetic index, weighted by the market capitalization (the number of a company's issued shares multiplied by their market price) of its constituents, which represents some 80 percent of the market value of all issues traded on the New York Stock Exchange. It comprises 500 shares, mainly NYSE listed firms. The CME trades futures and futures options on the index. Index options are traded at the CBOE.
▥ **www.spglobal.com** ▥
▶ **See also** CBOE, CME, NYSE.

S&P/IFCI The International Finance Corporation's indices of investable emerging stock markets, now known as the S&P/IFC. They measure in dollar terms the performances of markets deemed reasonably open to foreign investors. The IFCI Composite is the broad, all-region benchmark.
▶ *See also* IFC, Standard & Poor's.

Sarbanes–Oxley Act US legislation which created a federal accounting supervision board and introduced criminal liability for executives who knowingly file false financial reports.

SARL Portuguese and Brazilian company title: abbreviation of Sociedad Anonima de Responsibiliade Limitada. French company title: abbreviation of Societée à Responsibilitée Limitée. Also used in Luxembourg.

SAS Italian company title: abbreviation of Società in Accomandita Semplice.

Savings Rate The proportion of income that is put aside and not consumed immediately.

S/B Sell after Buy limit order. Two orders treated as one, the first order being to buy. If done, the sell order becomes valid.
▶ *See also* B/S (Buy after Sell limit order, which is the reverse).

SC French company title: abbreviation of Societé en Commandité. Also used in Luxembourg.

Scaleup To sell at regular price intervals in a rising market. Opposite of scaledown, which is purchasing at regular price intervals in a declining market.

Scalpers Traders in the options and futures market who hold their positions for a very short time. Their aim is to make small gains frequently.

▶ *See* Day Trading.

Scatter Chart In technical analysis, these charts illustrate the degree of correlation in a market between two different financial instruments, such as two shares or two bonds, by showing the value for one plotted against the value of the other. The X axis has values for the first instrument and the Y axis portrays corresponding values for the second instrument. Scatter charts cannot be combined with other analyses on the same graph and limit minders cannot be set for them.

▶ *See also* Technical Analysis.

Schatz German government debt with a two-year maturity.

SCL Spanish company title: abbreviation of Sociedad Cooperativa Limitada.

Screen Trading Trading conducted via an electronic system. In contrast with floor trading which is conducted face-to-face on an exchange trading floor.

Scrip Issue A free issue of shares to shareholders when a company transfers money from its reserves to its permanent capital. Changing reserves into permanent capital, or into new shares as part of the long-term funding of the business, makes the reserves more obviously and more accountably part of the shareholders' equity. The new shares are distributed to the existing holders in proportion to their existing holdings. Also known as a capitalization issue.

▶ *See also* Capitalization Issue.

SDR Special drawing rights or SDRs are a form of special currency created by the International Monetary Fund and its member countries to supplement the Fund's existing reserves of currencies, and are contributed to by member states. The value of SDRs is based on a basket of the major traded currencies – the dollar, euro and yen – and fluctuates as the currencies themselves change. They serve as the unit of account of the IMF and a number of international organizations. SDRs are not a useable currency nor are they a direct claim on the IMF. But holders of SDRs can exchange them into these currencies.

▧ **www.imf.org/external/fin.htm** ▧

▶ *See also* IMF, ODR.

SEAQ Stock Exchange Automated Quotation. The screen-based system used by the London Stock Exchange to trade its shares.

Seasonal Adjustment An adjustment made to certain economic indicators to allow for predictable peaks and troughs caused by seasonal factors. Seasonal adjustment to an economic indicator makes it easier to discern the underlying trend. Adjustment is made by deducting an average of the change in a set number of previous years from the current change, showing whether a rise or fall is unusual or purely seasonal.
▶ *See also* Economic Indicators.

Seasoned Offer An offer of shares or bonds by a company that is already listed on a stock exchange. In contrast to an initial public offering by a company which is being listed for the first time. A seasoned offer can be in the form of an offer for sale to the public as a whole or a placing with a restricted set of institutional investors.
▶ *See also* IPO.

Seat Term used in derivative markets. A seat is the membership right to trade on an exchange. A seat can be bought or sold and its price reflects the underlying prosperity and prospects of the exchange itself.

SEC Securities and Exchange Commission The US regulatory body responsible for overseeing and administering rules associated with all sectors of the securities industry. Its main aim is to protect investors and maintain the integrity of the markets by full public disclosure.
■ **www.sec.gov** ■

SEC Filings In the US, companies are required to make SEC filings on their corporate activities. Some of the forms must also be filed with the appropriate stock exchange. The filings can be accessed electronically through the SEC website. ■ **www.sec.gov/edgar.shtml** ■
▶ *See also* SEC.

Secondary Market The secondary market is where securities are bought and sold once they have been issued in the primary market. The secondary market gives a continuing opportunity for buying and selling and price discovery, and provides the liquidity that allows the primary market to function.
▶ *See also* Primary Markets.

Secondary Metals Product of refining scrap or alloys as opposed to primary metals produced from ore.
▶ *See also* Primary Metals.

Secondary Offering Offering to the public of a large block of privately held shares, often by the institution that sponsored the overall deal into the market.

Sector Fund A type of mutual fund which invests in one industry or in one geographical area only.

Sectoral Analysts Market analysts who focus on one particular industry. They research specific companies in that sector and make buy and sell recommendations based on that research.

Sector Index A stock exchange composite index that reflects the market activity of a particular industry.

Secular Trend A persistent trend in a single direction. A market movement over the long term which does not reflect cyclical seasonal or technical factors.

Securities and Exchange Commission ▶ *See* SEC.

Securitization Creation of financial instruments by combining other financial assets and then selling them to investors in the new form. Mortgages can be securitized, as can future royalties from a pop star's song portfolio. The new instruments can then be traded.

Security A certificate issued by a company, government or any organization which offers proof that investors have invested money in the organization's equity or debt.

Seignorage Revenue, or spending power, which a government acquires by printing money. The act of printing money increases the money supply at very little cost without increasing the supply of goods, so it can be regarded as an inflation tax.
▶ *See also* Printing Money.

Selloff When severe market pressure depresses prices, causing the sale to avoid further falls of shares, bonds, options, futures or any other form of commodity or financial market instrument.

Sell-side Used to describe financial institutions whose primary business is trading. The opposite of buy-side, where financial institutions make investments either for themselves or on behalf of other investors.

Senate Finance Committee Key US Senate committee responsible for tax and other revenue bills.

Senior Secured Debt Secured debt that is paid first in the event of a default.

Senior Unsecured Debt Securities that have priority ahead of all other unsecured or subordinated debt in ranking for payment in the event of default.

Settlement Payment for securities or commodities in exchange for their delivery. Usually takes place some time after the deal itself.

Settlement Date ▶ *See* Value Date.

Settlement Price ▶ *See* EDSP.

Settlement Risk The risk of an expected settlement amount not being made on time. The establishment of netting systems is an effort to minimize settlement risk.
▶ *See also* Netting.

SETS London's Stock Exchange Electronic Trading System. An electronic order-driven trading system which handles all of the UK's FTSE Eurotop 300 equities, all equities that have a LIFFE-traded equity option and some Irish stocks traded in euros.
▶ *See also* LIFFE, Order Driven.

SGX The Singapore Exchange. ▣ **www.ses.com.sg** ▣

Share A share represents ownership in a company and the right to receive a share in the profits of that company. Also called a stock.
▶ *See also* Ordinary Share, Preference Share.

Share Capital/Issued Capital Shares that have actually been issued, or allotted, to shareholders. In contrast with authorized share capital, which is the maximum amount of share capital that a company is allowed to issue by its constitution or charter.

Share Discount The amount by which the market value of shares drops below par value. The par or nominal value of a share is an arbitrary figure which is set when a share is first sold or issued. It usually has little or no significance because shares usually trade far above par value. However, a share discount to par value can be significant for preferred shares, which pay fixed dividends based on par value.
▶ *See also* Par Value, Preference Shares.

Share Dividend ▶ *See* Dividend.

Shareholder An individual who holds shares or stock in an organization or company.

Shareholders' Equity ▶ *See* Shareholders' Fund.

Shareholders' Funds Net assets (shareholders' funds plus retained reserves) of a company minus the minority interests. Also known as shareholders' equity or shareholders' capital employed.
▶ *See also* Minority Interests.

Shareholder Value Describes the ability of a company to deliver value to shareholders in terms of both dividends and growth in the company's share price. It focuses on a company's investments and its capacity to generate cash flows from its capital.

Share Premium The market value of shares in excess of their par value.

Share Register A central register containing details of a company's share ownership. Shareholders and the public usually have a legal right to inspect a company's share register, which is usually kept by a bank or institution which acts as the official registrar. Investors are rightly suspicious of jurisdictions which do not insist on accurate and easily accessible share registers.

Share Repurchase ▶ *See* Buy Back.

Shares Per Warrant Ratio A ratio measuring the amount of shares available through the exercise of a warrant.
▶ *See also* Warrant.

Sharpe Ratio A way of deciding whether returns are produced by intelligent investment decisions or by accepting excess risk. It measures the return of an investment compared with investment in government bonds, which are regarded as virtually risk free because the government in theory always repays its debts. The Sharpe Ratio is calculated by subtracting the rate of return on government securities from the rate of return on a portfolio, and then dividing the difference by the standard deviation of the portfolio's returns.
▶ *See also* Excess Portfolio Returns, Sortino Ratio, Standard Deviation.

Shelf Registration The US method of registering new share issues in advance and having the issue documentation prepared so the stock can be issued quickly.

Shell Company A non-trading company with a stock market quote. Also a dormant unquoted company.

Sherpas Senior officals from the leading industrial democracies of the G7/G8 organization who meet three or four times before each of the G7 summit comferences to agree topics to be discussed and to draft the final communiqué. Named after the porters on mountain-climbing expeditions.
▶ *See also* G7, G8.

Shogun Bond Public offering in Japan of a non-yen bond by a foreign borrower.

Short Investors are 'short' when they sell borrowed assets in the hope that they can buy them back when prices have fallen. A short position is the opposite of a long position, when investors buy assets in the hope that they can sell them when prices have risen.
▶ *See also* Long.

Short Bill A bill of exchange that is payable on demand or within a very short time.

Shortcovering The buying back of a security or asset previously sold so as to close out a short position. Also known as bear covering.
▶ *See also* Short Position.

Short Dated Forwards/Deposits Transactions in bank deposits or in exchanging currencies which extend for a period of up to a month. They are designated by letters that show the duration of the deal, such as O/N for the period covering today until the next working day. Similarly T/N is tomorrow/next working day, S/N is spot to the next day following spot and S/W is spot to one week following spot. For most markets spot is the technical term for a transaction that starts two days from today.
▶ *See also* Forward, Swap.

Short First Coupon The first interest payment on a recently issued bond which is less than the normal semi-annual or annual payment.

Short Hedge The sale of a futures or option position to protect against a fall in price in the corresponding cash market. Losses in holdings of cash instruments or commodities will be offset by the profits from the futures or options which can be realized by meeting those obligations at the new lower price of the future of option. Opposite of long hedge.
▶ *See also* Cash Markets, Futures, Hedging, Option.

Short Margin Account An account requiring a margin deposit from investors who are involved in short selling, as opposed to buying on margin.

Short Position A position showing a sale or a greater number of sales over purchases in anticipation of a fall in prices. A short position can be closed out through the purchase of an equivalent amount. Buying back from a short position is known as shortcovering. Selling into a market without a prior long position is called short-selling.
▶ *See also* Long Position.

Short-selling The selling of instruments that are not held in anticipation of a fall in prices. The action of buying back to cover the short position is known in the market as shortcovering.
▶ *See also* Shortcovering.

Short-term Borrowing Loans that a company needs to pay back within 12 months.

SICAV Société d'Investissement à Capital Variable. In France and Luxembourg, these are investment funds similar to mutual funds and unit trusts.

SICOVAM Société Interprofessionnelle pour la Compensation des Valeurs Mobilières. Former clearing organization of the Paris Stock Exchange, absorbed into Euroclear.
▶ *See* Euroclear.

Sideways Market/Movement A market trend where price rises and falls are small and restricted to a narrow range. Often referred to as a trendless, congested or ranging market.

Sight Draft ▶ *See* Bill of Exchange.

Sight Money/Sight Deposits ▶ *See* Call Money.

Signalling When a company sends out signals about its future performance. Typical signals would be advance information about expected future earnings and dividend payments.

SIM Italian company title: abbreviation of Società di Intermediazione Mobiliare.

Simple Interest The cost of borrowing, or the return on lending money. It is calculated on the amount borrowed or lent (the principal), the length of time the funds are borrowed for, and the market general interest rate level.
▶ *See also* Compound Interest.

Simple Moving Average An unweighted moving average.
▶ *See also* Moving Average.

Simple Stock Future A futures contract which gives the right to purchase shares of a single company at a set price. This contrasts with an index future which gives the right to buy all the constituents of a specific share market index. Single stock futures offer a more highly geared way of investing in a stock because the holding can be initially controlled by just the cost of the futures contract.
▶ *See also* Futures, Gearing.

Sinking Fund Mandatory prepayments by a borrower to redeem a certain amount of an issue, thus reducing the principal amount due at maturity. The prepayments are made regardless of price movements in the secondary bond market, through payments to a special account.
▶ *See also* Pro Rata Sinking Fund, Purchase Fund.

SL   Spanish company title: abbreviation of Società Limitada.

S/L   A stop loss order. A limit order to buy or sell which operates only when a given price is reached. Such an order is normally placed to cut losses on an existing position. Once the stop loss level is reached, the order is often executed at the next market price (particularly in volatile markets).

SMI   Swiss Market Index. The SMI consists of 24 securities (bearer shares and participation certificates) from 20 major Swiss companies quoted on the Basel, Geneva and Zurich Stock Exchanges. It is weighted by the market capitalization of its constituent securities. The SMI is the basis of the index options traded on EUREX.
   ■ www.eurexchange.com ■
   ▶ See also EUREX.

S/N   Abbreviation for spot/next. Used in swap and deposit transactions when the first value date for the transaction is spot value (which in most markets is the value two days from today) and maturity falls on the next working day.
   ▶ See also Short Dated Forwards/Deposits, Swap.

SNC   Italian company title: abbreviation of Società in Nome Collectivo.

Society for Worldwide Interbank Financial Telecommunication
   ▶ See SWIFT.

SOFFEX   Formerly the Swiss Options and Financial Futures Exchange, which merged with the German exchange DTB to create EUREX.
   ▶ See also EUREX.

Soft Loan   A loan with an interest rate below the real cost of borrowing, or with no interest rate at all. The Internation Development Association, an affiliate of the World Bank, provides soft loans to developing countries for long-term capital projects.
   ▶ See also IDA.

Softs   Soft commodities such as sugar, coffee and cocoa. In contrast with commodities such as metals, grains and oilseeds.

Sogo Sosha   Very large Japanese trading companies which handle a major part of the country's imports and exports. They include Marubeni and Mitsubishi. Sogo Sosha played an important part in rebuilding the Japanese economy after the Second World War.

Solvency Margin, Solvency Ratio The level of an insurance company's spare capital in excess of its projected liabilities, effectively a measure of its financial health. There are often statutory minimum solvency margins, which are sometimes known as the resilience test. In a bear market insurance companies may face problems maintaining their solvency margins because their equity investments are falling in value. Also known as solvency ratio.

Solvent When a company can meet all its debts as they fall due.
   ▶ *See also* Insolvent.

Sortino Ratio A way of measuring the relative performance of an investment portfolio. Similar to the Sharpe Ratio, but it uses the downside standard deviation rather than the overall standard deviation, to distinguish between bad and good volatility.
   ▶ *See also* Standard Deviation.

Sovereign Immunity The right of a state not to be sued and its protection from seizure of assets in the event of a loan default.

Sovereign Issue A bond issued by a government-backed agency.

Sovereign Risk Risks associated with lending funds to, or making an investment in, a particular country. Also known as country risk.

SpA Italian company title: abbreviation of Società per Azioni.

Special Drawing Rights ▶ *See* SDR.

Specialist Market makers in one or more selected securities listed on an exchange. Found at a trading post on the floor, they earn their income from commission when acting as a broker, or from the spread in their quoted prices when acting as a dealer.

Specifications Refers to properties of a given crude oil or refined petroleum product. Properties are specified because they often vary widely, even within the same grade of product. The properties affect the price and end-use of the crude or petroleum product.

Speculation Taking relatively high risks in financial markets in the hope of making large gains. Speculation involves trying to anticipate the future when making investments.

Speculator An investor who practices speculation. A speculator tries to anticipate price changes with a view to making profits. Generally, speculators have no long-term interest in the securities or assets they trade in.
   ▶ *See also* Hedging.

Speedline In technical analysis, speedlines measure the rate of rise or fall in a trend and are constructed by dividing trends into thirds and drawing trendlines at key levels.
▶ *See also* Technical Analysis.

Spinning The favourable allocation by an underwriter of shares in a desirable initial public offering to selected clients in the expectation of winning their investment banking business in return.

Spin Off Method used by a company to split its operations and assets by creating a new company. It proportionately distributes shares in the new company to its own shareholders. Also termed hive off.

Split Capital Investment Trust An investment trust, or collective investment company, that sells shares and then pools together the proceeds to buy shares in other companies, thereby creating an investment portfolio. Investment trusts contrast with unit trusts and mutual funds, which do not make specific share offerings but sell and redeem their shares on a continuing basis according to investor demand. Split capital trusts sell more than one class of shares to their investors, with some offering higher dividend income and others higher capital growth, to meet the varying risk preference and tax position of the purchasers.
▶ *See also* Investment Trusts.

Sponsor Term used for the investment bank, or the merchant bank, which advises a company on how to issues new shares or bonds. It then finds out the level of potential demand for the new shares or bonds, prices them and sells them in the market.
▶ *See also* Investment Bank.

Spontaneous Lending New lending that is not intended to provide funds needed to repay interest and principal on existing loans.

Spot Immediate settlement, which in most markets is two working days after the trade.
▶ *See also* Settlement.

Spot Market A market whose trades deliver and settle immediately (normally two working days after the trade). Also known as cash market and physical market.

Spot Month The nearest dated futures contract.
▶ *See also* Contract Month, Futures.

Spot Next ▶ *See* S/N.

Spread The word 'spread' has several different meaning:

1 The difference in a price quotation between the bid, the price at which a dealer is prepared to buy, and the ask, the price at which a dealer will sell. A large spread usually means the market lacks liquidity. When a market lacks liquidity dealers often cannot buy and sell quickly and so they widen the spread to avoid being caught on the wrong side of the market.

2 Spread can also be used to express the difference in yields between two fixed income securities of the same quality but different maturities, or of different quality but the same maturities.

3 Often 'spread' refers to the difference in yield between a bond and a reference government bond, which is regarded as relatively risk-free.

4 A futures spread is the difference in prices between delivery months in the same or different markets.

5 Spread can also refer to the difference between borrowing and lending rates by which a financial intermediary makes profits.

Spread Betting A form of betting that depends on the establishment of a spread, or a buying and selling price, for a particular market or instrument at a certain time. For example, a bookmaker may offer a spread for next week of 120 to 130 on a market index which is now standing at 125. A bullish punter would buy the spread, or accept the offer price of 130, placing an up bet that the market will rise above 130. He would gain additional winnings for every point rise above that level. A bearish punter would sell the spread, or accept the bid price of 120, placing a down bet that the market will fall below 120. He would gain extra profits for every further point fall below that level. Bets can be closed out at any time by making a matching but contrary trade at the current spread. Prices for spread bets are usually set in line with the underlying market, but the advantage to the punter is that there are no commissions or trading taxes to pay, and often no taxes on capital gains. Spread betting also allows highly speculative small investments. The bets are highly geared. Spread betting is offered on sporting events and on almost every underlying financial instrument and market.
▶ *See also* Bid, Offer, Spread.

Spread Trading The purchase of one futures contract and the simultaneous sale of another in order to take advantage of expected price discrepancies.

Square Position ▶ *See* Flat.

Squeeze When prices are being forced up or down as investors rush to cut their losses. A short squeeze is when prices rise sharply as investors cover short positions by buying shares. A squeeze is also used to describe when any commodity is in short supply or a period when monetary policy is tight.

SRL Italian company title: abbreviation of Società Responsibilità Limitata.

Stability and Growth Pact A European Union budget pact designed to underpin monetary union and the euro. It aims to prevent any one Eurozone member from racking up large government budget deficits that would raise the cost of borrowing for the whole club. The pact requires countries to keep their budget deficit below 3 percent of their gross domestic product and to wipe out their budget deficts altogether in the medium term. Extensions can be granted when growth is significantly weaker than expected, but fines are imposed for breaking the rules.

Stag Operator who applies for a new security hoping to sell it as soon as it is allotted, at a premium over the issue price.

Stagflation A state of the economy where high inflation is accompanied by high unemployment and stagnant economic activity.

Standard & Poor's A leading credit rating agency. Its assessments of the creditworthiness of borrowers are widely watched in the capital markets and can affect the price of bonds and the cost of borrowing.
   ■ www.standardandpoors.com ■
   ▶ See also Credit Rating, Moody's.

Standard Deviation A statistical measure of the amount by which one value in a range of values is likely to vary from the mean value. It is used as a method of assessing how variable or volatile a price is likely to be. The bigger the standard deviation the more widespread are the price movements and the more volatile the performance of the stock or financial instrument.

Standby Credit Arrangement with a lender (a group of banks, or the IMF in the case of a member country) whereby a fixed amount of credit will be available for drawing during a given period, if required.

Standby Loan The basic IMF sovereign loan, usually over one or two years, aimed at overcoming short-term balance of payments difficulties. Loan conditions are focused on macro-economic policies.

Statement of Cash Flows A financial account that shows the cash flows generated by a company's operations, investments and financing activities. Sometimes called the flow of funds statement or the source and applications of funds statement.

State Planning Government regulation of a sector of the economy using state-appointed administrators who do not bow to free market forces.
▶ *See also* Market Economy, Mixed Economy, Planned Economy.

Ste Cve Belgian company title: abbreviation of Société Coopérative.

Stochastics Used in technical analysis, stochastics is a momentum indicator which identifies possible changes in trends in sideways moving markets. Closing levels consistently near the top of the range show buying pressure and closing levels consistently near the bottom of the range show selling pressure.
▶ *See also* Technical Analysis.

Stock
1 The amount of money employed by a company in its work-in-progress, in raw materials and in finished goods. Also known as inventory.
2 A stock represents part ownership of a company and the right to receive a share in the profits of that company. Also called a share.
▶ *See also* Ordinary Share, Preference Share.

Stock Average An arithmetic average also referred to as an index.
▶ *See* Stock Index.

Stock Broker A company or individual, executing trades and/or providing investment advice to institutional customers, but not acting as a principal.

Stock Dividend A dividend paid to shareholders in the form of authorized but hitherto unissued shares.
▶ *See also* Dividend.

Stock Exchange A trading-floor or screen-based market where exchange members buy and sell securities.

Stock Exchange Automated Quotation ▶ *See* SEAQ.

Stock Index A market index is a numerical representation of the way an entire market has performed relative to some 'base' reference date in the past. They are calculated in two ways – weighted or unweighted. Unweighted indices are simple arithmetic or geometric averages. An arithmetic average adds up all the percentage changes in the prices of the constituent stocks and then divides that by the number of stocks in the index. The geometric average is a very precise measurement, calculated by multiplying all the prices of the shares in the index and taking the nth root where n is the number of shares you are averaging. It is much less frequently used than an arithmetic average. In weighted indices, certain stocks carry a greater weighting than others, usually based on their market value or capitalization.

▶ *See also* Capitalization-weighted Index, Market Capitalization.

Stock Index Fund A fund that invests in a group of securities from a particular stock market index.

▶ *See also* Tracker Fund.

Stock Index Future A futures contract on a share market index.

▶ *See also* Futures.

Stock Index Option A call or put option on a stock index.

▶ *See also* Option.

Stock Lending Lending of shares by long-term holders such as pension funds or insurance companies when shares are in short supply. Often an investment house will not actually take delivery of the stock but will use it as an underlying instrument in a derivatives strategy.

Stock Option ▶ *See* Equity Options.

Stock Split The break-up of a share into smaller units without affecting either the total share capital or reserves. The main effect is to reduce the unit price of each quoted share, making them easier to trade in small lots and more attractive to small investors. Opposite of a reverse stock split.

▶ *See also* Reverse Stock Split.

Stop Loss/Stop Limit Order ▶ *See* S/L.

Straddle An option strategy involving one call and one put with the same strike and same expiry date. The strategy allows the buyer to take advantage of large price movements in either direction, by exercising the call in a rising market and the put in a falling market. The risk is that prices move only slightly and the change is not enough to cover the costs of the two options.

Straight Bond ▶ *See* Bullet Bond.

Strangle An option strategy involving one call and one put with different strike levels but with the same expiry date. The strategy produces a profit if prices break above or below a given range, effectively a bet on volatility.

Street Name ▶ *See* Nominee Account.

Strike Price The price agreed in an options transaction and at which the option may be exercised. Also known as the exercise price.

Structural Adjustment Reform of the structure of a whole economy. Mostly used in the context of structural adjustment programmes promoted by the IMF and the World Bank. Designed to bring about open markets, liberalized trade and to lower budget and current account deficits.

Structural Deficit The portion of a country's budget deficit that is not the result of economic swings.
  ▶ *See also* Cyclical Deficit.

Student Loan Marketing Association ▶ *See* Sallie Mae.

Subordinated Debt Debt that in the event of a default is repaid only after senior debt has been repaid. It is higher risk than the senior debt.

Subsidiary A company of which more than 50 percent of its voting stock is owned by the parent company.

Sunk Costs Costs that have already been paid for and can therefore be ignored in calculating the future profitability of a project.

Sunshine Laws Laws in the United States that ensure maximum disclosure of the business of government agencies, including those responsible for regulating securities trading.

SuperMontage The NASDAQ Stock Market's trading-and-order display system, which both shows orders and executes them, in a manner similar to trading on ECNs, electronic communications networks.
  ▶ *See also* ECN, NASDAQ.

Super-voting Share A type of share capital structure not often seen outside the United States in which certain shares, on being issued, give the holder increased voting rights.

Supply/Demand The amount of sellers providing supplies to a market and of buyers creating demand. Supply and demand is a major influence in generating the market price.

Supply-side Economics A theory in economics that says tax cuts, liberal employment laws, deregulation and similar measures to ease constraints on companies, will boost investment in production and increase the supply of goods in the economy. Also seen as a way of controlling inflation, by concentrating on increased output rather than on controlling prices or money supply.

Support Support is a level, usually identified on a price chart, where buying interest is strong enough to overcome selling pressure so that the price does not fall beyond the support level.
▶ *See also* Resistance, Trendline.

Supranational An agency which raises money in world capital markets to fund investment in developing countries or large projects. Supranationals are owned by a consortium of national governments. They include the World Bank and the European Bank for Reconstruction and Development.

Surplus The difference occurring when income or revenue is greater than expenditure. Opposite of deficit.
▶ *See also* Deficit.

Suspension A company's shares can be temporarily suspended, either voluntarily by the company or by the relevant stock exchange, when a key announcement is expected. Longer or permanent suspension can be imposed by a stock exchange for failure to comply with listing requirements or numerous other reasons.

S/W Abbreviation for spot/week. Used in swap and deposit transactions when the first value date is spot value and maturity falls a calendar week from then.
▶ *See also* Short Dated Forwards/Deposits, Swap.

Swap An exchange of cash flows between two counterparties designed to offset interest rate or currency risk and to match their assets to their liabilities. For example, a company may have costs which it must pay in Swiss francs while its revenues are in US dollars. Another company may have the opposite requirement. A bank, in exchange for a fee, arranges a currency swap which meets both requirements. The same is true of interest rate swaps, which allow two parties to exchange fixed rate for floating rate risk to their mutual advantage. A key point is that parties to a swap do not exchange principal, or the underlying fixed amount of debt, but just cash flow, or the interest payments.

Swap Spread The difference between the swap interest rate and the underlying benchmark government bond yield at any given maturity. The swap spread is seen as a barometer of risk appetite, and represents the premium investors' exposure to future interest rate fluctuations. The narrower the spread is, the greater the appetite for risk.

Swaption An option on a swap, giving the holder the right, but not the obligation, to enter into an interest rate swap as either the payer or receiver of the fixed side of the swap.
▶ *See also* Swap.

SWIFT The Society for Worldwide Interbank Financial Telecommunication. Operates a standard network for making international banking transactions. ▪ **www.swift.com** ▪

SWIFT Codes The coded instructions used by SWIFT for effecting international banking transactions over its network.
▶ *See also* SWIFT.

Swing Line A credit facility allowing borrowers to take money overnight.

Swiss Market Index ▶ *See* SMI.

Switch The exchanging of one security for another. A switch is often used to improve a portfolio, perhaps to enhance the yield or quality.

Syndicate A group of institutions responsible for issuing debt. A syndicate is formed to share the risk of an issue and split it into manageable amounts.

Syndicated Loan A large loan arranged by a group of banks that form a syndicate, headed by the lead manager.

Synthetic A financial instrument that is created by combining two or more instruments to create a new asset with distinct attributes. For example, the purchase of a call option on a share and the simultaneous sale of a put option on the same share artificially creates an asset which has the same characteristics as the underlying share and the same risks and potential rewards.

Systematic Risk Risk that cannot be diversified away because it is the risk of movements in the overall market or in the relevant market segment.
▶ *See also* Diversification.

Systemic Risk The risk associated with an adverse change in the overall financial system.

T

T+1 Settlement of a share deal one day after the transaction takes place. Regarded as the ideal, reducing the delay in the exchange of cash and securities to a minimum. Some markets work on T+2, T+3, etc.
▶ *See also* Settlement, Rolling Settlement.

Takedown To receive and accept an allotment of securities in the primary market.

Takeover Acquisition of a controlling interest in a company through the purchase of its shares.

Takeover Bid The initial offer by a predator company for another. The bid can be in cash, shares or a combination. Bids usually have a closing date for acceptance. The bid can be hostile (without the acceptance or cooperation of the target company), or friendly (accepted by the target).

Taking a Position The act of buying or selling to establish a long or short position.

Tan Book ▶ *See* Beige Book.

Tangibles ▶ *See* Assets/Liabilities.

Tankan The Bank of Japan's quarterly corporate survey of companies, which provides a wide range of corporate data. It includes the closely watched diffusion index for major manufacturers, which compares the ratio of those who expect business to improve to those who expect it to worsen. The lower the index, the gloomier the outlook. The tankan is an important reference for the central bank in formulating monetary policy. ■ **www.boj.or.jp/en/siryo/exp/faqtk2.htm** ■

Taxation Risk The risk that tax laws relating to dividend income and capital gains on shares might change, making stocks less attractive.

TECHNICAL ANALYSIS

The **words in bold** are explained more fully under their individual entries.

Technical analysis is a method of predicting the future direction of prices by studying charts of past market action. Technical analysts, or chartists, try to predict future prices on the basis of how prices move up and down, rather than why they have moved.

They pay close attention to recurring patterns in charts of price action and look at trends, and at the speed of change and the momentum.

The analysts use four basic types of charts – line, bar, candlestick, and point and figure – and a large number of technical theories and indicators including **Elliott wave theory, RSI, moving average convergence/divergence and stochastics**.

1   A **line chart** is the simplest form of chart. It is a plain record of a price charted against time with the changes marked as dots and joined together by a line.

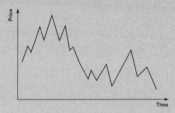

2   A **bar chart** represents price information on a vertical bar. The top of the bar is the highest price and the bottom of the bar the lowest. A dash on the left-hand side of the bar denotes the opening price and a dash on the right-hand side the closing price.

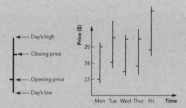

3   A **candlestick chart** captures the same price information as a bar chart: the open, high, low and close. A thick box (known as the body of the candle) joins the open and close values. Thin lines on either end of the body (known as shadows)

join the high and low prices. If the opening value is higher than the closing value, the body of the candle is solid or coloured. Conversely, if the close is higher than the open then the body of the candle is clear, white or unshaded.

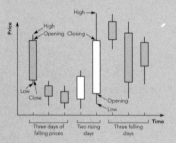

4 A **point and figure price chart** captures pure price movements with no regard for time or volume. Rising prices are denoted by a column of Xs and falling prices by a column of Os. Subsequent columns are placed to the right of earlier columns.

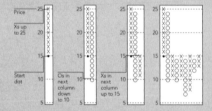

Chartists make particular use of trendlines, which connect areas of specific price action. Both uptrends and downtrends are defined as trends that can be drawn on a chart by joining a minimum of four points. Chartists also look for peaks and troughs and for patterns in price behaviour, such as **head and shoulders**, **double top** and **triple bottom**.

They watch for speedlines, which measure the rate of change, and patterns in price lines which form **flags** or **pennants**. They also check for areas of resistance and support in price patterns, signs of corrections or breakouts, and for gaps when prices have jumped or fallen so quickly that there is a gap in the price points on a chart.

Channels can be drawn on charts to provide clear guidance when prices have moved outside a trading range. Chartists also look for patterns in the number of rises and falls in a market, using retracements to provide evidence to support **Dow theory** and **Gann**, **Fibonacci** and **Elliott wave** analyses.

Chartists rely heavily on **relative strength indices, momentum, moving averages** and on **MACD** or moving average convergence/divergence. The following definitions of technical analysis terms are defined and explained under their own entries.

Accumulation/Distribution Analysis	Line Chart
Alexander's Filter	Momentum
Alpha	Money Flow Index
Bar Chart	MACD Moving Average
Beta	Moving Average
Bollinger Bands	Moving Average Crossover
Breakout	On Balance Volume
Broadening	Oscillator
Candlestick Chart	Patterns
CAPM	Peaks/Troughs
Channel Lines	Point and Figure Chart
Charting	Price Channel
Chart Points	Quantitative Analysis
Chartist	Rectangle
Continuation	Relative Performance
Convergence/Divergence.	Relative Strength
Correction	Retracement
Correlation	Reversal
Counter Clockwise	Reversal Day
Cylinder	Relative Strength Index
Double Top/Bottom	Sharpe Ratio
Downtrend	Sortino Ratio
Exponential Moving Average	Speedline
Failure Swing	Stochastics
Fibonacci Numbers	Support
Flags/Pennants	Three Box Reversal
Floor	Top Reversal
Gann	Trendline
Gap	Triangles
Geometric average	Triple Top/Bottom
Head and Shoulders	Uptrend/Downtrend
High Low Open Close, HLOC	Wedges
Kairi	Williams Percent R

TED spread Abbreviation for Treasury Eurodollar Spread. This is the yield difference between US Treasury bills and Eurodollar futures contracts and is a widely followed spread trade.

▶ *See also* Futures, Spread Trading.

Tender Meaning varies greatly according to context. In a securities market it can mean that all allocations are at the same price. It can also mean the act of offering securities in response to a takeover bid or a tender offer. In the money market it can be an offer to buy Treasury bills. In commodities and futures markets it is the notice of intent to deliver physical goods against a futures contract.

Tenderable Grades Grades designated as suitable for delivery to settle a futures contract. Also called deliverable grades.

Tender Offer A company making a tender offer requires applicants to state the number of securities they require plus the price they are prepared to pay for them. Once all applications have been received, the company fixes a single 'striking price' at which the securities will be allotted to applicants at that price or higher. Also known as an offer for subscription.

Tender Price Price offered by investors at which they are willing to buy a new issue. The issuing house usually sets predetermined limits within which the tender price can be made.

Term CD Certificate of deposit that carry maturities from two to five years.
  ▶ See also CD.

Terminal Onshore installation designed to receive oil or gas from a pipeline or from tankers. Not a refinery.

Terminal Market Commodity market where physicals are exchanged for cash and are deliverable against maturing futures contracts.

Terminal Value The assumed value of a business at the end of a forecasting period, usually after 10 years of projected earnings.

Term Repo A repo lasting for 30 days or longer and used to hedge a position for a similar amount of time.
  ▶ See also Repo.

Term Sheet A document that legally defines the details of a loan or rescheduling agreement, signed by all participants.

Theta A measure of change in the value of an option compared with the continuous decrease in time to expiry. Also known as time decay.
  ▶ See also Option.

Thin Market A market where there is little buying or selling interest, with low volume or activity. Can apply to a whole market or a single instrument.

IDJIA 8,259.84 + 223.81 I DJTI 2,263.39 + 62.09 I DJUI 172.45 + 2.571

FIGURE 14 Ticker tape

Three Box Reversal In technical analysis, a much used point and figure chart for intermediate analysis, which needs only the high and low prices for the day.
▶ See also Point and Figure Charts, Technical Analysis.

Throughput Total volume of raw materials processed in a given period by a plant such as an oil refinery. Also, the total volume of crude oil and refined products handled by a storage facility or pipeline.

Tick The minimum movement possible in the price of a financial instrument. A tick is one hundredth of a percentage point for bond yields and interest rates.
▶ See also Basis Point.

Ticker Symbol Letters that identify a stock traded on a stock exchange. A short and convenient way of identifying a stock, e.g. RTR.L for Reuters quoted in London.
▶ See also Ticker Tape.

Ticker Tape An electronic display showing prices at which each successive trade is executed on a stock exchange, together with the trading volume and the share's identifying symbols. (Figure 14.)
▶ See also Ticker Symbol.

Tier One Also known as core capital, this comprises equity, disclosed reserves and retained earnings. Under capital adequacy standards set for commercial banks by the Bank for International Settlements, at least half of the 8 percent of capital required to be set against risk-weighted assets must be tier one or core capital. Supplementary capital, or tier two, constitutes the rest. This includes undisclosed reserves, general provisions against loan losses, subordinated term debt and hybrid capital instruments combining characteristics of debt and equity. Also known as core capital.
▶ See also BIS, Capital Adequacy.

Tier Two ▶ See Tier One.

TIFFE The Tokyo International Financial Futures Exchange. The exchange trades interest rate and currency futures. ■ **www.tiffe.or.jp** ■

Tigers Collective term used in the 1990s to describe fast-developing economies of South-East Asia including Indonesia, Malaysia, Taiwan and Thailand.

Time Decay ▶ *See* Theta.

Time Deposit ▶ *See* CD.

Time Draft ▶ *See* Bill of Exchange.

Time Series A series of values over consecutive periods of time. Used in financial markets to describe price histories.

Time Value The component of an option premium which takes into consideration the time to expiry and the volatility of the underlying instrument.
    ▶ *See also* Intrinsic Value.

T/N Abbreviation for tomorrow/next or tom/next. Used in swap and deposit transactions when the first value date is tomorrow (tom) and maturity falls on the next working day (spot). The T/N swap price is adjusted for the interest rate differential in that short period.
    ▶ *See also* Short Dated Forwards/Deposits, Swap.

Tobin Tax A tax on transactions in the foreign exchange market, aimed at reducing purely speculative trading. First proposed by James Tobin, a Nobel-laureate economist.

TOCOM The Tokyo Commodities Exchange, Japan's largest commodity exchange. ■ **www.tocom.or.jp** ■

Tokyo International Financial Futures Exchange ▶ *See* TIFFE.

Tokyo Stock Exchange ▶ *See* TSE.

Tombstone A public notice such as a newspaper advertisement announcing the details of a new issue including the names of investment and finance houses who have organized and provided the funds. A tombstone appears as a matter of record and is not an invitation to subscribe. The layout and list of names resembles the inscription on a tombstone. (Figure 15.)
    ▶ *See also* Bulge Bracket.

TomNext ▶ *See* T/N.

This announcement appears as a matter of record only

BMW Group

BMW US Capital Corp.
Wilmington, Delaware, United States of America

USD 250,000,000
7.375% Notes due 2003
Issue price: 101.177%

USD 400,000,000
Floating Rate Notes due 2003
Issue price: 100.010%

unconditionally and irrevocably guaranteed by

Bayerische Motoren Werke Aktiengesellschaft
Munich, Federal Republic of Germany

ABN AMRO		HypoVereinsbank
Bank of America International Limited	Bayerishe Landesbank Girozentrale	BNP Paribas Group
Credit Suisse First Boston	DG BANK Deutsche Genossenschaftsbank AG	Dresdner Kleinwort Benson
Merrill Lynch International	Nomura International	Warburg Dillon Read

FIGURE 15 Tombstone

Top Down An investment strategy that tries to achieve a balance in an investment portfolio by selecting various sectors or industries. If a fund uses a top-down approach it will look at general economic or market trends to find the best sectors to invest in. Then it will look for the best investments within that sector. A fund may also choose countries before it chooses sectors and finally the individual companies within those sectors. Opposite of bottom up.

▶ *See also* Bottom Up.

Top Line Net sales or total revenues of a company. Used as an adjective for any action aimed at increasing net sales or revenues. In contrast with bottom line, which is a company's profit or loss after all income and expenses have been accounted for. The terms top line and bottom line are roughly derived from the respective positions of those figures in a company's profit and loss account.
▶ *See also* Bottom Line.

Top Reversal A top reversal day is the setting of a new high in an uptrend followed by a lower close than the previous day's closing rate (sometimes the previous two days).

Total Return Total return is the dividend plus any capital gains or losses achieved by investing in a stock, expressed in annualized terms as a percentage of the amount invested.

Touch The best (highest) bid and (lowest) offer for a given security in the current market. This need not be the two-way price of one market maker but is taken by looking at the market prices submitted by all market makers.
▶ *See also* Bid, Bid-Ask Quote, Offer.

Toxic A very high-risk investment which is highly likely to be in default.

Tracker Fund An investment fund that tracks the performance of a particular stock index by investing in its constituent shares in the same proportion as the index itself. The fund's risk and returns will match that of the index.

Tracking Share A tracking share or stock is created by a company for a subsidiary. It trades separately from the parent company's stock but does not carry any voting rights. It enables the company to compensate staff or raise funds to make acquisitions. It is popular among established companies who risk losing staff to new start-ups, because it is a way of offering employees a stake in the business.

Trade Balance ▶ *See* Balance of Trade.

Trade Barrier Artificial restraint on the free exchange of goods and services between countries, usually in the form of tariffs, subsidies, quotas or exchange controls.

Trade Bill ▶ *See* Bill of Exchange.

Trade Figures The record of a country's trading relationship with the rest of the world, showing the balance between exports and imports of visible goods such as raw materials and manufactured items. The trade figures are relatively easy to collect and are usually published monthly. Also known as the balance of trade.

Trade Weighted Used in reference to foreign exchange rates, with currency movements weighted in accordance with their importance in a country's trade. This trade weighting is then formulated in an index.

Trading Band Formal exchange rate limits within which a government or central bank allows its currency to trade without intervention. Also known as an intervention band. It is sometimes coupled with a crawling peg system of gradual appreciation or depreciation.
▶ *See also* Crawling Peg.

Trading Floor ▶ *See* Floor.

Trading House A business that buys and sells futures and physicals for the accounts of customers as well as for its own account.

Trading Post In the US, the post is the structure on the floor of a stock exchange at which market makers buy and sell securities.

Trading Profit ▶ *See* Operating Profit.

Trading Range The high and low trading points of an instrument over a period of time. Often referred to as the hi/lo. Chartists watch to see if the price of a financial instrument breaks through its trading high or low since this can be a portent for its future trend.

Trading Volume A generic term used to describe the total number of securities or contracts traded in any particular period.

Tranche French word for a slice. Used widely to mean a portion, allocation or instalment.

Transaction Costs ▶ *See* Transaction Fees.

Transaction Fees Charges payable by investors on purchases and sales of securities.

Transition Management A specialized function within the funds management industry, handling switches of large portfolios from one market sector to another, e.g. from equities to bonds.

Translation Risk A form of currency risk associated with the valuation of balance sheet assets and liabilities between financial reporting dates.

Treasuries Generic name for government Treasury bills, notes and bonds.

Treasury Bill Short-term government security issued in domestic currency with maturities not exceeding one year and therefore considered to be a money market instrument. Treasury bills are sold at a discount from par and do not carry a coupon.

Treasury Bond Government debt security issued with a maturity of ten years or more, traded in the capital markets. Treasury bonds are issued with a fixed coupon.

Treasury Note Government debt security issued with maturities of two to ten years and traded in the capital markets. Treasury notes bear a fixed coupon.

Trendline In technical analysis, a trendline is a line connecting specific price action to identify the direction of the market. The longer the trendline has been in place, tested but not broken, the more significant it becomes. (Figure 16.)
▶ *See also* Technical Analysis.

Trend Reversal ▶ *See* Reversal Day.

Triangles In technical analysis triangles are price patterns usually interpreted as a continuation signal. They represent a pause in the existing trend, after which the original trend resumes. Triangles usually take between one and three months to form. (Figure 17.)
▶ *See also* Technical Analysis.

Trigger Option A type of barrier option.
▶ *See also* Options, Down and In, Up and In.

Trigger Price The price at which buy/sell mechanisms in commodity agreements take effect.
▶ *See also* Commodity Agreements.

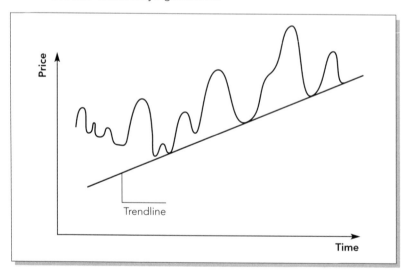

FIGURE 16 Trendline

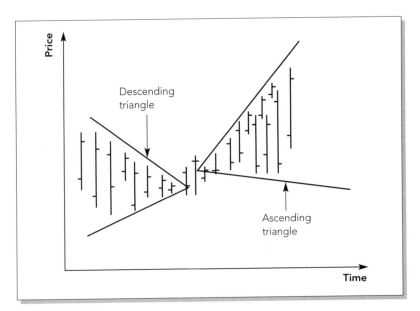

FIGURE 17 Triangles

Triple A Rated ▶ *See* AAA/Aaa.

Triple Top/Bottom In technical analysis, a price pattern similar to the head and shoulders except that the three peaks or troughs are at about the same level. (Figure 7.)
   ▶ *See also* Head and Shoulders, Technical Analysis.

Triple Witching The simultaneous expiry of stock index futures contracts, of stock index options and of options on individual stocks. Occurs every quarter and can often increase volatility, notably on the US stock markets. Double witching is similar to triple witching, with any two of the three contracts expiring at the same time.

Trustee Institution appointed to ensure all terms and conditions of the bond indenture are fully adhered to.

TSE The Tokyo Stock Exchange. ▨ **www.tse.or.jp/english** ▨

Turnover
   1 The amount of goods or services sold by a company in a given period. Also known as revenue or sales.
   2 Total volume of trades in a market during a given period.

Two-way Market Market where dealers actively quote both buying and selling rates.

U

UCITS Undertakings for Collective Investments in Transferable Securities. European Community regulation governing any collective fund, such as a unit trust, sold within the Community.

UNCTAD United Nations Conference on Trade and Development. An organization that promotes the trade, investment and development opportunities of developing countries and helps them to integrate into the world economy on an equitable basis. At one time it was a forum for most commodity price stabilization pacts.
■ **www.unctad.org** ■

Undercapitalized Term used when a business is not supplied with enough funds by its owners to support its activities and provide for any needed expansion.

Underlying Used in derivative markets to describe the financial instrument or physical commodity on which a futures or options contract is based.
▶ *See also* Derivatives.

Undersubscribed When a new issue is not completely bought by investors. Opposite of oversubscribed.
▶ *See also* Oversubscribed.

Undervalued When a security or currency is trading at a price lower than it should, relative to fundamental factors. Opposite to overvalued.
▶ *See also* Overvalued.

Underwriter ▶ *See* Lead Manager/Underwriter.

Underwriting A form of insurance whereby an underwriter agrees for a fee to take up a specific quantity of a new issue at the issue price if there is insufficient demand.

UNDP The United Nations Development Programme. One of the world's largest multilateral sources of grant funding for economic and social development.

Unemployment When people capable of working are unable to find work. There are two main types of unemployment. Frictional unemployment is the temporary unemployment caused by the time it takes people to find new jobs. Structural unemployment refers to the mismatch between vacancies and labour supply caused by structural economic change.

UNECE United Nations Economic Commission for Europe.
■ **www.unece.org** ■

Uniform Resource Locator ▶ *See* URL.

United Nations Conference on Trade and Development ▶ *See* UNCTAD.

Unit trust ▶ *See* Mutual Fund.

Unlimited Liability Where no restriction applies to an owner's losses in a business. In contrast with limited liability where the loss to owners, or shareholders, is limited by laws to the amount of capital they have invested.

Unlisted Stock A security that is not listed or traded on a stock exchange floor.

Unmatched Book One in which the maturities of assets and liabilities do not correspond. More specifically, when the average maturity of the liabilities is less than that of the assets. For a bank it can mean it has made long-term loans but has only short-term deposits, which may be withdrawn before the loan assets are realized. Sometimes known as lending long and borrowing short.
▶ *See also* Book.

Unrealized Gain/Profit Loss The profit or loss that would be reported, should a position be liquidated.

Unweighted/Weighted Indices Stock indices are calculated in two ways, either weighted or unweighted. The unweighted indices are simple arithmetic or geometric averages. In the weighted indices certain stocks carry a greater weighting than others, usually based on their market value or capitalization.

Unwinding a Position A long or short position is unwound, or reversed, by an offsetting transaction to result in a square or flat position.
▶ *See also* Long, Short.

Up and In A trigger option that is activated when the price of the underlying rises to a predetermined level.
▶ *See also* Option.

Up and Out A knockout option that is cancelled when the price of the underlying rises above a predetermined level.
▶ *See also* Option.

Upgrade An upward regrade by a credit rating agency of the credit status of a borrowing institution or its debt instruments. It usually means that the borrower will be able to obtain funds more easily and more cheaply because its credit risk has improved. The opposit of downgrade.
▶ *See also* Credit Rating, Downgrade.

Upstream Exploration for and production of crude oil and natural gas, in contrast with the downstream refining and marketing of oil products.

Uptrend/Downtrend In technical analysis both an uptrend and a downtrend are defined as trends that can be drawn on a chart by joining a minimum of four points.
▶ *See also* Technical Analysis.

URL Uniform resource locator. The address of a web page.

Uruguay Round World trade negotiations that created the World Trade Organization.
▶ *See also* WTO.

USDA US Department of Agriculture which implements agricultural policy and is a major source of forecasts and statistics on agriculture in the US and worldwide. ■ **www.usda.gov** ■

US Street Method The standard yield-to-maturity calculation used by the US market participants, apart from the US Treasury, whereby the yield is compounded semi-annually regardless of the coupon frequency.
▶ *See also* YTM Yield To Maturity.

US Treasury Bill Short-term US government bearer securities with maturities of three, six and maximum twelve months. Sold on a regular basis and commanding a dominating position on money markets. Nearly one-third of marketable US Treasury debt is concentrated in Treasury bills. The purchase and sale of such bills through open market operations forms a key part of US monetary policy.
▶ *See also* Open Market Operations.

US Treasury Bond Long-term US Treasury securities with maturities of ten years or more. Like Treasury notes, they pay a semi-annual coupon, so they are also known as coupon securities.

US Treasury Note US Treasury securities with maturities from two to ten years. Notes are non-callable. They pay a fixed semi-annual coupon and mature at par.

Utilities State or private-sector enterprises providing public services such as gas, electricity and water.

Value Date The date on which either the security or cash equivalent is settled on completion of a trade.

Vanilla Bond A bond with no unusual features, paying a fixed rate of interest and redeemable in full on maturity. The term derives from vanilla or 'plain' flavoured ice-cream.
  ▶ *See also* Bullet Bond.

Variable Costs A cost which varies with the volume of production or sales, such as the cost of raw materials or packaging. In contrast with fixed costs, such as rent, which stay the same regardless of the volume of production or sales.

Variable Rate A periodically adjusted rate, usually based on a standard market rate.

Variable Redemption Bond A bond whose redemption value is linked to a variable such as the dollar/yen exchange rate, the performance of the US Treasury bond, a stock index or the gold price.

Variation Margin Variation margin is collected on a daily basis by clearing houses or brokers to ensure margin requirements on a particular transaction keep pace with subsequent market movements. It represents a running profit or loss on a contract. It is calculated by revaluing all positions with reference to the closing prices each day.
  ▶ *See also* Margin, Mark to Market.

Vega The measure of change in the value of the option compared with a change in volatility.
  ▶ *See also* Option.

Venture Capital Funds used to invest in small companies that are considered to be in their first phase of growth. Funding is provided by private and institutional investors.

Vertical Spread An option strategy, using the simultaneous sale and purchase of two options of the same type and expiry date but with different strike prices.
  ▶ *See also* Option.

Virus Computer code or a program designed to have negative effects on the computer or computer network it infects.

Volatility Volatility describes the degree to which a value, such as a stock price or an interest rate, changes over a specified time period. High volatility means that the value changes dramatically, usually due to high market uncertainty. Traders thrive on market volatility because it presents many opportunities to earn a profit. Low volatility means values change minimally, as is the case when all news has been priced into the market. Professional investors tend to benefit from low volatility because they are better able to lock in stable returns. The financial markets distinguish between historical volatility and implied volatility. Historical volatility is a measure of volatility based on past price or yield behaviour, while implied volatility is implied by the price of an option.

Volatility Analysis Volatility analysis measures the rate of random change in market prices.

Volatility Index Used in technical analysis. A trend-following analysis that measures the average price movement in each set period of time.
▶ *See* Technical Analysis.

Volume-weighted Average Price ▶ *See* VWAP.

Voting Trust A trust set up by the company at a commercial bank inviting ordinary shareholders to deposit their shares for a fixed period in return for other privileges. This procedure is carried out if a company has financial instability and board members wish to concentrate voting power to make rapid policy changes.

VTC Voting Trust Certificate. A negotiable certificate proving that ordinary shares have been deposited into a voting trust, confirming that ordinary shareholders have relinquished their right to vote.
▶ *See also* Voting Trust.

VWAP Volume-weighted Average Price. VWAP is a method of pricing transactions and a benchmark to measure the efficiency of institutional trading or the performance of traders. VWAP represents the total value of stocks traded in a particular security on a given day, divided by the total volume of stocks traded in that security on that day. Calculation techniques vary: some will use data from all markets or just the primary market and may or may not adjust for resubmits and other error corrections. It is also known as dynamic time and sales.

WACC Weighted Average Cost of Capital. WACC is used to measure whether a potential investment will generate an adequate return. It is the cost of debt and equity, weighted by their relative contribution to overall costs both in the proportion of the funding and the cost of the related interest or dividend payments.

Wall Street Colloquial name for the New York Stock Exchange that has loosely come to mean securities trading generally in the US.

Wall Street Refiner A Wall Street investment firm that buys or sells crude oil and petroleum products – as futures contracts or paper barrels – on a scale similar to real refineries. Typically these investment firms do not own oil refineries and take no actual delivery of oil.

Warehousing Process whereby a group of investors independently buys shares in a company but each investor keeps his holding below the official notification of a stake holding. This can be a surreptitious method of mounting a takeover bid.
▶ *See also* Acting in Concert.

Warrant A type of financial instrument attached to a security that has a separate life and value. A warrant allows the investor to purchase ordinary shares at a fixed price over a period of time (years) or to perpetuity. The price of the shares is usually higher than the market price at the time of issue. A warrant is freely transferable and can be traded separately. Warrants are usually issued by companies for their own shares, or the shares of a subsidary. Covered warrants are issued by banks, for the shares of other companies, or for use as a trading instrument.

Warrant Bonds Bonds with an attached warrant which entitles purchase of a certain number of shares of the borrowing company for a certain period at a price fixed in advance. The coupon on the bond may be less than comparable bonds without warrants because of the possible benefit of buying shares at an advantageous price.

Watered Stock Shares which represent overvalued assets, usually because of inflated accounting values. Derived from the practice of giving cattle water before they were weighed in at the slaughterhouse.

Wedges Used in technical analysis. This pattern is similar to a symmetrical triangle. Wedges are usually seen within the existing trend and are generally continuation patterns. The wedge usually lasts more than a month but not more than three months.

Weighted Average Cost of Capital ▶ See WACC.

Weighted Average Coupon The weighted average coupon rate of all the loan rates of the underlying collateral in a pool of mortgages.

Weighted Average Maturity The weighted average maturity of all the loans making up the underlying collateral in a mortgage pool.

Weighted/Unweighted Index Stock indices are calculated in two ways, either weighted or unweighted. The unweighted indices are simple arithmetic or geometric averages. In weighted indices certain stocks carry a greater weighting than others, usually based on their market value or capitalization.

Weighting The weight, or importance, given to the various constituent components of an index or economic indicator.

Wet Barrels Term used in oil trading that means delivery of a product, with a shipping date, rather than the transfer of a tanker receipt, which changes ownership but does not usually involve delivery.
▶ See also Paper Barrels, Daisy Chain.

When Issued A conditional transaction because the security involved has been authorized but not yet issued.

Whisper Estimates Informal earnings forecasts for high-profile blue-chip companies. Whisper numbers are generally above the consensus estimates collated and published by earnings tracking companies. A company will often see its stock sold off if it fails to meet whisper numbers even though it matches the published consensus figures.
▶ See also Consensus Estimates.

White Knight A potential friendly acquirer sought out by a company to protect it from a hostile takeover.
▶ See also Poison Pill.

Wholesale Goods sold in large quantities. An intermediate stage in distribution, between the manufacturer and the final retailer. Wholesale price changes are one way of measuring inflation.

W/I When Issued, or more exactly When, As and If Issued. W/I trading starts immediately after the formal announcement or authorization of a planned issue of shares or bonds but before they are delivered. Trading takes place on what is known as the grey market. No interest accrues during this period. Also known as free to trade.

Wide Opening When the spread between buying and selling prices is unusually wide.

Williams Percent R Used in technical analysis. This oscillator is like a sto-chastic since it measures the latest close in relation to its price range over a set number of days. Named after its originator, Larry Williams.
▶ *See also* Technical Analysis.

Windfall Profit An unusual profit, normally as the result of a specific, one-off situation.

Window Dressing Dates Window dressing dates are ends of periods, usu-ally a year end but can be three or six months, when banks and companies aim to present their accounts in a favourable light, often helped by raising additional short-term funds.

Window Shortened A reference to a Federal Reserve Bank discount window.
▶ *See also* Federal Reserve System.

Withholding Tax Tax deducted at source on interest or dividend payments to investors.

Working Capital Working capital usually refers to net working capital and is the resource that a company can use to finance day-to-day opera-tions. It is calculated by taking current liabilities from current assets.
▶ *See also* Assets/Liabilities.

Working Control Theoretically more than 50 percent of all voting shares is needed to control a company. However, if the holder has a substantial minority interest then it could have effective (working) control if the rest of the company's stock was all held in small shareholdings.

World Bank The World Bank is an agency for channelling aid funds to poor countries for medium- and long-term projects. The Bank raises funds by selling bonds on world capital markets and makes loans from its own resources. ■ **www.worldbank.org** ■
▶ *See also* Bretton Woods.

World Trade Organization ▶ *See* WTO.

World Wide Web ▶ *See* WWW.

Write Down Book-keeping action that reduces the value of an asset on a balance sheet.

Write Off Book-keeping action that at one stroke depreciates an asset out of the balance sheet.

Written Down Value Fixed assets in a company's balance sheet which are listed at their historical, or original, cost, minus depreciation.

WTI West Texas Intermediate is a benchmark crude against which other crudes are priced. A light (40 degrees API) sweet blend of crude oils produced in fields in Western Texas, it is the benchmark for US crude oil.
▶ *See also* API Gravity.

WTO World Trade Organization. Based in Geneva and launched in 1995 to supervise existing international trade accords and provide a forum for negotiation of new agreements as well as to adjudicate in disputes. Absorbed the old GATT. ▓ **www.wto.org** ▓
▶ *See also* Doha Round, GATT, Uruguay Round.

WWW World Wide Web. A global system of servers that supplies the infrastructure for the internet.

Yankee Bond A dollar bond issued in the US, by a foreign borrower, registered with the SEC.
  ▶ *See also* SEC.

Yard Currency market term for one thousand million units of a currency. Based on the French word milliard.

Year Bill ▶ *See* US Treasury Bill.

Year-on-Year Rate A rate that compares the current reporting period (e.g. a month or quarter) with the same period a year earlier.

Yellow Strip In the UK share market the yellow strip that appears on price display screens shows the best bid and ask price among all those quoted by market makers. The difference between the best bid and best ask is known as the spread.
  ▶ *See also* Ask, Bid, Spread.

Yield Percentage return on an investment, usually at an annual rate.

Yield Curve The graphical representation of the yields of a set of bonds or other instruments with the same credit risk and currency, but different maturities. Yield is plotted along the vertical axis and time to maturity on the horizontal axis. There are many different yield curves, including government benchmark curves, deposit curves, swap curves and credit curves. Benchmark curves consist of securities that meet certain criteria for liquidity, size, price, availability, turnover rate and other characteristics. These securities set standards for the market against which other issues can be measured. A yield curve is not static and can change quickly at any time. For example, a word or two from a central banker can fuel expectations of higher inflation, which may cause longer-term debt prices to fall more than short-term prices. The nominal yield curve is positive, rising from left to right, because yields on longer maturities are higher than on short maturities to reflect the greater risk of lending money for a longer time. If the yield curve is positive sloping it will steepen as the longer yields move up more than the shorter ones. An inverted, or negative, yield curve slopes downward from left to right, with short-term yields higher than long-term yields. Investors may be expecting a reduction in inflation in the longer term or there may be expectations of sharply reduced supply of bonds, both of which will depress yields. (Figure 18.)

▶ *See also* Maturity.

Yield Gap Also known as yield ratio. This ratio compares the dividend yield on equities from the yield on long-term government bonds. It is used to assess whether equities are under- or over-priced compared with government bonds. The dividend yield on equities (expressed as

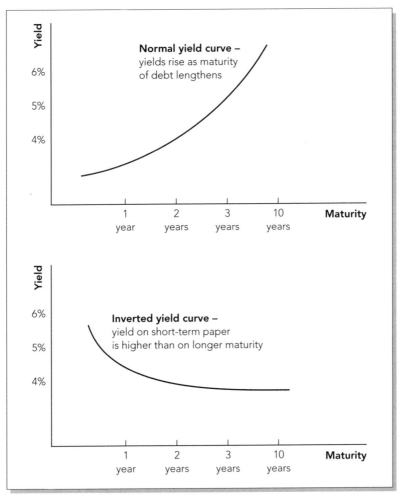

FIGURE 18 Yield curve

a percentage of the share price) is usually higher than the yield on bonds, reflecting the higher risk of holding equities. When equity prices rise, their dividend yields fall as a percentage of their price, thus reducing the yield ratio. When equity prices fall their yield rises. The thoery holds that if earnings yield is higher than bond yield then equities are cheap.

▶ *See also* Dividend Yield.

Yours Dealers' jargon used to confirm the act of selling. When a dealer accepts a bid, or the offer to buy from another dealer, he says 'yours' to confirm that he has 'hit the bid' and is willing to sell the requested amount at the requested price. 'Yours' must be accompanied by a specific number or amount to show how large the accepted deal is.

▶ *See also* Bid, Offer.

YTM Yield To Maturity. A key consideration when comparing bond investments. It is the annualized rate of return of a bond, namely the interest rate that makes the present value of the a bond's future cash equal to the present price of the bond. It assumes the bond will be held to maturity and that the coupons will be reinvested at the same rate.

Z

Zero Cost Option An option strategy whereby the cost of purchasing an option is totally offset by the premium generated from the sale of an option.

    ▶ *See also* Risk Reversal.

Zero Coupon Bond A bond that pays no coupon but is issued at a deep discount to face value. The difference between the issue and redemption prices creates a hefty capital gain that boosts the effective yield close to market levels. As it does not pay a coupon, investors do not run the risk of reinvesting interest paid at a lower rate if interest rates fall during the life of the bond. There may also be tax advantages to an investor from taking a one-off capital gain rather than a stream of income from coupon payments.

Zero Coupon Swap An interest rate swap in which one party makes regular payments while the other party makes one lump sum payment, typically at the end of the contract.

    ▶ *See also* Swap.

Zero Coupon Yield Curve A yield curve of zero coupon bonds. Market practice is often to derive this curve theoretically from the par yield curve and it is frequently used to derive discount factors. Also known as a spot yield curve.

    ▶ *See also* Yield Curve.

INTERNATIONAL COMPANY NAMES

AB   Swedish company title: abbreviation of Aktiebolag.

AE   Greek company title: abbreviation of Anonymi Eteria.

AG   German company title: abbreviation of Aktiengesellschaft, a joint-stock company.

AN   Norwegian company title: abbreviation of Ansvarlig Firma.

AS   Czech or Slovak company title: abbreviation of Akciova spolecnost.

A/S   Danish company title: abbreviation of Aktieselskabet.

ASA   Norwegian company title: abbreviation of Aksjeselaskap.

BA   Norwegian company title: abbreviation of Bergenset Ansvar.

Bhd   Malaysian company title: abbreviation of Berhad.

Bt   Hungarian company title: abbreviation of Beteti tarsasag.

BV   Dutch company title: abbreviation of Besloten Vennootschap.

BVBA   Belgian company title: abbreviation of Besloten Vennootschap met Beperkte aansprakelijkheid.

CRL   Portuguese company title: abbreviation of Cooperativa de Responsabilidad Limitada.

DD   Slovenian company title: abbreviation of Delniska Druzba.

Dd   Croatian company title: abbreviation of Dionicko Drustvo.

FA   Indonesian company title: abbreviation of Firma.

GmbH   German company title: abbreviation of Gesellschaft mit beschränkter Haftung, a limited liability company.

Inc.   Incorporated. A US and Canadian company title.

I/S   Danish and Norwegian company title: abbreviation of Interessentskab.

JD   Slovenian company title: abbreviation of Javna Druzba.

Kft   Hungarian company title: abbreviation of Korlatolt felelossegu tarsasag.

KG   German and Swiss company title: abbreviation of Kommanditgessellschaft and Kollectivgessellschaft respectively.

KK   Japanese company title: abbreviation of Kabushiki Kaisha.

Kkt   Hungarian company title: abbreviation of Kozkereseti tarasag.

KmG   Swiss company title: abbreviation of Kommanditgessellschaft.

K/S   Danish company title: abbreviation of Kommanditselskab.

Lda   Portuguese, Brazilian and Spanish company title: abbreviation of Limitada.

LLC   US company title: abbreviation of limited liability company.

LLP   US company title: abbreviation of limited liability partnership.

LP   US company title: abbreviation of limited partnership.

Ltd   UK company title: abbreviation of Limited. Generally replaced by public limited company or plc. Also used for quoted companies in Australia, Canada and New Zealand.

Ltée   French-Canadian company title: abbreviation of Limitée.

NV   Dutch company title: abbreviation of Naamloze Vennootschap.

Oy   Finnish company title: abbreviation of Osakeyhito.

Plc   A UK company title: abbreviation of public limited company.

Pte   Singapore company title: abbreviation of private.

Pty   Australian company title: abbreviation of proprietary.

SA   French company title: abbreviation of Société Anonyme. The term is also used in Belgium and Switzerland.

SA   Spanish company title: abbreviation of Sociedad Anonima.

SA   Italian company title: abbreviation of Societa.

SA de CV Mexican company title: abbreviation of Sociedad Anonima de Capital Variable.

SAE   Spanish company title: abbreviation of Sociedad Anonima Español.

SAL   Spanish company title: abbreviation of Sociedad Anonima Laboral.

SARL   Portuguese and Brazilian company title: abbreviation of Sociedad Anonima de Responsibiliade Limitada. Also, French company title: abbreviation of Societée à Responsibilitée Limitée. Also used in Luxembourg.

SAS   Italian company title: abbreviation of Società in Accomandita Semplice.

SC   French company title: abbreviation of Societé en Commandité. Also used in Luxembourg.

SCL   Spanish company title: abbreviation of Sociedad Cooperativa Limitada.

SIM   Italian company title: abbreviation of Società di Intermediazione Mobiliare.

SL   Spanish company title: abbreviation of Società Limitada.

SNC   Italian company title: abbreviation of Società in Nome Collectivo.

SpA   Italian company title: abbreviation of Società per Azioni.

SRL   Italian company title: abbreviation of Società Responsibilità Limitata.

Ste Cve   Belgian company title: abbreviation of Société Coopérative.

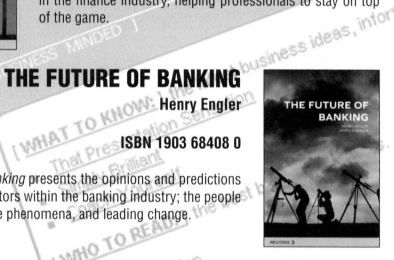